BEYOND ADHD

BEYOND ADHD

Overcoming the Label and Thriving

Jeff Emmerson and Robert Yehling

ROWMAN & LITTLEFIELD
Lanham • Boulder • New York • London

Published by Rowman & Littlefield
A wholly owned subsidiary of The Rowman & Littlefield Publishing Group, Inc.
4501 Forbes Boulevard, Suite 200, Lanham, Maryland 20706
www.rowman.com

Unit A, Whitacre Mews, 26-34 Stannary Street, London SE11 4AB

British Library Cataloguing in Publication Information Available

Library of Congress Cataloging-in-Publication Data

Names: Emmerson, Jeff, author. | Yehling, Robert, author.
Title: Beyond ADHD : overcoming the label and thriving / Jeff Emmerson and Robert Yehling.
Other titles: Beyond attention-deficit hyperactivity disorder.
Description: Lanham : Rowman & Littlefield, [2017] | Includes bibliographical references and index.
Identifiers: LCCN 2017000124 (print) | LCCN 2017005620 (ebook) | ISBN 9781442275102 (cloth : alk. paper) | ISBN 9781442275119 (electronic)
Subjects: LCSH: Attention-deficit hyperactivity disorder—Alternative treatment. | Behavior modification.
Classification: LCC F3101.4.B33 C47 2015 | DDC 320.0820983—dc23 LC record available at http://lccn.loc.gov/2015034023

∞ ™ The paper used in this publication meets the minimum requirements of American National Standard for Information Sciences Permanence of Paper for Printed Library Materials, ANSI/NISO Z39.48-1992.

Printed in the United States of America

CONTENTS

ACKNOWLEDGMENTS

I want to thank the following people for helping me turn my dream into reality, making *Beyond ADHD* come to life:

To Robert Yehling, my co-author and friend of five years, who worked tirelessly and polished my story and the rest of the writing into something to be incredibly proud of. I simply wouldn't be where I am today without you, Bob. I also appreciate all the time you've taken to hear my thoughts and teach me the ropes when it comes to the publishing world (and beyond). Bob has now written about autism, Asperger syndrome, and ADHD; his dedication to neuroscience and mental health and fitness is pretty obvious.

To Dana Newman, my agent. I am incredibly fortunate to have you with us, and I'll forever be grateful for your faith in my vision. Thank you for your efforts in finding a book deal for *Beyond ADHD*. Thank you just as much for your kindness and support throughout this journey. Big things ahead! Your guidance has been instrumental. Thank you for caring about mental health like you do.

To everyone at Rowman & Littlefield, especially Suzanne Staszak Silva, who wanted *Beyond ADHD* to come to life, and pitched it to her team. You changed my life with that decision. I'll never forget that.

A hearty thank you to everyone who contributed to this book! Your help has been crucial in opening eyes across the world through raising life-changing awareness around these symptoms and the bigger picture as well. Special thanks to those who directly helped us along the way with their insights, interviews, and comments: Dr. Marianne Kuzujanakis, Dr. Susannah-Joy Schuilenberg, Dr. Andres De Los Rosas, Dr. Tim Royer, Dr. Patrick Quaid, and Erica Damatto.Thanks also to certified functional medicine coach Karin Yehling for assisting in the fact-checking on the material pertaining to functional medicine.

Thank you to Everyday Health, Additudemag, AOL Health, and other online publications that helped me build a name for myself and raise empowering awareness in this world. I never forget who helped along the way.

To Jane Friedman—thank you for introducing me to Dave Malone. Our interactions and time together played an important role early on in the concept of this book coming to life. Cheers to both of you! Thank you, Dave! I'm very glad our paths crossed.

To the United Way of Guelph, Ontario, Canada—thank you for helping me to afford therapy sessions when I was unemployed and struggling. I'm speechless other than to say thank you for all that you do for the community!

To the Honorable David G. Carr, the judge who sentenced me in a Kitchener, Ontario, Canada courtroom on November 8, 2000. Though your ruling broke my heart, it also lit a fire within me that became a freight train of its own—one I'm incredibly grateful for in hindsight. You did the right thing, I now realize. Thank you, and I aim to personally hand you a copy of this book (if I'm allowed to do so).

To Kevin McIntyre (my former probation officer)—I hope you'll actually get to read this, wherever you are. I will definitely leave a copy at the probation and parole branch as a "thank you" for all that probation officers like yourself do. You are truly unsung heroes doing God's work with the resources you're given. I won't ever forget you, Kevin. You saw potential in me when I felt horrible about myself. For that I'm eternally grateful, and I aim to pay it forward.

To Rebekah Labelle (Waterloo Regional Police Service)—Thank you for your help and kindness as I worked hard to pursue my goals from the past. I had a lot to learn, but you were always kind. Thank you for your help and a listening ear when I really needed it.

To my grade 9 and 11 (I think) English teacher, Jim Majer—thank you for being the single best teacher I remember. You often threw me out of class for goofing off, but you and I had an unspoken connection that transcends time. You always "got it." Thank you for sending me out to ponder life on my own terms. I learned so much more by walking the streets and working things out in my head than being in class, frankly. What a lesson. P.S.—Thank you for always having the soul-provoking music of Enya playing in the background during class! Genius move. Thank you for being human as well, and swearing when necessary. That showed me that you don't have to be "perfect" and play a "holier than thou" fake role to be successful. Authenticity: check!

To the John Howard Society of Kitchener-Waterloo—thank you for your teenage and adult diversionary programs such as anger management and restitution. As a former "client," I'm grateful for the seeds these programs planted in me, even though I'm a late bloomer of sorts. Yet again—better later than never.

To the adult mental health unit at Grand River Hospital in Kitchener, Ontario, Canada—thank you for helping me help myself after committing myself in early 2013. Seeing my deceased brother Ryan's former room haunted me, but meeting Rick Lauzon (a former high school classmate) was both humbling and wonderfully empowering at the same time. Thank you to the staff who kept an eye on me and were kind to me. I look forward to returning with a copy or two of *Beyond ADHD* as a thank you and a reminder that you *do* make a difference.

To my friends (both old and new) on Twitter and other social media channels—thank you for reading, watching, listening to, and interacting with me over the last few years. Wow, what a powerful experience it's been to share with you, learn from you, and raise such crucial awareness and empowerment together. Building my platform has been a godsend, and you play a *big* role in all of it! If I wasn't doing this, I'd be in trouble, so thank you from the bottom of my heart for helping me spread the word in the hope that others will be helped.

To any and everyone from my past, from friends to my first wife (who I made mistakes with, but had some amazing times with and learned a lot from), to former hockey teammates (love you guys!) and anyone else I shared time with—thank you for teaching me in some way, shape, or form. I wish all of you only the best in this life, this sometimes-crazy journey. I wasn't always easy to be around, that's for sure, and I know it, but thank you for sharing your journey with me. Greg—I hope you find a way to live with inner peace and fulfillment. I'll always love you and remember the amazing moments we shared. Please, if you ever read this, know that I'm grateful for you—for us.

Finally, to *you*, the reader—thank you, and I mean it when I say it. You mean the world to me, whatever your opinion is about ADHD, my story, and all that's in this book. I'm grateful for you for taking some of your precious time to read this book (or listen to it in audio form).

Please know that you truly aren't alone, that others *do* care, and that as rushed and crazy as the world around you may get at times, a deep breath is almost always available. Stop and look at the sky and be grateful for the simple things that end up being the big things in the end.

If I'm near your town or city doing a book signing, speaking engagement, or you happen to recognize me on the street, please do stop, reach out to me, and say hello. It would mean a lot to me, since I do so much behind a computer but treasure face-to-face engagement as well. You know—the way people used to do it more before the 24-7 smart phone world.

To anyone I may have left out, I have this to say—as read from a CD liner cover some time during the 1990s, "charge it to my head and not my heart." You are forever appreciated for playing a role in my life, whatever it was. "Everything is everything," to quote Daryl Hall of Hall and Oates.

See you out there, online, and stay tuned for more in the future! Until then . . .

Yours in purpose and massive gratitude,

Jeff Emmerson, Ontario, Canada, 2017

JEFF'S THANK-YOUS

Sitting down to write this, I suddenly take a deep breath and see my life flash before my eyes, sort of like sitting in a very dark movie theater, hearing very stirring, emotional music start to play as the screen begins to show photos of key moments in times that have passed.

I (frankly) never thought I'd make it here. As tears start to well up in my eyes (tears of gratitude for this life and all the lessons that have been sent my way), I want to dedicate this book, this "first child" of mine, to several real-life angels who have been in my midst over the years, angels who have had a crucial impact on my life.

First, I've got to give thanks to the music group Hall and Oates, who reignited my creative fire and inspired me to start writing this, my first book (though I had no idea what the book's topic would be way back then, way before my foray into the mental health system) after seeing them live in concert on August 30, 2006. I was deeply touched by seeing Daryl Hall and John Oates live for the first time with my dad (he raised me with their music) to the point that I felt a massive fire within that I'll never forget. That's the power of the arts—we've got to keep funding them in public schools! They offer a world of hope and possibility for expressive students, which is an investment in society as a whole. Anyway, thank you to Hall and Oates and to Daryl Hall's solo work, which has been a big part to the soundtrack of my life growing up. I hope to personally hand you a copy of this book, Daryl. Let's see if I can make that happen . . .

Dad—You adopted me at eight weeks old and you never gave up on me—not once. This first book is dedicated to you as a way to say, "See, Dad? I did make it to being a success like I always told you I could!" I never did achieve that original goal of being a National Hockey League goaltender and buying you that brand new Corvette to say thank you as I said I was going to, but I'd say that this is an even more meaningful achievement, given the journey you've witnessed before your own eyes. I thank God that you're still here, that Aimee and I moved back across the country to be with you in your remaining years, and that I now savor every single moment with you more than I ever have before. I'm actually in the present moment way more now than I used to be. Better later than never, I suppose. I love you. Thank you for your selflessness, for your superhuman levels of patience with me, and for giving me a soft place to land when Mom and I would butt heads in violent ways, either verbally or physically. Because of you I'm here to a very large degree. Never forget that.

Mom—First off, I know you did the very best you could have done, and I love you for that. I also forgive you for the rest, just as I finally learned to forgive myself (though regrets still punch me in the stomach from time to time, but that's OK, that's part of being human). Though we no longer talk (a choice I made a few years ago for my own health, something I needed to do to help heal and grow up in ways), I will always appreciate all that you did for me, and there was a lot—make no mistake. From endless travel to and from my all-star hockey games to buying me things I needed when I was unemployed as a young man at times—I certainly won't forget. You only wish me peace, as you said yourself, and I want the same for you, of course. Your son went on to do rather big things, if I may be so bold. It feels incredibly good to have proven myself in my own eyes and in society's eyes as well! That's truly all I ever wanted after being badly scarred early on in ways (especially as a highly sensitive and driven boy—driven when I was interested and passionate about something, anyway). Everything has come to pass, and I wish you well for the rest of your days, whatever comes.

This book is also dedicated to my grandmother, or "Nan," as I grew up calling her (and always will). Nan, you are a true angel to me, and your traditions now live on in our house, whether it's holiday time, or snow blowing (I just bought the same brand of snow blower you had, Nan!), or standing by my principles stubbornly. You were so kind and selfless to my sister Kim and me; we could never repay you, but we are who we are today due, in large part, to your love and guidance. You were more of a mother to me than your daughter was, and I thank God for your strong yet loving female example as a young man who had a rather warped sense of what a "healthy" male/female relationship actually looks like. I love you more than ever, and I know I haven't yet visited your grave site—I'm waiting for this book to be released to come and say hello and read to you a while. I love you beyond space and time.

Aimee—my wife and my best friend in this partnership called marriage, I also dedicate this book to you. From when we met, I knew I had met my match—you wouldn't let me push you away as was my habit of doing. No—you stayed there and helped me break through my massive commitment and fear issues, even seeing the rage in my eyes at moments as we worked through my inner demons. I love you in a way I never thought I could. Having you support both of us financially for several years bothered me to no end, but I thank God that I didn't succeed at hanging myself during that fateful late-August day in 2011. Not only would you have been the one to find my dead body, I wouldn't have had a chance to truly show you how much your faith in us would pay off, and I sure as heck wouldn't have been able to experience all that we've lived through since! God, what a ride it's already been for us. I'm very grateful for the love and kindness your grandmother, uncles, cousins, parents, and brother have shown me as well. They are amazing human beings. Thank you for loving me so selflessly, and for sticking with me as I committed myself in January of 2013. The darkest moments have brought us to a place where nothing can stop us now—ourselves included. I love you and our furbabies! You are my happy ending, so to speak. I'm so at peace now, and I have you to thank. You are clearly another angel in my midst.

Sean—I also dedicate this book to you for all you've done for me, and for all we've done together. As a young man, finding a male friend who saw life as I did and felt just as deeply about it has literally been a lifesaver at times. You and I have enjoyed late night and wee hours walks and discussions that have helped me stay sane in a rushed, seemingly "asleep" world at times (consciousness-wise). It will always be food for my soul to return to the streets we grew up on every few months or so to walk with you, talk with you, and reflect on just how far both of us have come. (You signed a book deal right before I did! Who would have thought?) From traumatic backgrounds of childhood trauma and early struggles to successful authors—God, what a blessing! From then to now and beyond . . . Memory Lane Forever! (Update regarding Sean: Though we've gone our separate ways, you will always hold a special, sacred place in my heart and soul. We shared so many heartfelt, vulnerable moments together. They are a significant part of my history. To take from a poem I once read, "Friendships: For a reason, season, or lifetime—all are normal." Life goes on and those streets will always be a safe place to walk in and reflect in, even if I'm on my own. No doubt that will make the experience even more hauntingly beautiful.)

To my deceased brother Ryan—this book is dedicated to your memory. You may no longer be with us physically, but I always feel you cheering me on from afar. You and I always shared a very cool bond, even if we didn't see each other a lot (as we grew up in different families). I thank God and the universe that I got to take you out to see that Meatloaf concert at the movie theater for your thirty-third birthday on May 9, 2008, because that was not only an amazing time for both of us, but the last time I would see you alive. I'll also never forget growing up with you, how you saved many a frog from my "curious scientific mind" and grasps at the creek, and I sure won't forget the nights we played video games, and later on shared a few beverages with Meatloaf, Chicago, Rik Emmett, Aerosmith, and Rush playing on the stereo as we'd talk about life at the time. I'll be returning to your grave site to read to you and leave a copy of this book for whoever might come across it.

Finally, Ryan—pouring my heart out to you with tubes down your throat in the ICU during your first suicide attempt (and being in a near three-day coma as a result) and having you wake up literally fifteen minutes later is something I'll never forget as well. You said later that you didn't remember any of what I said, but I sure feel you with me now. You battled with things I'll never know, and you had the heart and spirit of a gentle lion, which I shall always remember. I have never gotten over the sheer terror and haunting of losing you in the way that we did, and I promise you that I will always speak openly about suicide prevention in your honor, wherever my journey takes me. May you rest in the truest of peace, knowing that your daughter Kaylee carries on and is loved! I will hold you close for the rest of my days and beyond. I love you, man. You're always with me.

Beyond ADHD is also dedicated to the universe and all who I have and will cross paths with in some way, shape, or form. Whether you're dealing with mental health challenges or not, no matter who you are, you're human and so am I, and therefore, we're connected in a journey of hopes, dreams, struggles, despair, anxiety, and lessons to always be learned (among other things).

Do your best and remember to be grateful for the simplest of things, as I remind myself to do at times. This, the book that took me (literally) to hell and back, onward to triumph, is dedicated to you. If you see me at a book signing, a public-speaking event, online, or anywhere else, please don't hesitate to say hello, no matter how busy I might look. It means a lot to hear from you, my reader. After all, if there weren't any books to write, I wouldn't be where I am. I thank you for believing in me and for believing that this book can make a difference for others in some way, shape, or form.

Enough from me—let's get to the reason you're reading this. I promise you that I've poured my heart and soul into these pages. Let me know what you think when you're done, and please read with an open, empathic mind. In the end, as long as this book made you take a deeper look at the diagnosis and label of ADHD and the bigger picture of reasons for these symptoms appearing more and more, then I've done my job. I also seek to inspire through my fierce desire to take my pain, mistakes, and challenges and turn them into something positive. I ached to make it to this point—my soul ached for years, through days and nights where I never thought I'd see success. My point? Don't EVER give up. You never know what's coming around the corner when you work hard and ask for help when you need it, come hell or high water. I'm proof that dreams *do* come true. If I'd been successful in my 2011 suicide attempt, none of this success would be happening! To anyone who feels depressed or suicidal, please re-read that last sentence as many times as you need to. That's my heart reaching out to yours!

Jeff Emmerson, 2017

Part I

1

A NEW DOCTOR'S OFFICE

Happiness and excitement filled our hearts as we drove across the 401 highway in Ontario, Canada, destined for the U.S. border. Our happiness was borne by the anticipation of the answers I might receive at our destination, answers that would explain and perhaps present new directions in a life I'd had such a hard time understanding, right down to my ADHD diagnosis five years before.

Our excitement sprouted from how much greater my life could become as my wife, Aimee, and I began to explore these possible new directions, and share the news with my social media followers, the thousands of medical and health-care professionals, educators, professors, parents, and others whose lives, like mine, revolved to some degree around either living with an ADHD diagnosis or caring for those with one.

During the drive, Aimee and I discussed our five-year personal odyssey with ADHD and shared notes that pertained to the man we would be visiting, Dr. Timothy G. Royer, Psy.D., founder of the Neurocore Center in Livonia, Michigan, near Detroit.[1] Through our correspondence on Twitter and subsequent phone calls, Dr. Royer had shared a number of powerful experiences he'd encountered and witnessed while division chief of pediatric psychology at Helen DeVos Children's Hospital in Grand Rapids, Michigan, during the 1990s.

THE LEGO BOY

One of those experiences concerned the "Lego Boy," aged sixteen. The boy came to him seriously challenged and behaviorally disruptive, years after being placed in a special home. His IQ measured out at 93, low average, but his brain processing speed scored 65—special education territory. When Dr. Royer looked at the file and then the hardly responsive teenager, a shiver ran through his spine, the shiver of cold realization: this was the same kid he'd first tested ten years earlier, when his school recommended he be evaluated for ADHD! At that time, Jimmy preferred drawing complex pictures in class to coursework, hence the teacher's snap determination he was unfocused. They weren't ordinary stick-figure pictures, either, but well-conceived drawings. When Dr. Royer gave the boy an IQ test, he scored off the charts, at 152—genius range.

Here is what happened next, which Dr. Royer allowed me to share from his as-yet unpublished book, *Burning Out Rembrandt*:

> I sat down with Jimmy's mom to share the results. In the corner of the meeting room was a box of Lego blocks, and she told him to play while we talked. I explained to her that Jimmy needed to change schools. He was more like a special education student, in that the normal school curriculum wasn't designed for a brain that worked like his. Neither the teachers, administrators, nor other students would ever be able to understand or meet his needs.
>
> The mom told me that the school wanted her to put him on drugs to treat ADHD. They all said that they weren't supposed to diagnose or recommend treatment, but off the record, they were putting a lot of pressure on her. It seemed obvious to them: if Jimmy can't focus on the teacher and what the rest of the class is doing, he must have ADHD. Isn't that what ADHD means? The teacher had a classroom full of kids and didn't have the time to deal with a child who couldn't pay attention.
>
> "No way," I said emphatically. "Don't do it. There is nothing wrong with him. Far from it. His brain is gifted."[2]

When the mother and son left the office, Dr. Royer was convinced they would take the conventional path—go to a clinician, get diagnosed for the behavioral symptoms of ADHD, and receive a prescription of methylphenidate. He walked toward his office sadly, stopping in his tracks at what he saw next: "On the floor was what I can only describe as a Lego city," he recalled in *Burning Out Rembrandt*.

> Not a Lego village, or town, but a complex city. There were towers of different shapes and sizes. The designs were eclectic; some of them looked futuristic and some ancient. Some towers floated above the rest of the structure, connected by cantilevers and flying buttresses. There were streets and multileveled buildings joined by walkways. It was color-coordinated. It had style. It took my breath away, not only for its imagination, but also for the engineering and artistic skill it took to pull it off.
>
> *"What the hell?"* I thought. Jimmy had sat there quietly, for maybe twenty minutes, and built that? What was he drawing while the teacher droned on? Someone should be keeping those papers. From that point on, I thought of him as my Lego Boy.

Instead, as Dr. Royer recalled, the boy was diagnosed and prescribed methylphenidate. He never picked up a block again, nor did he draw anymore. The mother gushed with happiness that he now listened to the teacher and did what he was told, but in reality, he was sliding into a shell from which he would never truly emerge. When his behavioral problems returned and became truly disruptive and violent, he was admitted to a special needs facility. When your measured IQ shrinks by sixty points in ten years, your engagement with the world—and your creative mind—is greatly reduced.

The story ran through my head over and over again. What went wrong? It sure wasn't the Lego blocks! If that was what happened to gifted, creative, lively minds after an ADHD diagnosis and prescription, when what they most needed was to be creatively and intellectually challenged, well, I wanted to get as far beyond it as possible. In that spirit, Dr. Royer and I eagerly looked forward to our visit, even though, at thirty-nine, I was well beyond the need for pediatric psychology or a children's hospital.

ANTICIPATION AND EXCITEMENT

Because of the way anticipation and excitement tend to foreshorten long drives, our three-and-a-half-hour drive felt like twenty minutes.

We delighted in a typical spring day. It was warm enough for me to wear cargo shorts and a golf shirt—a good thing, since I was really nervous, which often makes me sweat. We rolled the car windows down slightly, Aimee keeping her eyes on the road while I read and fidgeted, increasingly excited about seeing Dr. Royer in one of his many Neurocore centers throughout Michigan.

Once we crossed the border into the United States, I sensed that feeling of being in a very different place, a totally different landscape. It is amazing how a quick drive across the Detroit River can change things. The roads and store chains look different, and the sheer sizes of the cities dwarf those in Ontario. The huge highway billboards, massive volume of traffic driving at feverish speeds, and sun beating down on us were all stressors. We weren't in Kansas anymore—or Guelph, where we lived.

Road tension and anticipation spiked my heart rate a little more. So did the questions chattering away inside my mind. What degree of ADHD would Dr. Royer find in my body/brain? Was I heading in the same direction as young Jimmy? Would this long-awaited get-together with my new social networking friend bring a desired closure of some sort—or open up a new can of mental health worms?

I bounced in the passenger's seat as fear, anxiety, excitement, and my inquiring, need-to-know mind fired enough adrenalin and cortisol through my system to turn the familiar "flight-or-fight" response into a series of wind sprints. "What if Dr. Royer uncovers something other than ADHD through his tests?" I asked Aimee. "What if the months of hard work I've put into building my platform as a man speaking out about having ADHD aren't real?"

"Just take it as it comes, hon," Aimee replied in her calm, even-keel manner. *How does she do that?* "It will be what it will be. After all, you're all about honesty and authenticity online, so remember that people will appreciate that."

My mission created this appointment in the first place. My mission is to motivate, empower, and educate others navigating the ADHD maze, and the challenges and struggles they face. I have dedicated myself to talking with people throughout the world about living with attention deficit hyperactivity disorder, both adult-onset and child ADHD. What started as a quest to find others to share our common stories led me into a world of confused patients, bewildered parents and loved ones, uncertain diagnoses, treatment plans that ranged from effective to prescriptive to bizarre—with powerful stimulant drugs causing all sorts of unintended consequences. I also noticed a lot of fighting between medical and other health-care professionals over how to properly diagnose and treat ADHD, which I found astounding, since, in the United States alone, they've diagnosed 6.4 million children and 10 million adults (4.4 percent of the total adult population), according to the Centers for Disease Control and Prevention.[3] Many of these patients often had more questions than answers—like me.

It didn't seem right. How could a behavioral disorder that impacts so many still be so mysterious? Shouldn't doctors have ready answers and clear-cut diagnoses for something so pervasive, along with clear-cut treatments—with prescriptions given as a last resort rather than the first?

As I developed and produced my *Beyond the Label of ADHD* video blog, and started micro-blogging on Twitter, I was stunned by the variety of experiences, diagnoses, remarks, and concerns. I'm not alone: therapists, clinicians, psychologists, pediatricians, psychiatrists, neuroscientists, neurologists, and behavioral experts are expressing their grave concerns with the way we diagnose, treat, and regard ADHD. Soon, my little initiative grew into a community of a quarter-million Twitter followers and thousands of video blog viewers. Among them was Dr. Royer, a neuroscientist and expert in the use of biofeedback and autonomic nervous system testing in the assessment of and treatment of ADHD, anxiety, and sleep disorders. He also happened to be well-versed in the use of long-term, non-invasive (read: non-prescriptive) solutions to tackle the problem at the core.

MEETING WITH DR. ROYER

Finally, we arrived at Neurocore Brain Performance Center, where Dr. Royer presides as a principal and chief science officer. Dr. Royer followed the content of my network, knew its size, and read or watched many of my blogs, so he entered our meeting with a much better picture of me than I had of him. But one thing kept jogging my mind: *I'm not ending up like little Jimmy.* I wanted answers, and wouldn't be too patient if his testing didn't yield them.

Dr. Royer greeted us warmly. He was a bit shorter than me, in great physical shape, and very friendly. He made us feel at home right away. His smile and positive energy became immediately obvious, so I gravitated toward him comfortably. He instructed members of his staff to set up in a room where we could chat and get down to business. One thing that struck me about the staff—they were just as awesome as their leader. There was nothing brusque or clinical about them, like I'd found at most other doctors' offices during my twenty-year quest to find out what the hell was wrong with me.

We sat around a circular table. Dr. Royer began by telling Aimee and me about his experience in the field, recounting his time at the children's hospital in the 1990s, the thousands of brains he'd scanned and observed over the years, and how and why he created Neurocore. He went into great depth in explaining his testing procedures and teaching us about the autonomic nervous system. I didn't remember any other doctor breaking down tests like this, so I started to relax. He really knew his stuff. He spoke in a very gentle, calm tone, and excelled at making things easy to understand. He would make an amazing teacher, I thought to myself.

Aimee was just as interested, for good reason. She has lived with me since 2010, witnessing my behavior/thought patterns and struggles first hand, such as my suicide attempt in 2011 and committing myself to a psych ward briefly in early 2013. Thankfully, she saw something *beyond* those dark places into which my mind plunged and into which my entire consciousness shifted. She never stopped believing in me. I needed someone to believe in me!

Dr. Royer told us he would test and scan my brain, heart, breathing, nervous system, and sensory abilities to obtain a true picture of how my body was working. We wanted to know how my physiological body might be relating or contributing to my ADHD and its first cousin, anxiety disorder. They had turned my adult life into a roller-coaster ride of emotions, events, hospital stays, impulsive behaviors, doctors' opinions, and medicines that did not work.

As we talked, and Dr. Royer started sharing his skepticism about the true prevalence and diagnostic accuracy of ADHD, new questions rolled into my mind like a set of ocean waves: *What if I really don't have ADHD? What if the doctors were wrong all these years? What if this is something else? Will I make a good impression? I'm just a guy from a* *small city in Canada! Can I really face people with confidence? I'm so damn shy, and my social anxiety will be through the roof! What tests will I be put through? What the f*** am I going to do if I have something other than ADHD? Jesus—I've devoted so much of the last few years to building my online platform and pouring my heart out publicly!*

I tried hard to shut off the inquisition valve, but it's not easy when you have Jeff Emmerson's mind, and that mind veers in all directions with the slightest scary nudge.

Dr. Royer finished explaining his testing process, also sharing with us the history of the quantitative electroencephalography (QEEG), an amazing brain-mapping technique that first started hitting neurology centers in the late 2000s, and his testing/process. Among other things, the QEEG advanced autism diagnoses and treatment, particularly at the Amen Clinic in Southern California.[4] Its ability to read into the subtlest workings of the brain was known. Today, it is finding its way into more and more neurological settings. Perfect timing, given the epidemic rate of PTSDs, traumatic brain injuries, and various mental health and behavioral disorders tied to the neurology of the brain, of which ADHD is listed as one. I would have never imagined using this machine for ADHD, but that's why we were in his office—to try something different.

I was happy as hell, but nervous about the possible outcome. I had been down this road so many times that my excitement and hope of finally pinpointing my situation clashed squarely with memories of bad diagnoses, bad meds, and very bad resulting experiences. Plus, I remembered something that Dr. Jane Tanaka, once the California child psychiatrist of the year, had told my co-writer about social and behavioral disorders when he was working on *Just Add Water*, the biography of autistic surfing star Clay Marzo: for many behavioral/mental health disorders, it takes ten years on average to get a correct diagnosis. *Ten years.* You know how much distress that creates in a mind like mine? Or in an adult's life? Imagine two rivers colliding—and looking into the resulting muck to figure out which debris came from which river.

Then something else hit me: what if my years of seeking answers had been a waste? What if I simply had textbook ADHD and was wasting Dr. Royer's time? But what if I didn't have textbook ADHD? Or ADHD at all? What then? The questions crashed inside my skull like pissed-off rams, along with a comment Dr. Royer made about misdiagnoses: "They are usually with you for the rest of your life. There are huge implications." Don't I know!

As we sat there, I thought of how I'm one who digs to find the truth about something, no matter how big the effort or where it takes me. Give me the challenge, and I'm on it, along with my obsessiveness to "get it right." There is something else, too: my irritation over what I perceive as a health-care system focused more on medicating than prescribing proactive behavior and life strategies for those whose brains are wired differently. Before I could lay these perspectives on the line with others around the world, I needed to gain an even deeper understanding of what lay behind the ADHD diagnosis I had received. That's what brought me to Dr. Royer's office.

Finally, I thought about the countless parents who give up trying to find answers for their kids. Or, they unwittingly turn the wrong way with their kid, such as Jimmy's mother did in the Lego Boy story. I considered the equally numerous adults who give up hope for themselves. I also hurt inside for the day when the diagnosed kids become adults, and then give up because nothing seems to work—jobs, relationships, friends, family members—all due to an apparent inability to cope. The stigmatic ADHD label, in many walks of life, might as well be a scarlet letter. A correct diagnosis for these families and individuals is more imperative than ever. But how do we weigh reasoned diagnosing against a superheated climate when ADHD diagnoses are rising alarmingly? What about those swept into the ADHD tsunami, even though they may not *have* ADHD? Like the 45 percent to 50 percent of people that, Dr. Royer told me, are misdiagnosed in the first place?

Like so many millions, I felt the ADHD label stick to my public and private identity after specialists diagnosed me in 2011. Only I did something else with the label: I built a large online platform and reputation for being "the adult ADHD guy" on Twitter, YouTube, LinkedIn, and elsewhere. I was deathly afraid to be wrong in the public eye—and in my own life, for that matter. I had to get this right.

Dr. Royer introduced me to tests, protocols, and a wholesome overview of my body and its systems that I'd never heard before from any doctor, in any office. He sought a history of my brain, heart rate variability, and the autonomic nervous system. While we discussed this, he also explained the functions of each of the five different brain wave types (gamma, beta, theta, delta, and alpha). No one had done that for me before! He also pointed out how another battery of tests he planned, auditory/visual testing, would be geared toward uncovering my vigilance, focus, and speed levels/responses. "What we've found is when we do actual physiological screening—cardio, respiratory, brain, adrenals, and so on—it brings the accuracy of the diagnosis up to an average of 88 percent, instead of a 50 to 55 percent average based on checklists and observed behaviors alone," he said. Works for me!

Aimee sat directly behind me while Dr. Royer hooked me up to a blood pressure cuff, heart rate monitor, and a "belt" that monitored my breathing, the type used in lie-detector (polygraph) tests. That was weird, since I had a polygraph test a year earlier as part of the hiring procedure for an armored car company—a very traumatic experience. This time around, I was a guest, not a job applicant trying again to fulfill a personal mission upon which I'd first embarked more than a decade earlier.

As Dr. Royer explained his procedure, I found myself consciously breathing deeper in an effort to relax. I was on blood pressure medication, and suspected that the smaller "standard" cuff would register a high reading, which had happened before, scaring the hell out of me. It did register high, but he felt confident that the reading wasn't accurate. I'd recorded a lower reading a week or so before, so all was good.

I submitted to the rest of his regimen. It included several in-depth brain and body tests/scans, including auditory and visual recognition (speed) testing, an EEG (electroencephalogram), cardio/respiratory system scans, and blood pressure/heart rate monitoring. I also had to fill out a survey on overall health, which was put into a database and compared to thousands of others to help determine my results.

TEST RESULTS

Aimee returned to the front waiting room, since I needed total privacy. I sat in front of a computer with a staff member in the corner behind me to make sure everything ran smoothly. I wondered how I'd perform, and the anxiety mounted from my desire to do as well as possible. I was dealing with two other factors that typically make any experience more anxious: I was a bit tired from the drive, and my adrenalin was elevated from my excitement over these tests. Even in this moment, the former youth hockey star's competitive mind was kicking in—hardly a normal reaction to a medical test.

I passed through the barrage of visual and auditory prompts on the computer, answering as fast and controlled as I could. It felt like about twenty straight minutes on high alert. After I finished, I took a deep breath, wondering what Dr. Royer would find.

When I saw the results, my eyes bugged like a cartoon character's. The results were stunning. First, I learned that I was breathing at approximately eleven breaths per minute, five more than the ideal range. That suggests a hyperactive autonomic nervous system, basically a full-body battle with anxiety. Then came the EEG brain scans, the results I anticipated more than any other. Dr. Royer measured my results against approximately ten thousand brain scans on file at Neurocore, scans taken by him and his team. They showed that while the center of my brain was working at the 58th percentile, the right side of my brain struggled in the 29th percentile and my left in the 33rd percentile. Put them all together and I was using 40 percent of my brain's capacity with a measured, above-average IQ! *How could I be running at so much lower capacity than normal when my brain never seemed to stop cranking with thoughts and perceptions?*

"I suspect you may possibly be in a higher IQ range, perhaps even the gifted range, once your brain use is optimized," Dr. Royer said. He looked more intently at me, focusing the conversation on finding ways to help my brain function more optimally—and helping me learn practices, exercises, and other activities to get there. "This is going to involve a process of teachings and sessions."

Later, Dr. Royer further explained the percentile scale, starting with the obvious question we all want to know on a perfect day: what does a brain operating at 100 percent look like to a neuroscientist? His specific description had the effect of making me want to settle down my brain waves and reach for the stars—quickly:

"One hundred percent full functioning would be a high beta, which is the fast brain wave; from a clinical standpoint, we want that number to be less than .14."

The best we've ever seen is .55, an extremely low volume of stress brain wave activity. Then you align the beta waves with those that allow you to focus and sleep, which need to be around a ratio of 2.4. If you had 2.4 and .55 in all three areas of your brain, you're gonna be pushing up against the high 90s, probably the 98th or 99th percentile.

We have a client who was the MVP of his sports league a few years ago. His beta number was very low, which is very good; the amount of actual stress in his brain versus made-up stress is about .7. If you give him the ball with three seconds left in the game and he's got to make the shot, to him it's the same as if he's shooting out on the practice court because his brain isn't overfiring. Jeff's reference point on that same number was 2.5. So that's picking up the stress versus the calmness in the brain. You want that ratio to be lower and lower.[5]

As I pondered that big-time difference—my brain was affected by stress three and a half times more than the athlete he mentioned—Dr. Royer shared another story:

I worked with a lady who was the number one tennis player in the world for many years in a row. Her beta number was also .7. Every time you see these iconic people, you see high beta readings. I have a guy who's a multi-billionaire, about the 120th richest man in the world; his high beta is .75. These are people that, no matter what we would interpret as a stressful or a lion-chasing-me moment, they become unbelievably calm and focused and extremely efficient. They only see life-and-death situations when there are really life-and-death situations. These are the people who operate at near ideal brain capacity.

I quickly wondered, *what would happen if we ran these tests while diagnosing for ADHD?*

As a stubborn former athlete, I will work at something—and work at it again—until I improve or create a similarly positive outcome. What could be better than *improved brain performance*? This excited me. It also opened my investigative floodgates. I was floored by the science Dr. Royer shared with me, not to mention seeing where my brain function and usage stood in comparison to the previous brain/body scans he had performed.

Finally, Dr. Royer funneled everything into his diagnostic opinion of me: "Compared to the thousands of other minds in his database, you don't have what appears to be classic ADHD based on the test results," he said.

That stunned me. "If it's not classic ADHD, then what is it?" I asked.

"An anxiety disorder might be an alternate diagnosis, but we need to do more testing and treating to be sure. You may have ADHD, yes, but it isn't the 'textbook' ADHD that I've come to see a pattern for biologically."

Dr. Royer's tests also confirmed something very significant. He said that my ANS (autonomic nervous system) was in "overdrive," closer to the fight-or-flight reaction than poised calmness when presented with stressful situations (I'm an intensely driven, emotional man). Even such a simple statement, that my ANS was in overdrive, exceeded what I'd been told during my ADHD diagnosis. What did "overdrive" mean? What could I do about it? For the first time, I found a new answer popping up: *Something.* I could do something about it. Now I needed to find out what it was.

I knew I showed these exact traits. In years past, I'd undergone exhaustive testing from specialists that ruled out bipolar disorder, cyclothymia, hypomania, depression, and many other causes. Nothing fit. Anxiety disorder and ADHD are common co-partners, so I was good with it. It confirmed for me there isn't one "textbook" cookie-cutter approach to diagnosing ADHD. If you have the traits, and other factors are ruled out, then you go with what fits. That's pretty much how it goes for most people with the diagnosis.

THE TRIP HOME

We said our goodbyes to Dr. Royer, vowing to meet up again and continue this mutually beneficial work. On our trip home, Aimee and I talked excitedly over how awesome it had been to speak with Dr. Royer and members of his staff, as well as forming a feeling for the work at Neurocore. Clearly, his work was changing lives by shedding light on the strengths of individuals, as well as their innate power to live *with* mood, mental, and behavioral disorders, rather than *in spite of* them. I felt a huge sense of relief.

"I'm so proud of you with all you're doing, raising awareness, and sharing your story so honestly and putting yourself out there," Aimee said.

Tears welled up in my eyes. She had financially supported us for most of our time together, even cleaning toilets once to make ends meet during my emotional struggle, a cut-throat inner battle in which the victor was my life and the loser could have been—well, my life. She has been patient, supportive, and an amazing human being. I am forever in awe with how she never let me push her away early on (God knows I tried), as I'd pushed away countless other women in my past. My success is her success as we continue to provide a global online voice for those striving and struggling to overcome inner and outer trauma to find their most authentic, powerful selves. Whenever I think of the people who have been kind enough to take a chance on me and allow me to show them my potential, such as Aimee and Dr. Royer, I come to tears fast. I always will.

Still, I was unsettled for weeks after our meeting. As the afterglow of this eye-opening get-together waned, it occurred to me I may never receive that "perfect" piece of proof to explain the emergence and development of my symptoms and what caused them. For one thing, as I began to learn more, I realized there was no cookie-cutter list of symptoms, only guidelines based on observed behaviors. Nor did the medical community agree entirely with the classification of ADHD. Faced with this overload of opinions, I chose my old friend—the hard way—to find answers that would make sense for me. I'd move through my life, see what created the stress and anxiety I continuously feel, and work on changing those things.

Dr. Royer and I agreed to exchange services and, through our work together, focus on three tasks: (1) to get to the bottom of ADHD; (2) to erase the commonly held beliefs about ADHD, the "label," and liberate those suffering from mood disorders to be far less limited by a diagnosis that may or may not have been accurate in the first place; and (3) to rise beyond ADHD, and again participate in a society and life of balance, kindness, and accomplishment, where uniqueness is celebrated and disruptive behavior explored for its deeper cause—every day.

We got to work.

2

PEEKING BEHIND THE ADHD CURTAIN

After we returned home to Guelph, I continued to be blown away by Dr. Royer's first tests and initial findings. I now found myself in the hands of a specialist who seemed to deeply care about me as a person, as well as someone trying to figure out what lay behind my diagnosed ADHD.

THOUGHTS ABOUT MY INITIAL VISIT

The first surprise was that he'd cast major doubt on the diagnosis itself. This really made me think for weeks, mulling over my childhood, the verbal and physical violence I witnessed in the home with Mom and Dad, wondering if the actual root was environmental and behavioral and not ADHD at all. The sensory tests that showed my brain's "processing speed," the EEG, and the multiple questionnaires all pointed to a much bigger picture.

My afternoon with Dr. Royer was a case of tearing myself away from the tether of my previous ADHD diagnosis—along with a large part of the identity I'd created from that diagnosis, further developed and shared with family, friends, and my growing online community presence. He took his time with the testing and was very thorough in explaining the biology behind my behaviors, a first for me. The most anyone else had done was to give me checklists for bipolar disorder, depression, and anxiety, and draw blood for diabetes, thyroid issues, cholesterol, and so on. Dr. Royer got "under the hood" and looked much deeper, from various angles. Instead of the subjective assessing done in doctor's offices across North America that relies heavily on an ADHD checklist from the fifth edition of the American Psychiatric Associate's *Diagnostic and Statistical Manual of Mental Disorders* (known as DSM-V),[1] he worked directly with scientifically proven biological tests. This was completely foreign to me, but incredibly welcome. I was desperate for answers, whatever they might be.

NEW FINDINGS AND A NEW TREATMENT PLAN

After the appointment, I spent the next days chattering up a storm on my *Beyond ADHD* video blog, breaking out subjects I'd never even considered before. I started doing research designed to steer me into the grander scheme, the bigger picture. This avalanche of new findings to which I'd been exposed could help us gain a better understanding of ADHD, and ultimately, an understanding that would take me, and the people who looked to me for answers, *beyond* the medical diagnosis.

First, I had to follow up with the treatment plan. I noticed how Dr. Royer strongly advocated self-effort over medication, though the latter serves the former when prescribed appropriately. In my case, we did forty neurofeedback sessions with a video to measure my brain wave activity. We also worked on calming my breathing. While Dr. Royer has included medications in his plans, he refrains in the majority of cases— including mine. Furthermore, his tests and findings came with a "do-it-yourself" component. Why rely exclusively on medication when we can learn ways to improve, sharpen, and focus our minds and attention, and in so doing, perhaps rise *beyond* what we thought possible in the first place? If he prescribed breathing treatments to further calm and balance patient's/client's bodies, he immediately backed it up with a "do-it-at-home" schedule to enforce the self-effort discipline. It also caused me to ponder this: why not receive training on proper breathing *before* we actually need treatment?

Something else deeply impressed me about Dr. Royer's approach: he didn't stick purely to modern psychology, modern medicine, or even the latest findings in neuroscience and neuropsychiatry. When it came to working with me (as with his thousands of other patients), the world's various healing and medical modalities were his oyster. Take the deeply relaxing, energizing breathing exercises he gave me. For those, Dr. Royer turned to a yogic technique known as diaphragmatic breathing. I noticed quickly how it calmed the high-speed train running inside my mind while also slowing my heart rate. It also helped neutralize my "fight-or-flight" response, common in those with behavioral and anxiety disorders such as ADHD, ADD, or obsessive-compulsive disorders.

Put simply, those of us wired to the "fight-or-flight" response tend to freak out more quickly and intensely than others. My overly high beta brain wave readings confirmed this. Adrenaline and cortisol shoots into our brains more rapidly than those with more balanced biochemistries and calmer demeanors. When that happens, *look out*: our instincts are to either fight the person, situation, circumstance, or challenge; or to run for the hills, physically and emotionally. I know many people whose brains are "wired" into this fight-or-flight response, and I can tell you one thing: we all dread it. Why? Because the outcome is rarely good, almost always damaging, and sometimes destructive. Jobs, families, relationships, personal property, and much more often crumble. It's like being in an earthquake between the ears. If ever you could point to one across-the-board positive of the ADHD medications prescribed for calming, it would be neutralizing this fight-or-flight response.

I was tired of that. In Dr. Royer's diaphragmatic breathing exercises, I found a way to get beyond "fight or flight" through self-effort. When I inhaled through my nose and exhaled through my mouth, I *felt* the cleansing breath relaxing my body and mind. This was a "self-care" gift, to borrow a term I heard while admitted temporarily to a psychiatric ward in January 2013.

It didn't take long to notice results. Almost immediately, my fight-or-flight response receded. I was deeply relieved, because when I act out, I can cause myself tremendous stress and anxiety, feel wild mood swings, and harbor equally wild projections about events or comments that really happened or will happen—or never happened and will not. I do not have a good relationship with "fight or flight." It often ends in self-sabotage, which, when I look through my life, is what defined many of my earlier adult years.

Five years after my ADHD diagnosis, I could practice and see the benefits of this new way, which didn't necessarily need lifelong medical prescriptions to succeed. I also noticed how diaphragmatic breathing helped me with "racing, catastrophic thinking," a pattern for many years. I am learning to "sit with the panic that brings despair into my mind" and breathe deeply through it, allowing it to gradually pass so I don't make impulsive decisions I later regret, as I once did. Catastrophic "what if" thinking drove me to my suicide attempt in 2011; I remember the feeling *very* well. I hope I never come close to that feeling again.

QUESTIONS ABOUT MY PAST MEDICAL TREATMENT

Dr. Royer handed me a golden key. With it, I found myself asking skeptical questions about my past medical treatment. Why hadn't a doctor talked to me about conscious breathing? Did I go to doctors unfamiliar with healthy breathing practices? That's hard to believe; most clinicians are well schooled in breathing exercises—maybe not yogic breathing, but certainly exercises designed to strengthen our pulmonary systems, calm our emotions and nerves, and bring more oxygen and energy into our bodies. That led to my next question: Why weren't my doctors, or countless others about whom I'd heard, prescribing breathing practices as a treatment for ADHD, alongside prescription-based treatment and therapy?

That is the million-dollar question—rather, the $20-million question, if you assign a dollar to each adult or child diagnosed with ADHD, or living with it, in North America.

I asked this question more and more as I passed through, evaluated, and worked through the after-care portions of Dr. Royer's courses of action for me. I received training on how to apply EEG probes to my head and ears for the next level of treatment. Dr. Royer had arranged for EEG probes to be sent to my house, something that wouldn't happen in the medical world. The probes measure electrical activity in the brain, electrical activity that can be altered by seizures, blackouts, temporary loss of oxygen, traumatic events—or that ever-concerning anxiety that accompanies "fight or flight."

EEGS, BRAIN CHEMISTRY, AND HOW THE BRAIN WORKS

We further explored the EEGs, my brain chemistry, and how my brain worked. Dr. Royer also taught me about two types of cerebral channels we can manipulate:

1. Ligand-gated channel—When we introduce a chemical to the brain to manipulate behavior/symptoms. The ligand-gated channel has huge relevance, since meds are sometimes temporarily (ideally) needed while we simultaneously train the brain to learn new concepts; and
2. Voltage-gated channel—Used for learning any new concept, such as anxiety coping mechanisms, driving a car, learning a new language, and so on.

We observed my creativity brain waves, anxiety, and focus levels from the EEG scan on the screen. Dr. Royer explained that, with the EEG training, I could insert a movie into the computer and literally train my brain/body to perform optimally over time. The movie would stop playing when my brain waves were at undesirable levels, and resume once I brought my body and brain back to optimal states of calm and clarity. "This is a form of *operant conditioning*," Dr. Royer said.[2]

MY HISTORY OF MEDICATIONS

Not only was I relieved, but fascinated—really fascinated. For one thing, medications were the last thing on either of our minds. The list of medications I have been given on my mental health diagnosing "journey" could hold their own in any medicine cabinet: it started with lorazepam, which stopped my racing mind, I must admit. I slept a lot better, but realized how dangerous opiates are, and my new doctor was very quick to tell me this as well. Then there was escitalopram, one of two antidepressants, which seemed to help temporarily. The other, bupropion, made me feel weird, worsening my mood and anger at times. Also in my medicine chest was quetiapine, an extremely powerful antipsychotic, which helped me sleep while in the psych ward after committing myself in early 2013. However, I gained a lot of weight and suffered through horrible, severe mood swings into dark anger, which Aimee remembers all too well. Next up was amphetamine and dextroamphetamine, a staple prescription for ADHD, which did nothing for me; I stopped after two months of use.

In 2015, my general practitioner prescribed lurasidone, along with lithium, since she thought (as opposed to concluded beyond the shadow of a doubt) that I might have rapid-cycling bipolar disorder. These led to horrible anger and depressed feelings, and I switched doctors soon after; my wife and I were so furious with her lack of competency. In her defense, I went to the emergency room yet again and was told I couldn't see a psychiatrist unless I committed myself. I was still in control of my own safety, and this was infuriating—there was an *eight-month* waiting list to see a psychiatrist.

To bring this list to conclusion, I circle back to the beginning: sertraline was the first drug I was ever given for mental health, in 2010. It did nothing for my anxiety. Aripiprazole, another antipsychotic, did nothing for me, either.

Dr. Royer wasn't infusing me with more meds, but with the knowledge and confidence that I could now train my brain and body to rise *above and beyond* the unpredictable ways of my moods and behaviors. I had never heard that potential future outcome conveyed or described anywhere else. Even the best ADHD literature of the time focused on living the "best possible" lives within the accepted ADHD protocol, which combined medications and combinations of behavioral, occupational, and relationship therapy. But did we really need all this medication? And why couldn't "best possible lives" become "living at our highest potential"? I viewed Dr. Royer's perspective as part of a novel way to approach this disorder.

We live in a time of "diagnose-and-prescribe." If something is wrong with me, I need to be prescribed a medication. More and more, this has been our reaction process socially, to uncover something "wrong" with us, and then to get a prescription. In my opinion, that reaction has been partially fueled by the media and pharmaceutical companies, in concert with overwhelmed doctors.

ANOTHER APPROACH

I have harbored major concerns with this quick-to-prescribe approach for a few years now. Through Dr. Royer's work, I began to understand *why:* An overreliance on medication takes away our power and ability to train our bodies and minds to manage and possibly conquer ADHD symptoms with self-will and discipline (along with a well-balanced diet with plenty of calming foods, among other things). I wanted to opt for another approach, to reclaim my highest and best self in an engaging, powerful way. When I lift weights and swim laps in the pool, I feel *good* about myself; that's how I want to feel when dealing with my neurological issues. My body releases endorphins and adrenalin for all the right reasons. "Fight-or-flight" transforms into "focus and create." There is always an important place for medication in treating many mental and behavioral disorders, including ADHD, but it is not the only way. And it certainly doesn't help us get beyond the effects of ADHD. In my eyes, my work with Dr. Royer validated all of the above.

As Dr. Royer pointed out, I definitely live with "textbook *traits* of ADHD/ADD" (note the difference in wording between *traits* and *behaviors* or *disorder*). However, there was always an unstated "but" when we spoke. But *what?* That's what I wanted to know, not only for myself, but also for those who communicated with me on social media and through other channels for support, advice, a helping hand, or simply a virtual shoulder to lean on. My loyal base of followers connected with my sincerity, authenticity, and brutal honesty, even when I felt embarrassed. I could not let them (or myself) down—I had to keep digging!

Then there was the steadfast woman at my side. Aimee has always been a big believer in science, not to mention her vested interest in my mental and emotional stability. She's witnessed (and, a few times, dealt with the brunt of) my mental battles during our nine years together. She visited me each night in the psych ward, anchored me during the up-and-down mood swings that come with the territory, and witnessed me start and stop this book several times—then helped nudge me through. She made it a point to mention the higher purpose of sharing a story like this with readers who, in most cases, can take what I've discovered and broken out (such as Dr. Royer's revolutionary tests), and apply it to their own situations, whether it concerns their children, friends, significant others—or themselves.

We realized we had nothing to lose and everything to gain by remaining open to Neurocore, Dr. Royer's new, evolved scientific approach to assessing brain and body. It made sense: Neurocore goes way beyond the usual behavioral checklist that diagnosticians use in this particular field.

Meanwhile, I lost some online followers while I questioned whether ADHD existed at all, or if it was wildly exaggerated. I felt like an eighteenth-century pioneer getting waylaid off the trail at times, but every bold experiment was valid and crucial to my learning. I was out there doing it, and I was going to share it—beginning with the tests, results, discussions, and outcomes in Dr. Royer's office. Most importantly, several big names in neurology, pediatrics, psychology, children's psychiatry, and neuroscience started stepping into my discussions.

All of this has left me holding a mixed bag of feelings concerning ADHD and society—and the label attached to my original diagnosis. I can't stand labels to start with, because they tag and limit you. Ask any school kid who's been diagnosed only to have it somehow become public (which happens far too often). Let's go back to Clay Marzo, the world-class autistic surfer I mentioned earlier. It took twelve years of clinics and diagnoses for Clay to learn, at age seventeen, that he was on the autism spectrum. Know what those twelve years were like on the school grounds, especially being a Caucasian living on the Hawaiian island of Maui? You got it—rough. He was bullied, often. His mother, Jill Marzo Clark, resisted all attempts to label him until his primary sponsor, Quiksilver, required him to be examined and diagnosed in order to retain his large athlete endorsement contract.[3] Even so, in the film documentary *Just Add Water,* Jill is quoted as saying, "You can't put a tag or label on someone like Clay. He lives in his own world. We should celebrate that, not limit it with a label."[4] She's right. Tags can hurt us; they affect our relationships with classmates and teachers, and later on, may impinge on college admissions and work opportunities.

THE ADHD DIAGNOSIS

Back to the ADHD label. Now that I have received access and direct experience with the scientific protocols of Dr. Royer's assessment processes, from a man who directly studied more than ten thousand brains (as of late 2016), I'm validated even further in questioning the veracity of the ADHD diagnosis for these reasons:

- With at least 44 percent of Americans sleeping less than six hours each night (per a 2010 report in *National Geographic*),[5] and 40 million Americans on anti-anxiety medication (according to Alice Boyes, PhD, the author of *The Anxiety Toolkit*),[6] the potential for misdiagnosis is alarming.
- We're spending more and more time in front of computer screens, mobile devices, Playstations, flat screens, and so on. These screens emit positive ions that charge up our electrical fields and speed up our biochemistry—not good for any of us, but especially those with ADD or ADHD. It's getting in the way of play/social/relaxation time. Even more frightening is the continued cutback on physical education and playground recesses, and reduction of work lunchtime, work breaks, and vacations.
- The general food supply is less nutritious and more filled with harmful chemicals and sugar than ever.[7] Even the fast-food chains are trying to improve, to a point. Processed, prepackaged, and fast food is the norm, and with it, high-fructose corn syrup, the addictive, unhealthy sugar additive that has wreaked havoc on public health since the FDA made it a U.S. food supply staple in 1972. "I cannot underscore how destructive high-fructose corn syrup has been to our national health," Dr. Aruni Bhatnagar of the University of Louisville's Diabetes and Obesity Center told my coauthor for *Innovation & Tech Today* magazine in 2014.[8] "As long as we're subsidizing high-fructose corn syrup over healthier sugars, it will be a very hot-button issue. The problem is, it decreases natural insulin production *and* gives us empty calories. If you drink a soda, you will eat more. The appetite is driven by carbonated beverages and drinks with high-fructose corn syrup." When it comes to the causative agent in common between diabetes, cardiovascular disease, obesity, ADD, ADHD, anxiety disorders, some

cancers, and lack of good health, you can stick a pin right in the center of sugar.

- Finally, the big one: the *laissez faire,* "this is just how it is." This takes two forms: (1) we are becoming more dependent on medical solutions to ADHD; and (2), we are not following up with other well-documented, increasingly available ways of changing our lives to increase concentration and reduce anxiety. Consequently, we either feel powerless to move forward, or *render ourselves* powerless. I believe we need to change both—now. This needs to be reversed for everyone's sake. Yes, we're all busy and living in a stressful society, which seems to move faster by the minute, but we can't keep waiting for the magic ADHD cure or try to ignore what prevents us from concentrating properly, acting out on impulses, and the other diagnostic markers. We need to take charge—a core part of this book.

I'm ready to get beyond my forty years of mentally battling it out with parents and grandparents, teachers, girlfriends, doctors, employers, and police, and a life with hundreds of major ups and downs. If I don't have another roller-coaster ride in my life, I'll be the happiest person in the world—well, next to having Aimee by my side. How about you? This is why the focus of *Beyond ADHD* is squarely on peeling away the label and reaching beyond it, through the prism of my experience and the pioneering work of astute men and women whose views inform much of the story to follow.

3

OPTIMAL HEALTH, INTERRUPTED
Decoding ADHD (Part One)

Optimal personal health is a dance between our self-awareness and self-care, genetics, and the care and treatment provided by doctors, nurses, therapists, and/or alternative care providers. How successfully we dance our way through wholesome, healthy lives relies on our ability to take care of ourselves, understand our own mental, physical, and emotional strengths and weaknesses, take care of any medical needs, and adapt to and thrive in our surroundings. This includes eating right, sleeping enough, relaxing whenever possible, and reducing stress to a minimum—or at least a manageable level. That specific level differs with each person.

CONDITIONED TO CONFORM

But what happens when society and its expectations interrupt this dance? When we are conditioned to conform to certain behaviors, thoughts, laws, works, or actions that don't match what we feel and believe to be right? When outside stimuli bombard our nervous and immune systems—stimuli like television and media, overcrowding, loud noise, video games, fast-moving apps and features on our mobile devices, a food supply loaded with sugar and preservatives, or the need to interconnect with every device known to man through the "Internet of

Things"? What happens when the very qualities that make us distinctly, beautifully human—self-determination, the ability to reason and create, compassion, emotional depth and love, willpower, spiritual insight, assessing right from wrong, holding different opinions and ideas while respecting those of others—are muted to the point that we look in the mirror one day and wonder who we've become?

In a way, that's where we stand socially today. We see the results all around us, beginning with a giant split in political and social sentiment—always a sign of unease in our collective hearts and souls. Millions are addicted to opioids, alcohol, gambling, sex, various drugs, work, and a host of other unhealthy outcomes. For many others, their senses of imagination, willpower, insight, *out*sight (seeing the world with clear eyes), and drive to succeed as individuals, families, and societies have been deeply impacted. More and more, we turn outside ourselves to look for quick fixes or solutions for our physical and emotional pain, feelings of alienation, loss of purpose and meaning, and loss of confidence in our social and political leaders. Why can't *they* improve the situation?

I am not a pessimistic person, but I am realistic. I find it really troubling, even dangerous, that institutions (such as education, industry, the government, schools, infrastructure, and corporations) pressure us to fit into their narrow conceptions of "normal" behavior and thought. This tough tug-of-war with our instinctive sense of self-expression plays out every day. While we struggle to express ourselves and make our mark in the world, daily life costs more, provides less, moves faster, takes up more of our time, cares less, bombards us with more messages, and leaves us with little time or energy to do what we need emotionally and physically—exercise, pray, be with family, read a book, vacation, eat properly, interact socially, and get outside more.

Consequently, nearly 120 million people in the United States take prescribed painkillers, stimulants, tranquilizers, and sedatives, according to the 2015 National Survey on Drug Use and Health.[1] Just a generation ago, that number was 30 million. A half-century ago, less than 1 percent of the population held prescriptions for what we now know as ADHD; now, that number is north of 7 percent for both children and adults, according to the CDC.[2]

THE UNDERLYING CAUSES

We're moving into a dire situation, which raises the question: When are we going to explore the underlying causes of ADHD and how they impact us, many of which I just listed out? The first stage is to dive deeper into the series of specific behaviors and conditions consistent with the diagnosis, rule out any other possible diagnoses or outcomes, and whittle down to a certain, conclusive diagnosis. That's what good medicine is about, right? Well, it is not quite happening like that; we're diagnosing and prescribing at an increasing rate. Note what behavioral psychologist Dr. Philip Hickey says in a May 2016 article, "ADHD: The Hoax Unravels," which appeared in *Behaviorism and Mental Health*: "At the risk of stating the obvious, ADHD is not an illness. Rather, it is an unreliable and disempowering label for a loose collection of arbitrarily chosen and vaguely defined behaviors. ADHD has been avidly promoted as an illness by pharma-psychiatry for the purpose of selling stimulant drugs."[3]

In 2015, AbleChild.org, an organization of parents for label- and drug-free education, put out a stunning list: "50 Conditions That Mimic ADHD."[4] Fifty conditions? I was highly skeptical at such a long list until I looked at it and realized something: it doesn't even cover everything! Some claim the figure is closer to one hundred comorbid conditions, to use the medical term. But let's stick with AbleChild.org's official list of fifty. When I overlay that list against the DSM-V checklist of nine predominant ADHD characteristics, I feel like I'm trying to identify distant constellations with a blurry telescope. It's no wonder many feel that ADHD, while a medically accepted mental health disorder, is also quite vague. As Dr. Hickey noted in his piece, "ADHD is defined by the presence of six or more habitual behaviors from either or both of two checklists of nine items each."[5] According to DSM-V, those items are

- excessive talking;
- trouble waiting his or her turn;
- constantly "on the go";
- often interrupts or intrudes;
- often unable to play or quietly take part in leisure activities (calling attention to oneself);

- easily distracted;
- inattentive;
- does not seem to listen when spoken to directly; and
- reluctant to do tasks that require sustained mental effort (lack of focus, concentration).

Now, let's look more closely at just ten of the fifty comorbid conditions cited by the CDC to illustrate the degree of overlap:

1. **Anxiety:** Anxiety, borne by stress, is one of society's biggest maladies. Inattentiveness, lack of focus, easy distraction, and excessive, nervous talking are typical signs. "Anxiety is often misdiagnosed as ADHD," says Dr. Jeffrey Hirschfield, a pediatrician for nearly twenty-five years at St. Petersburg General Hospital and Bayfront Medical Center in Florida, "but they are treated entirely differently."
2. **Autism:** Inattentiveness, and lack of focus/concentration, on all but one or two subjects or objects, regular social anxiety (see above), trouble waiting his or her turn, and not seeming to listen when spoken to—all part of a very real disorder that impacts one in sixty-eight North American children.
3. **Learning Disabilities:** Inability to focus at school or concentrate for long periods on schoolwork and homework, acting out, easily distracted, nervous talking, and frequent interrupting or intruding are typical.
4. **Vision Problems:** Convergence insufficiency (CI)—the inability to focus and coordinate both eyes on an object, such as a book page—disrupts kids and adults to the point that they mimic up to seven or eight of the nine ADHD characteristics. An eye exam and therapy can curtail CI—and spare years of living on ADHD meds. We'll get into this later.
5. **Hypoglycemia (low blood sugar):** What happens when you crave sweets? Typically, lack of focus, inattentiveness, anxiety, not waiting your turn, and distraction result. When it's full-blown hypoglycemia, these conditions are more present—and look a lot like ADHD.
6. **Sleep Disorders:** Since 1942, the average nightly sleep for North Americans has dropped more than a full hour, from 7.9 to

6.8, according to a December 2013 Gallup Poll.[6] If eight hours is recommended (many doctors consider seven hours a necessary minimum), then we're operating in a sleep-deprived culture. Sleep deprivation can affect us in ways that include nervous talking, inattentiveness, lack of concentration, impatience, frequent interruption, lack of listening, moodiness, and trouble focusing on long-period mental tasks. Sound like it could also be ADHD? Yes—except, it's not.

7. **Allergies:** This might not seem so obvious, but I list it because 15 to 20 percent of us suffer from some sort of allergy. When we're allergic to, say, food, our behaviors are often badly affected, displaying similar characteristics to those on the ADHD checklist. In 2010, when the Institute for Functional Medicine published a case study on an ADHD patient, one of the most exhaustive studies of the inner workings of an ADHD case I've ever seen, they directly cited food, home, and environmental allergies as a causative factor in the diagnosis.[7]

8. **Post-Traumatic Stress Disorder (PTSD):** One of the great medical stories of the past ten years (though sadly spurred on by war injuries, spousal and child abuse) has been the increased ability to diagnose PTSD. However, six of the nine ADHD characteristics are present in those with PTSD—and it's very hard to tell the difference between an agitated person with PTSD and one being treated for ADHD.

9. **Vitamin B Deficiencies:** Let's look at the central problem of poor eating habits—or lack of nutrients in our food. Inattention, hyperactivity, impulsivity, sleep disorders, lack of focus/concentration, acting out, and the inability to play or take part in leisure activities can quietly result from faulty neurotransmitters in the brain, the outcome of vitamin B deficiencies. If you noticed, I just wrote almost the entire ADHD checklist. I cover nutrition more in chapter 15.

10. **Early Onset Bipolar Disorder:** This is a very serious chemical imbalance in the brain and is sometimes life-threatening. Medication is not only required but often means the difference between life and death for more serious bipolar disorder cases. Yet, did you know that 85 percent of children with early onset bipolar disorder also meet the criteria for ADHD? And that ADHD

stimulant medication is the *worst* thing one with bipolar disorder can take?[8] The biggest trip wire between the two concerns mood swings. We often think of adult bipolar disorder, where manic periods can last hours, days, or weeks—but in a child, it can happen many times within a day, a condition known as rapid cycling.

Now, I'll go another step deeper into my own life and show how just two of these indicators—impulsive behavior and lack of focus—have hampered me at various times. Do they mean I have ADHD? No. Would they be cause for writing an ADHD prescription? Easily. In fact, as we lay out further, many parents get ADHD prescriptions for their school-aged kids specifically so they can focus and work better at school.

I've been an impulsive person at times. I have spontaneously ended relationships, quit jobs, switched from college to university in Canada (from practical learning to more of an academic setting) and taken many other impulsive actions during mood swings that drove me into literal exhaustion and my loved ones nearly out of my life (a couple of times, they did). We all have moments when we're stressed or realize that something just isn't the right choice, but I have definitely been more impulsive than the average person. I've had dozens of jobs and relationships, and declared a lot of things I was "going to achieve," yet most efforts end with a snap decision to do something else, or see someone else, due to boredom or a lack of self-confidence and identity.

Another classic symptom is "daydreaming," being distracted easily. Ever since I can remember, I've shown a lack of interest in tasks I wasn't passionate about, focusing instead on those that I loved. The daydreaming came into play when I was forced to sit through classes in which I had no personal interest. Often, I got into trouble by joking around with a classmate or reading bodybuilding magazines in class (I was an avid weightlifter). Teachers often didn't know what to do with me, nor did my family—when they weren't busy fighting with each other, which contributed to my feelings of high anxiety and lack of security, major challenges unto themselves.

Finally, "hyperfocus" is another common trait of ADHDers—yet any of us can be very focused on a task, even to the point of obsessing over it. For over ten years, I was obsessed with my goal of going from a jail cell to proving myself, clearing my name, and being an armored car guard. When self-worth is sought externally (as opposed to a healthy sense of self), people tend to focus on "outward" goals measured by degrees, salary amounts, size of home, money in the bank, the type of person we date, and the car we drive—all that superficial, materialistic stuff that can't truly bring us peace.

All of the traits I just described come from early trauma, the resulting anxiety, and an obsession with proving myself to everyone *but* myself. I now know this—but it took forty years to figure it out. That's a long time, but it didn't have to be that way. Did I hear about it from a doctor, or discuss it during the exam when I was diagnosed with ADHD? No. It never came up. I had to figure it out on my own, which I was able to do through a lot of trial and error, but I believe our doctors should be better versed in the deeper issues that lie beneath behaviors or symptoms. While I realize it is a tall order in today's hyperactive ADHD diagnostic environment, it's precisely *through* slowing down the rapidity with which we diagnose new cases that we can help people recognize what lies within them. If we don't start working from this more thoughtful, humanistic approach in the doctor's office, these causes will become so deeply ingrained, so insidious within us, that we may never fully work through them. The key is to adopt a practice in which we learn more about ourselves, never stop learning, and continually grow. I address this further in the book, but it serves society and this ADHD "epidemic" for this process to begin when a child or adult visits a doctor when he or she feels they can't concentrate or pay attention—rather than a quick "diagnose-and-prescribe" visit.

THE ADHD UMBRELLA CHECKLIST

No lasting solution to our "ADHD explosion" can be found in these checklists, or in how diagnoses are rendered or prescriptions written. What *can* result is getting lost between disorders, at the expense of finding out the causes. Take this response by Anne Schuchat, principal deputy director of the CDC, to a *Washington Post* reporter's question about using applied behavior analysis (ABA) therapy—a therapy for autism patients—to address many ADHD behaviors: "We don't believe the same interventions for autism should be used for children with

ADHD."[9] While ABA therapy is not prescription-based, it still squares with our central problem: distinguishing ADHD from other conditions. But what if we *can* use ABA and other compassion-based behavioral therapy to treat ADHD without involving medication?

I had a very frustrating experience dealing with doctors until 2015, when I met Dr. Royer, as well as a cutting-edge optometrist, Dr. Patrick Quaid. They helped me begin to dig into the greater truth of my life struggles. I can tell you that the DSM-V checklist, the main ticket to ADHD diagnosis for clinicians, *does not provide insight into the root causes at all*. However, the way we have functioned as human beings since our beginnings on this planet does. So does the way our society and world function today, in a hurry and driven by technology, living in what Tony Schwartz, coauthor of *The Way We're Working Isn't Working*, calls "our addiction to distraction."[10] When studies like the one from the University of Virginia, presented at the Human-Computer Interaction Conference in May 2016, and a University of British Columbia study with 221 millennials, tie smartphone notifications to ADHD-like symptoms,[11] reviewing cross-hatched checklists alone gets us nowhere. And yet, that's where well-meaning parents, educators, doctors, and employers start and stop. I'd like to change that.

THE WAY WE'RE WIRED

How do we function as human beings today? Have you thought about that? And how did we function as human beings before we domesticated animals and food? Before we created communities and built structures? Before ships, wagons, trains, and cars? Before the Age of Reason and the Industrial Revolution? Before the Space Age? Before the Internet? Ever since we separated from our prehuman ancestors by standing on two legs and developing reason, intellect, willpower, and the ability to separate right from wrong, we've navigated this world with some basic skills that have served us well.

While the generations, their achievements, and ways of life have differed tremendously, one thing always remains the same: what lies at the heart of our every moment, a state of presence, in-the-moment awareness. "When we were hunter-gatherers, we were astutely aware of ourselves and everything around us, constantly present, constantly alert," Thom Hartmann told my coauthor in a 2003 interview. "We had what I call a 360-degree worldview. Everything existed in relationship to everything else. I believe the 360-degree worldview is our natural way of being."[12]

Another way to describe this is *complete attentiveness*. You're paying attention to everything around you, yet focusing on the very next thing that needs to take place. It is the state of *presence*, of being present. Writers, poets, artists, and musicians exhibit this constantly when they work, as do great athletes. One of the greatest tributes given to music superstar Prince after he died in April 2016 (sadly, of an accidental opioid overdose) was recognition of his undivided attention to his craft. Many things changed in Prince's life, but never his devotion to music. In a society that practices 360-degree awareness and thinking, such as a tribal culture or artistic community, this ability to remain attuned to one's personal mission and excellence while life circumstances swirl about is worth celebrating. It's also worth remembering and adapting into our own lives. For all but our most recent history on Earth, though, this is how we lived, survived, and evolved. *All of us* exhibited complete attentiveness. We had to. We were prey if we didn't.

That changed when we began compartmentalizing. The first stages took place thousands of years ago, when we shifted from hunter-gatherer to agricultural societies and began forming communities with shelters, fences, and later, walls. Nomadic encampments became communities. We built structures that separated us from the elements—and one another. We conveyed our thoughts into pictures and words. We gave names and labels to medicines, diseases, plants, animals, objects, and everything else under the sun. Once deeply attuned to nature and those around us—socializing for the sake of the group or community and playing until our legs gave way—we began to fragment our attention. We formed societies, wrote laws to govern our tribes and those outside them, and created religions based on our interpretations of spiritual law. We systematically detribalized. And here we are, deeply fragmented as a culture, society, and within ourselves. No wonder we need something to improve our level of focus!

Next, we created schools—first one-room, all-subjects schoolhouses (there's that 360-degree mind-set), then the Industrial Age formula of shaping schools to educate tomorrow's factory workers. That was (and is) the core model of public schools. Our ability to play and communicate with each other eroded as social demands increased. Our most essential structure, the tribe, began to fall apart, including its present-day model, the family.

What was the net psychological and spiritual result of becoming a more "civilized" society? We might have gained organized religion, convenience, intellect, technology, and other spoils of the twenty-first century. However, we have lost connection with something much more vital—our essential nature, our spirits, our souls. It suggests a plunge into the Biblical admonition in the Gospel of Matthew, "Ye cannot serve both God and mammon." We cannot feed our deeper spiritual selves if we continue to pour ourselves into the million and one things that catch our eyes and fetch our attention in everyday life. We are innately spiritual beings, fed by the same force that grows the universe. When we lose touch with that, we become fragmented, always yearning for "something else" or "something better" or "the next great thing."

Rather than diving deeper into our inner spiritual beings, where so many of our forebears found solace, we individually and collectively adjusted to the increasing regimentation of our lives. We also turned over some (or all) of our authority, our personal power, to others (employers, religious leaders, government officials, teachers, doctors, etc.). Some did not. Others fragmented in a major way from doing so. They tried to live in today's world and its demands in that 360-degree mindset, and because they couldn't adjust, it did not work. People with ADD and ADHD often find it difficult to fit into our cultural norms and especially school structures. Does that mean they have a disorder? A disease? Or are they, to revisit the phrase uttered a century ago by poet Robert Service, "a race of men who can't sit still"?[13]

In backtracking our journey to the beginning of humankind, we can see a few subjects I will address in the next chapter: loss of core tribal/family structure; reduced parenting time; reduced movement and exercise; an ever-changing environment that makes forming attachments and deep attentiveness difficult; addiction to distraction; and an increase in pent-up energy. Out of them, a truly troublesome picture emerges, one we're now feeding with medication despite the fact that a more lasting solution, the one that can lift us from this mess, is something far different.

4

OPTIMAL HEALTH, INTERRUPTED

Decoding ADHD (Part Two)

"Get a snack, do your homework, then go out and play until dinnertime!"

Most of us over thirty-five can still hear this command from the memory banks of our childhoods, along with the voice of the mother or father who delivered it. We came home from school, dropped off our books, raided the refrigerator, and then unleashed ourselves into neighborhoods or towns filled with backyard fences, friends, basketball courts, bicycles, garden hoses to drink from, friends' parents and siblings, and the like. We played, talked, rode bikes, built forts, rode skateboards, listened to our favorite music, told or read stories, or any one of a hundred other things. We ran in and out of friends' houses and yards almost like they were our own. If dinnertime came and we were still playing—which happened, since time often passed unnoticed—our parents simply called neighbors' houses until they'd tracked us down. Then we went home. On other days, we played multiple sports, attended dance or music classes, Boy Scouts, Girl Scouts, the Boys and Girls Club, YMCA, or other extracurricular programs that contributed to the upbringing of generations of societies.

Nothing special, right? It's a typical childhood, repeated one generation to another. You find within it core, ordinary values: consistent family life, sense of community (friends and neighbors), face-to-face interaction, flexibility and adaptation (play activities can change a dozen

times a day), playing with others, working with others, forming attachments and friendships, fresh air, and exercise.

KIDS TODAY

So, where has all of this gone? Today, kids spend more time looking at
screens of various types and less time beneath or climbing trees of
various types. While many kids of the 1970s through the 1990s were
latchkey kids, staying home alone and entertaining themselves while
one or both parents worked, more and more of today's kids are *never*
left alone. Or, if they are alone, they are consumed by their devices.
Many lack the basic skills of being responsible for themselves, but
they've learned to tune out parents as well—again through staying at
home and resorting to screens, video games, and the like. The time they
spend on screens almost boggles the mind. In October 2015, *The Atlantic* magazine reported on a *BMC Public Health* journal report,[1] an
Australian study of more than two thousand students; it was the first
time scientists looked at kids' use of media. It stated 46 percent of third-
grade boys spend more than two hours a day on screens—the American
Association of Pediatrics (AAP) recommendation for maximum screen
time. Jump to ninth grade, and the number is 70 percent. Girls were
even bigger users, going from 43 percent of third graders to over 90
percent of ninth graders tuning in for more than two hours a day.

How much more? A lot. In 2015, British market research firm
Childwise reported that children ages five to sixteen spend, on average,
six and a half hours per day in front of screens—more than double the
1995 figure of three hours, when TV was still the primary screen. Teenaged boys spend *eight hours* per day in front of screens, with teenaged
girls right behind them at seven hours.[2] Later in 2015, CNN reported
the teen screen-time rate was nine hours per day.[3] Worse, their multi-
screening has gone way up, watching two or more screens (mainly TVs,
mobile devices, video game consoles, and computer screens) at the
same time, a sure indicator of divided attention or "split focus," as some
psychologists call it. This data only gets more troublesome: a 2011 *New
York Times* article reported that kids aged two years and under spend
fifty-three minutes per day on screens, and 24 percent of children aged
two to four work on computers daily. It also found that 64 percent of

eight-year-olds from poorer homes (average income under $30,000) had TVs in their rooms, while 30 percent of those from higher-income homes did. This rapid rise in screen time comes despite ten years of warnings from the AAP, added the *New York Times* report.[4] And still we wonder why our kids don't pay attention as much, behave as well, focus as strongly, complete tasks as thoroughly, play as much, or remain in good physical condition.

When I speak on social media networks and in person with thought leaders in child care, psychiatry, and behavioral and mental health issues (on both sides of the ADHD argument), I can't help but ask over and over, Why have we relinquished our sense of community? Why have we given up on our kids' playtime? How is this impacting our kids today?

A single statistic that should concern all of us: in 1980, when the playtime scene that opened this chapter was as common as January snowfall in Toronto (and when ADHD was first classified and defined in DSM-III), the percentage of kids being medically treated for hyperactivity (as ADHD was previously known) was just climbing north of 2 percent. Ten years later, in 1991, when methylphenidate began to take off as the ADD/ADHD prescription of choice, that number was 2.5 percent. Flash forward to 2003: the number jumped to 7.8 percent—*it tripled in twelve years!* In 2015, according to the National Center of Health Statistics, it sat at 13 percent, with no decline in sight. "There was an almost 8-fold increase in ADHD prevalence in the United States compared with rates from 40 years ago," *The Psychiatric Times* reported.[5] Why is this happening? Are we diagnosing better? Noticing it more readily? Understanding symptoms better, as is the case with the autism spectrum?

Certainly, we have a standard diagnostic checklist that is part and parcel of every clinician's or pediatrician's office—the checklist put out by the American Psychiatric Association in DSM-V. As *Mother Jones* noted in a 2015 article on skyrocketing diagnoses, that checklist makes it possible for doctors to diagnose the patient with a "10- to 15-minute [doctor's office] visit," which leads to a long-term diagnosis and prescription.[6] Also, much of it is attributed to the changes in 1999 that allowed pharmaceutical companies to directly advertise their products to consumers and sell directly to doctors in addition to their usual market, the pharmacies. Advertising sells—and has it ever! We not only accept the advertising claims, but adopt a belief that we cannot improve without these pharmaceutical solutions. Many *need* medication—but many really do not. We are also quick to determine that "something's wrong" and label it if our health or behavior is less than perfect.

In my opinion, all of these attributes behind the rapid rise in ADHD diagnoses blur a deeper truth. Yes, there are kids and adults who really do possess problematic attention deficit and/or hyperactivity disorder. Medication does help them focus better and stabilize their behavior. However, medication should *never* be the only intervention or treatment, since the other 90 percent (so to speak) is day-to-day lifestyle and self-awareness. However, millions more—what Dr. Royer believes to be half the diagnosed cases—have been swept up by one of the biggest medical tsunamis we've ever seen: the rush to diagnose and prescribe on the ADHD label.

Along with this rise comes a corresponding decline in the dynamics and qualities that define families, tribes, communities, and neighborhoods. While crime has largely dropped in North America, as I just pointed out, TV, video game, computer, and mobile device usage has shot through the roof, and with that, socializing and interacting has plummeted. Why talk with someone face to face when you can text, email, FaceTime, or Skype them? Many corporations find themselves holding seminars in basic communication skills to incoming millennial workers, skills that kids of earlier generations learned naturally by talking to each other and playing together. Child and adult obesity has gone from "a few overweight kids in class" to a North American epidemic, with rates exceeding 35 percent in some states.[7] Parents have less time than ever to spend with their kids. A Department of Commerce statistic bears this out: in 1980, 32.4 percent of two-parent families had both parents working full or part-time; in 2009, that figure was 53.9 percent. Furthermore, the percentage of single-parent families jumped from 18 percent in 1980 to 25.8 percent in 2008, according to the U.S. Census Bureau.[8] Consequently, outside playtime, sports and extracurricular participation, and parent-child quality time have fallen. Their replacement? Screens that both babysit and endlessly enthrall and stimulate kids' minds, with pictures and scenes that change every few seconds. Folks, when a kid absorbs that kind of stimulation with such short-burst intervals, guess what happens to their attention span? And what are their reactions when people try to turn them off?

Here's the part that scares the hell out of me, and should scare anyone raising kids today: *You can plot the decline of playtime and sense of community, and the increase in working parent ratios, to the rise of ADHD diagnoses and prescription sales.* It is that obvious, that startling, and, until quite recently, played down by the medical profession and media. That has frustrated me to no end, since I try my best to help people from all walks of life recognize the quickly increasing trend of seeking a "quick-fix" that does all of us a disservice.

REDUCED MOVEMENT LEADS TO PENT-UP ENERGY

From childhood into my early teen years, I played organized youth hockey at the highest level. Besides the thrill of competition, of being good at my national sport, and of winning and losing, organized hockey kept me out of trouble for several years. It also taught me invaluable life lessons I still hold dear: the value of working as a team toward a common goal, sportsmanship, patience, determination, and appreciation for travel—not to mention getting out of the house on a regular basis. The activity interested me, an escape of sorts from the boring, mundane existence of junior high, and, even more, high school. Then, when I was in grade 10, something else seized my attention—weightlifting. So I jumped into that headlong, and it became my home-away-from-home, my community, my network of friends and positive influences. It was my way of moving forward.

Focus is everything in ice hockey, as with all other sports. So is movement, constant movement. When I was on the ice, moving and being in sync with my teammates, that was my world. During a game, my attention was absolute, every thought connected to a movement, every movement to a decision, every decision to an outcome. If I slide left, I'll stop the puck. If I try to dive and make a glove save, I might not—and I had a tenth of a second to decide. I loved that!

Hockey also put me into a positive, healthy, team-oriented environment, away from my often-toxic home life. During practices and games, I could focus on something other than the emotional abuse I was suffering at home. I wasn't obsessed with trying to please my mother while fighting the self-doubt inside me. While my growing anxiety and super-intense nervous system, worsened by ongoing trauma and my mother's genetics, eventually prevailed, hockey was my healthiest activity for many years.

In the end, that same anxiety caused me to overthink things, to stress to no end, paralyzing my mind (paralysis = no movement) to the point that I was exhausted and allowing bad goals at times. That fed my self-loathing, resulting in a pattern I would come to repeat time and time again: self-sabotage. I hurt my progress and burned tons of bridges in life before finally recognizing, at a deeper level, what I had done. In every case, I can say that my life stopped still, and I forgot how to move forward in a healthy, empowering way.

My point is that getting into the habit of movement and physical activity early in life often leads to lifelong health, just as instilling the love of learning in a kid leads to a high-achieving, constantly learning adult. Not only is it needed for physical health, but it also helps us weather the storms that inevitably come our way as adults.

Take a friend of mine from the United States. He excelled in youth baseball and tennis, ran track, spent his twenties and thirties surfing, skiing, and hiking mountain ranges. He then returned to running in his early forties and ran five Boston Marathons. He now coaches high school track and cross-country and teaches worldwide. All of this after being bounced from school psychologist to psychiatrist as a young teen by his loving, well-intentioned parents, and from prescription to pre-scription (a stimulant, then an antidepressant, then a tranquilizer, then drugs for severe mood disorders and even *schizophrenia*). Why? His parents had no idea what to do with his seeming hyperactivity, shifting moods, creative and emotional intensity, and *pent-up energy*. Doctors didn't provide any answers that didn't involve medication—which his parents were always skeptical of.

His grandmother, however, knew what to do: channel his creativity and energy into positive actions. In the past forty-plus years, he's had *two* medical prescriptions, one for an inflammation, the other a post-surgery pain med. In today's diagnostic culture, my friend most certain-ly would have been diagnosed as ADHD, and put on meds.

Our need to move and to play goes back a long, long way. In his 2009 bestselling book *Born to Run,* Christopher McDougall made a compel-ling scientific case that the separation point between early human be-ings and protohumans—including Neanderthals—came from how we killed our prey.[9] We used crude weapons, to be sure, but mainly, we ran it down, literally, by exhausting it over hours of pursuit. Those traits have stayed in our DNA ever since, which explains how, out of virtually every species in the animal kingdom, we are the most naturally active.

Zooming forward, we find in activity and movement important dynamics that fly in the face of our ADHD profile. They include total engagement and attention to the activity at hand, release of nervous energy, healthy bodies, fueled by diets that sustain them, and self-esteem and self-worth. We are also largely more focused on our jobs or in school. (Teachers, have you noticed how students pay better attention in class after recess, usually a quick burst of physical activity, rather than lunch, when they eat and tend to sit around?) Where there's movement, there's focus. Where there's movement, there's a release of anxiety, tension, and stress—leaving body and mind freed up to hold onto less and achieve more. Finally, where there's movement, there tends to be community—people working out together, sports teams hanging out together, social lives enhanced.

Now let's look at pent-up energy, which can hatch all sorts of outcomes, many of them negative and all of them featuring some characteristic of clinical ADHD. I'll start with my own experience, which, like most of us, begins at the beginning of school. From elementary school to my first couple years of high school, I was known for talking and "doing my own thing" during class. In grade 3, I used to laugh uncontrollably with a classmate. For whatever reason, we'd look at each other, and that was it—his smiling face made me laugh, as horrible as that sounds. (He was funny to me!) The same thing happened a couple years later with my best friend. I got a real kick out of making him laugh, because I loved the sound he'd make, which would in turn make me "lose it." Then the teacher would yell at both of us (but mostly me, since I had quite a reputation by then).

My lack of interest in classes resulted in several failing grades, detentions, and even a couple schoolyard fights. There were subplots happening in school all the time, which provided me with the distractions I sought from unbearably boring classes such as math, English, and others. This led to a worsened sense of self-esteem and self-worth.

My case is more the norm than the exception. It outlines the first challenge we face with pent-up energy: do we start school too early? To me, this can become a primary cause of early behaviors that fall under the ADHD label. I'm not alone, either. "The Gift of Time? School

Starting Age and Mental Health," a study by the National Bureau of Economic Research[10] released on October 26, 2015, opened by stating, "In many developed countries, children now begin their formal schooling at an older age. . . .We find that a one-year delay in the start of school dramatically reduces inattention/hyperactivity at age 7. . . . We also find that this large and targeted effect persists at age 11." The study was funded after a 2013 article in *The New Yorker*, "Youngest Kid, Smartest Kid?," brought renewed focus onto the subject. The report goes on to say that kids who start school later (known as "redshirting") perform better on standardized tests *and* pay greater attention in the classroom. (This is not to be confused with the other form of "redshirting," when college coaches hold back athletes for a year so they will grow bigger and be more competitive in sports.) "The capabilities of a child's brain increase at a rapid pace; the difference between five- and six-year-olds is far greater than between twenty-five and twenty-six-year-olds," the article states.[11]

Yet, the same article goes on to say that evidence is strong that starting school *younger* produces kids with greater academic and eventual life standing. When it comes to academic achievement, this argument breaks both ways.

What about *social* skills? *Developmental* skills? The ability to handle stress and anxiety? We send kids into supercharged preschool environments at ages two and three, places where enrollment competition can be as fierce as any private school or college. Everybody wants to raise a superstar, and these young upstarts certainly launch in that direction early on—but at what price to the kid?

Here is where pent-up energy comes in. We spend our first few years growing, developing, playing, and exploring our world. We're open-ended. We play until we're exhausted and learn by discovering and figuring out things (and watching our parents and older brothers and sisters, of course). Our parents will add to the experience by reading books to us until we can read them ourselves—and what are we doing when they're reading to us? Stretching our legs, grabbing our toes, maybe running around to emulate the character in the story we're listening to. *Always moving.* We're on a pretty simple schedule: When we're hungry, we eat. When we're tired, we sleep. When we want to read, or be read to, it happens. When we play alone in our rooms, or with our playground friends, it can go on for hours.

Then, at age five or six, *wham!* The door closes. The classroom door, that is. Suddenly, we're dropped into a regulated environment. We're made to sit in desks that are not so comfortable. We're told to sit until the teacher says it's OK to stand, go to recess, or go to the bathroom. And, if we can't see or hear as well as the kid next to us, we're really screwed. Suddenly, instead of sitting, running, jumping, sleeping, eating, reading, or otherwise playing to the natural rhythms of our bodies, we're on a regimented schedule where we sit for four to seven hours during the day—and can only release ourselves in small blocks of time, for example, recess and lunch. Some of us adjust. For others, our ability to function ideally is impaired, and teachers do notice. One of the bellwether "tells" for a potential ADHD situation is impaired functioning; it often supersedes all the other items on the DSM-V checklist. Why? Because when our function is impaired, we become frustrated, irritable, and lose our confidence. Our work suffers; our behavior suffers; our social abilities suffer. Numerous parents have reported getting their kids on low doses of ADHD meds, not because their kids are nine-point matches, but because their normal function is impaired. I would say much of that is the inability of a small child to make that abrupt adjustment from constant playtime to sitting still for four to six hours every day in a regulated environment.

Think about it. What happens when you bottle up energy not meant to be bottled? It puts pressure on the container—which then explodes. What happens to the five-, six-, or seven-year-old faced with this situation? Exactly what happens to millions of young schoolchildren diagnosed with early ADHD—fidgeting, talking and acting out in class, a growing lack of focus and attention, surly behavior, a growing inability or unwillingness to follow directions, the early effects of pent-up energy, and impaired function.

According to a 2016 article in *ADDitude* magazine, boys with ADHD move around the room eight times as much as "normal" kids, and are four times as fidgety when seated for psychological testing.[12] What do you think is behind this? I'll hazard a very educated guess: pent-up energy, along with dietary concerns, which I discuss later.

I know this feeling all too well—even today, some thirty years after I was one of those kids. When I was bored with a subject, I would go nuts mentally—I still do. So do many of us in our own ways. That sure doesn't mean we have ADHD, but when you're seven, or you're the concerned parent of a fidgety seven-year-old, try telling that to a school nurse, doctor, or administrator in today's diagnostic climate! Chances are, they've already bagged and tagged your kid as ADHD, and they may well put pressure on you to medicate the kid *so he or she can stay in school*—all because of pent-up energy with no release. That's a sad cop-out, for many reasons. Yes, something needs to be done about constant disruptions in class so that kids of all ages can learn, but the rushed labeling has got to go; it has become as much of a problem as the acting out itself—a dangerous problem to the health of millions of kids and adults, frankly.

Pent-up energy is also behind so many behavioral and social problems for adults, including those medicating for ADHD. If left unchecked, or without the right release strategies, it doesn't just go away. Instead, a preponderance of pent-up energy in the body slows down our metabolism, allows toxins to build in the body (unable to flush through sweat pores from exercise, for example), and, over time, creates health risks we never imagined having. According to the CDC and American Psychiatric Association, health issues such as obesity, heart disease, diabetes, hypertension, anxiety and mood disorder (ranging from moderate to life-threatening), lack of productivity, relationship issues, and antisocial behavior derive from lack of proper exercise and diet, and undue build-up of stress—the result of not moving and exercising, and allowing stress and toxins to build inside our bodies. Of course, there are genetic factors, but I'm focusing on what is preventable by each of us. Pent-up energy has turned millions of people into walking mini-volcanoes. Put them together, and you have a huge "supervolcano," such as the sleeping mega-giant beneath Yellowstone National Park in Wyoming. People vent individually, of course, but imagine what would happen if they all vented at once? I don't know if you watched the 2016 U.S. presidential campaign, but without casting opinions on either candidate, it's safe to say we saw America venting en masse.

You want to see ADHD diagnoses decline and prescription mania settle to a low roar? We have to get a handle on pent-up energy, or rather, educate thoroughly on how to release it. That begins with *moving again*. Long-time educator Susan Dermond, author of *Calm and Compassionate Children: A Handbook* (a staple in many progressive classrooms), put it succinctly when we spoke with her, "The enemy of depression and ADHD is *purposeful movement*. It's like lighting a candle in a dark room. The darkness flees. Depression and fidgeting flee with purposeful movement."[13]

How do we release the pent-up energy? Let's go back to solutions proposed by the *ADDitude* article: "The number one thing teachers can do to help ADHD students squirm and fidget less is to provide *physical outlets* (emphasis mine) that let them regularly release pent-up energy and improve focus."[14] The article lists a few easy activities that benefit everyone involved: sending the kid on more errands; letting them stand and walk around between lessons; using exercise balls instead of chairs and handling objects like squish balls, to keep the mind focused on class while part of the body moves. In other words, *bring movement back into the equation.*

Note how closely that corresponds to positive ways we can release pent-up energy as adults, now being presented as a way to offset sedentary behavior and lifestyle: stand and move at least once an hour; work at standing desks; exercise at lunch; walk ten thousand steps a day; get outside more and practice moving meditations. See the resemblance?

What about pent-up *mental energy?* One characteristic of those diagnosed with ADHD (among other disorders) is the nonstop motor running in their brains. Not only are our brains like the drum-pounding bunny from those memorable battery commercials, but we also *outlast* that iconic bunny! We can dream up, concoct, brainstorm, imagine, and cook up infinite possibilities and tangents in these universes contained between our ears—and then we can analyze and overanalyze them until we become pent-up, frustrated messes. Part of why we can't sit still is that our brains never take a break! If we don't have substantial outlets for that energy, we are in big trouble. Look at a man who surely would have been an ADHD kid in today's world, Thomas Edison. Imagine if he'd never expressed the ideas that led to his thousands of inventions— and the tens of thousands of failed experiments that came before? Would we have lights? Recorded sound? Motion pictures? Probably, but it wouldn't have happened as soon.

WHY BRAINSTORMING IS A SOLUTION, NOT A PROBLEM

This leads me to brainstorming—and how it's viewed. Smart, creative teachers and bosses see brainstorming as our chance to unleash an idea with reckless abandon and take it on the grand tour of its possibilities. This is where innovations, major changes, scientific and creative break-throughs, and disruptions in thought, technology, science, the arts, and society come from—brainstorming without being held back. Most often, though, we're told to "stay on subject." Color between the lines. Get from point A to point B—and don't deviate. Complete the assignment as instructed. Only read what's on the approved reading list. As adults, we hear this cautionary, limiting language in other ways: "Follow the rules." "Stick to the job description." "Management comes up with the ideas." "Think you have a better approach? Go somewhere else."

Consequently, millions of us are socially and professionally conditioned not to brainstorm. We're told to "bottle it up," "keep your ideas to yourself," "stay inside the box," "play within the system" and "leave it to the experts." Talk about the ultimate case of pent-up energy! Somehow, those who want to keep a lid on us as a people and society have succeeded in large measure in turning "brainstorming" and "creative expression" into four-letter words. The ADHD stimulant meds tend to bottle up human creativity, that which makes us unique, distinctive, and different from others. So are the brain-drains and distractions of our daily world—almost anything with a screen, for example. Then we have the messaging of many government officials, corporate executives, educators, and doctors alike. Rather than promoting the mental acuity of those who think outside the box (really, most of us *are* outside the box; what is "outside the box" but a euphemism for "bringing my individual gifts and abilities to bear"?), we as a society prefer to play it safe, listening only to "conventional wisdom." We call those with great, wild, free-flowing, brainstorming minds who don't succeed "insane," while those who change the world are known as "geniuses." As Oscar Wilde once said, "The public is incredibly tolerant. It forgives everything—except genius."

We are messing with gunpowder and a match by bottling up a kid's (or an adult's) ability to brainstorm or to think in areas outside his or her comfort zone—especially those of us whose brains are always moving in fifth gear. And I believe that much prescribing of ADHD meds for adults is for precisely this reason—because we've got storms running through our brains, without the ability to creatively brainstorm. Meds stop the storm—but they can also mute the creative side. When we're in this "stormy brain" space, we're unhappy, depressed, moody, inattentive, unhealthy, often manic, and antisocial. There's that damned nine-point checklist rearing its head again! In fact, I believe we have millions of potentially gifted geniuses muted by ADHD meds—and very poor messaging when it comes to allowing them to express their minds.

I'll use myself as an example. I love to fidget when I'm brainstorming. Why do I love it? Because brainstorming is *really fun* and I do it better while moving around! All possibilities, outcomes, roles, rules, and levels are on the table. Think of the best books, pieces of music, video games, works of art, science-fiction epics, or things like walking on the moon, exploring the deepest part of the sea, creating great fashion lines—or building future-forward cars, like Teslas or driverless vehicles. All of it started with a thought, which developed an idea, which mush-roomed into a concept, which blew through a mind as a brainstorm— *and then was expressed.*

We all like to brainstorm differently. I've found that sitting in an office chair that offers movement (there's that word again), or sitting in a comfortable chair in a relaxed, non-pressured setting, is where I do my best brainstorming, my most significant creative work. That and the shower! In the office, I love whiteboards—and different colors of dry-erase markers!—and I either move around, or swing around slowly in my office chair while in meetings, pen in mouth, arms over my head, relaxed, and envisioning the next step in whatever we're discussing. Ideas pop up, take root, and flow; they "arrive" because I'm not forcing them. Even the title *Beyond ADHD* came while I was relaxed and contemplative. Sure, I was pondering a title for this book, but not in a self-pressured way. I know myself well enough not to even start forcing it. As far as paper goes, I love using mind maps, especially since I'm a big-picture kind of thinker.

Only when we're *relaxed* do our creativity brainwaves come out to play. I work best as long as I'm not pressured. Many people are not at their best creatively when the nervous system is amped up, another *huge* reason why ADHD stimulants can be damaging to those diag-nosed with the hyper- versus hypoactive variety of the disorder. They might focus us, but they also ramp up the nervous system, as Dr. Royer made clear to me during my work with him. He also pointed out the difference in brain waves between creative brainstorming—a good use of the overstimulated mind; and fidgeting and being inattentive—a neg-ative outcome of the same. Slow brain waves lead to tuning out, loss of attention, becoming unfocused. Give them something to brainstorm, something that impassions or excites them, and *presto*—the sensorimotor rhythm increases and the fast beta waves kick in.

That very thing happened with Dr. Joel Lubar and his team at Zone Performance Psychology in Edmonton, Alberta. They performed fifty-minute trainings with visual and audio feedback with 250 attention-deficit kids, using EEGs to monitor brain waves. More than 80 percent of those kids showed much higher concentration and performance levels from activities that stimulated their minds and triggered brainstorm experiences. In all cases, the kids were reported *to be relaxed*; after all, the exercises on the computer amounted to fun mental adventures! Their concentration increased, their hyperactivity decreased, their creative brain waves sped up, and their performance levels rose by an average of 1.5 grades. All from a guided exercise that promoted creative brainstorming.[15]

Playing, sense of community and belonging, moving, dealing with pent-up energy, brainstorming—such simple, natural things that, until the emergence of psychology and psychiatry, were never mentioned as something that could be "wrong." We practiced all of them naturally, every day. However, our very desire to limit them *has* created something very wrong—a society that, increasingly, can't sit still, can't pay attention, behaves more poorly than ever, and must always find distraction, not to mention medicating much of our future creative potential away.

5

SO EASY TO DIAGNOSE, SO TRICKY TO UNDERSTAND

Following my sessions and follow-ups with Dr. Royer, I found myself tracking back to the beginning, to what started my five-year roller-coaster ride with ADHD and eventually compelled me to drive to Detroit: my original diagnoses in 2010 and 2011, and how my doctors arrived at it. Then I asked myself a bigger question: how can 20 million people now be diagnosed with ADHD when, as recently as 2000, only a few million diagnosed cases existed?

THE CURRENT DIAGNOSTIC PROCESS

When you have so many people being diagnosed for a single disorder, and that diagnosis leads to prescriptions as a first-resort therapy in 75 percent of the cases, according to the Centers for Disease Control and Prevention (CDC),[1] both diagnosis and treatment should be clear and unambiguous, right? That's not the way it is with ADHD. In fact, the current diagnostic process, and its use by doctors, teachers, nurses, behavioral psychologists, psychiatrists, neurologists, neuroscientists, pharmaceutical manufacturers, and other concerned parties, reminds me of how widely we interpret the same piece of music. If you and I put on a Beethoven symphony or a rock album, we will listen and evaluate differently. We will have different experiences. We may begin with preconceived notions of the composer, musicians, or type of music. If we listen on headphones with a splitter cord in order to hear the piece simultaneously, you may pick up on tonalities and subtleties that I will not. If we're listening to Beethoven, I might define the piece by the piano, while you focus on the backing instruments. If it's rock, I may dive into the guitar solo while you enjoy the singing and lyrics. We emerge with two entirely different experiences—different diagnoses, if you will—of what stood out and moved us.

Welcome to the clinical reality of ADHD, circa 2017. DSM-V defines ADHD as "a persistent pattern of inattention and/or hyperactivity-impulsivity that interferes with functioning or development, has symptoms presenting in two or more settings (e.g., at home, school, or work; with friends or relatives; in other activities), and negatively impacts directly on social, academic or occupational functioning."[2]

Now, look at the difference between that definition, which became the lay of the land when DSM-V was published in 2013, and the DSM-IV version that doctors used for the twenty years preceding that: "A behavior disorder originating in childhood in which the essential features are signs of developmentally inappropriate inattention, impulsivity, and hyperactivity. Although most individuals have symptoms of both inattention and hyperactivity-impulsivity, one or the other pattern may be predominant. The disorder is more frequent in males than females. Onset is in childhood. Symptoms often attenuate during late adolescence, although a minority experience the full complement of symptoms into mid-adulthood."[3]

Before I break down the significance in differences between the two most recent diagnoses published by the DSM, a word about the DSM itself. Since the American Psychiatric Association (APA) began publishing the *Diagnostic and Statistical Manual of Mental Disorders* in 1952, the DSM has grown to exert tremendous influence on the psychiatric field and society at large. This is according to "A Brief Historicity of the *Diagnostic and Statistical Manual of Mental Disorders*: Issues and Implications for the Future of Psychiatric Canon and Practice," a paper published by the National Institutes of Health.[4] Most specifically, it has provided diagnostic parameters and treatment guidelines for the assessment and categorizing of mental health conditions and disorders in North America, and increasingly worldwide. The preparation of each edition is lengthy and exhaustive, usually taking a decade. For example, more than 160 top APA researchers and clinicians (psychiatrists, neuroscientists, psychologists, specialists, statisticians, etc.) put together DSM-V through task forces, work groups, and study groups. Highlights of a series of white papers and direct contributions from more than four hundred international scientists are included. Finally, a scientific review committee (SRC) approved the final contents and guidelines after reviewing (and sometimes incorporating) lists of proposed changes.[5] By any measure, it takes a village of our best medical minds to produce the DSM.

The APA's larger goal for its "36,000 physician leaders in mental health," as the DSM-V website describes them,[6] is to create specific definitions, diagnoses, and treatment guidelines for specific disorders. That it has certainly done for the most part. When DSM-I came out in 1952, it listed 106 diagnostic categories, up from the 22 assembled by its forerunner, *Statistical Manual for the Use of Institutions for the Insane*, first published in 1918 by the APA's predecessor, the American Medico-Psychological Association. Beginning with the title of the publication, it represented a quantum leap forward. The redefining, expanding of definitions, and determination of new disorders weaves right through the ensuing sixty-five years of DSM history, to the point that DSM-V has 297 separate, defined disorders. That number is so high that, after DSM-IV published in 1994 with the same number of disorders, APA officials vowed the number would not increase in the subsequent edition.

Of course, the editors have changed definitions and diagnostic recommendations along the way as the APA received and processed updated findings and research, and accepted results from medical testing over the ensuing years. Some definition expansions or changes have been universally accepted and applied, while others have not, such as the difference in DSM-IV and DSM-V on ADHD diagnostics. The chair of DSM-IV himself, Dr. Allen Frances, objects to some of the DSM-V criteria.

THE HISTORY OF HYPERACTIVITY AND ADHD

Up until 1952, no one really knew what to make of hyperactivity.[7] What we now know as ADHD was first mentioned in a medical write-up by British pediatrician Dr. George Still in 1902 when he described "an abnormal defect of moral control in children." More than a century earlier, in 1798, while writing the second of a landmark three-book series he published on mental illness and mental health, Scottish physician Sir Alexander Crichton described attention deficit: "When any object of external sense, or of thought, occupies the mind in such a degree that a person does not receive a clear perception from any other one, he is said to attend to it."[8] A quarter-century before that, in 1775, German physician Melchior Adam Weikard wrote a description of "the inattentive person" in a textbook he published, *Der philosophische Arzt*. The description matched parts of the DSM checklist, and his recommended treatment was quite broad—but reflective of whole-person medicine, which I really like: "The inattentive person is to be separated from the noise or any other objects; he is to be kept solitary, in the dark, when he is too active. The easily agile fibres are to be fixated by rubbing, cold baths, steel powder, cinchona, mineral waters, horseback riding, and gymnastic exercises."[9]

No one knew what to call it, either—which should tell you something about how vague and fraught with misinterpretation it really is. In the mid-1930s, when the FDA first approved Benzedrine (amphetamine sulfate) as a medicine—the first drug to be used for the condition—it was known as "minimal brain damage." In just the history of the DSM, it's been known as "minimal brain dysfunction" (DSM-I, 1952), "hyperkinetic reaction of childhood" (DSM-II, 1968), "attention-deficit disorder with or without hyperactivity" (DSM-III, 1980), and, finally, ADHD (DSM-III-Revised, 1987). To further parse the term, in 1994, DSM-IV broke ADHD into three groups: ADHD inattentive type; ADHD hyperactive-impulsive type; and ADHD combined type. These terms make up the living history of ADHD in medical terms.[10]

What this means, to healthy skeptics like myself, is that doctors can make diagnoses on disorders from a field of 297 options—and prescribe accordingly—even though they sometimes don't know for sure what is taking place with the patient. The number of common symptoms, traits, or characteristics between disorders is so high (as we noted, the characteristics of ADHD are present, in part, in about a hundred other disorders, diseases, and ailments) that, it would seem, pinpointing a correct diagnosis could (and probably should, in some cases) amount to rocket science. That would involve a team of specialists who compare tests, exams, and notes, and figure out exactly what the patient has and what he or she needs—right?

Then there is the garbled history of ADHD and its diagnostic process. An early voice in the do-not-prescribe camp, Hartmann, shook the ADHD diagnostic rafters at the turn of the twenty-first century with two books on ADHD itself, then his 2003 follow-up, *The Edison Gene*. The book's title is its departure point: in 1855, seven-year-old Thomas Edison was sent home three months after beginning public school, with a note that said his brain was "addled." Edison biographer Gerald Beals notes on the thomasedison.com website, "If modern psychology had existed back then, the genuinely hyperactive (Edison) would have probably been deemed a victim of attention deficit syndrome and given a prescription for Ritalin."[11]

MEDICAL STANDARDS FOR DIAGNOSING ADHD

What *are* the medically held standards for diagnosing ADHD? The official ADHD protocol includes a set checklist of nine traits and behaviors, as outlined in DSM-V. There are no visible medical symptoms (sore throat, runny eyes, cough, etc.), which is noteworthy:

- Often talks excessively
- Often has trouble waiting his/her turn
- Is often "on the go," as if driven "by a motor"
- Often interrupts or intrudes on others
- Often unable to play or take part in leisure activities quietly
- Often easily distracted
- Often does not seem to listen when spoken to directly
- Often fails to give close attention to details, or makes careless mistakes in schoolwork (or paperwork)
- Often avoids, dislikes, or is reluctant to do tasks that require mental effort over a long period of time

According to DSM-V, if a patient displays six or more symptoms of inattention, *or* six or more symptoms of hyperactivity and impulsivity, then by definition, he or she has ADHD. Problem is, several symptoms also show among characteristics of more than fifty different conditions.

To further explore that, it takes time, money, and testing to sort out—money that many parents and adult-onset patients don't have, and time that most doctors can't carve out of their overwhelmed schedules. The other issue is the prevalent attitude in today's classrooms and society in general: we want to know what the problem is and get a quick fix *now*.

And, on top of *that*, DSM-V greatly expanded the criteria of diagnosis, stating that "a minority experience the full complement of symptoms into mid-adulthood." Consequently, diagnoses of children older than seven have jumped markedly, all the way into adults being diagnosed in droves—something rarely the case in the entire history of ADHD until so stated in DSM-V. Why? Did millions of teens and adults suddenly shift from "normal" behavior to present the characteristics of ADHD, or were there other factors? I'll get back to that question.

So is this a condition? A brain chemistry issue? A matter of anxiety? A sweeping epidemic? Or merely a difference in perspective, making it hard to color within the lines of a society run inside square boxes, set rules, tight conformity, and with an emphasis on delivering at a factory-like efficiency? Wouldn't it be nice if we had solid answers to these questions before we began diagnosing by the millions?

As countless medical doctors and astute experts in human behavior have pointed out, in various ways ADHD is one of the more complex conditions in DSM-V. Yet, we don't diagnose it in a deservingly meticulous way at all. Honestly, it's more of a fast-food diagnosis in many doctors' offices, through no direct fault of the doctors themselves.

On top of that, and in spite of the stated definition in DSM-V, opinions vary in the medical, psychological, business, and educational worlds about what constitutes ADHD. What should be an airtight checklist of symptoms reads more like a catch-all for the energetic child who can't sit still, or the bored or disinterested child who can't (or won't) pay attention. As for the underlying causes, we're even further in the dark and not all that willing to drill down into deeper roots behind a diagnosis such as social, environmental, family, physiological, genetic, dietary, vision, stress-related, academic, or neurological issues (which we explore further in part II). When we should dig, we diagnose. Consequently, quick-hitting diagnoses, often rendered in half-hour visits to the physician, follow. Again, it's the fast-food mentality. We'd be much better off ascribing ADHD diagnoses to the approaches of Ayurvedic or functional medicine, which plunge several layers beneath the symptoms to find out what physical and environmental events, conditions, other health issues, nutritional, and prescriptive factors fed into those symptoms. However, in this pressure-cooker society, "better off" doesn't always reach the doctor's office, mainly because it requires something overwhelmed doctors in family clinics don't have—time to properly examine and diagnose.

"My advice to my fellow colleagues, physicians, and other mental health care experts charged in the evaluation of potential ADD diagnoses is that the most appropriate primary diagnosis and therapy needs to be critically analyzed," Dr. Hirschfield concurred. "Each patient has unique circumstances and standard diagnostic tools and interventions available for their situation. A highly qualified mental health analysis should be completely and adequately reviewed before any single diagnosis or comorbid diagnosis is definitively determined."

But that's not the reality on the ground.

PHARMACEUTICALS AND ADHD

An ADHD diagnosis, like any other medical diagnosis treated by powerful pharmaceuticals, should be clear in its primary characteristics or "symptoms." Instead, it seems to be a catch basin that funnels into a quick exam and a named conclusion. From there, an estimated 75 percent of ADHD patients are given prescriptions for powerful stimulants as a first-resort treatment and sent on their way, without the benefit of a more thorough exam that could address questions like these: What are the root causes? Is Jeff's stress an ADHD condition—or the effects of a tough job? Is Jeff not paying attention because he has inattention issues derived from ADHD—or because the class work is boring and he feels unchallenged? How can we channel Jeff's energy toward his work or creative gifts and prevent burnout through rapid frustration and anxiety? How can we get him to sleep better at night and slow down his brain? How is his diet? What supplements or other meds is he taking? How are they impacting him physically and mentally? How can we relieve the undying anxiety that stops him from embracing his innate greatness? What tools can help us funnel snap-thinking, boundless energy, endless mind chatter, and the inability to sit still and redirect it toward our highest potential?

The disconnect between careful diagnosing and the ADHD climate of today bothers more and more esteemed medical experts in the field. Dr. Allen S. Frances, chair of the DSM-IV Task Force, has become an outspoken critic of ADHD diagnostic practices, particularly in the post-DSM-V world. In 2015, Dr. Frances took to the media concerning the huge upswing in diagnoses of young children, including a spirited 2015 response to a Twitter post I'd made:

> *Jeff Emmerson @Beyond_ADHD Without science behind diagnosing for MANY, I suspect millions are wrongly labeled with #ADHD #ADD (&on possibly dangerous meds)! I was.*
> *Allen Frances: #ADHD overdiagnosis cause by greedy Pharma, careless docs, concerned parents & overwhelmed teachers*

Now, take another look at the list we just presented: How many small children *don't* display these characteristics? They are excitedly exploring a world brand new to them, testing, experiencing fully, trying to figure out how it all works. They do not know how to filter, categorize, label, or rein in their 360-degree "hunter minds." Most are playing and learning at the same time. This is *normal behavior*, not frontal clouds of a condition that, with one diagnosis, can and often does lead to a lifetime of prescription drug dependency, with social and professional stigmatization as well. The rise in diagnoses of children ages seven and under, those I'm describing, are downright alarming. According to the CDC, of the 6.4 million children ages four through seventeen diagnosed through 2011, more than 70 percent were seven or under. In addition, 75 percent of children ages two through five *were prescribed medication and receiving clinical care.* [12]

Dr. Frances is pointed about his thoughts on medicating small children like this. "Under no circumstances," he tells me in a spirited email exchange, "should a child 2, 3, 4 years old, be on psychiatric medications without the most urgent of indications and the most extensive evaluation. I would extend that recommendation to older children as well." [13]

"The developing brain is such an unknown and rapidly changing entity that unless there is a dire indication, medication should be used only after other natural approaches (both patient-directed and environment-directed) are all adequately utilized," Dr. Frances adds. "A pill may seem to be an easy path, but for the child it may sometimes be the most costly in the long run."[14]

Dr. Frances focuses on the developing brain, once a euphemism for "childhood development." However, in light of recent breakthroughs, which have established that brain development, synaptic and neural rerouting, and cell regeneration can occur at up to age ninety (through a process called neuroplasticity), the developing brain is a whole-life process. While most brain development occurs in the first thirteen years, no longer do neuroscientists and neurologists consider *all* development complete by then. In other words, we have many reasons to slow our roll, to put the brakes on this rush to diagnostic judgment, and to diagnose more slowly, carefully, and precisely, to make sure we get it right for the sake of young children with pliable minds, and older teens and adults who have plenty of cerebral growth still remaining.

OVERDIAGNOSING

Instead, the opposite is occurring: we're overdiagnosing at an alarming rate. According to the Centers for Disease Control and Prevention (CDC), by 2003, the 100th anniversary of Dr. Still's diagnosis of a patient for "a defect of moral control," now considered the historical genesis of the ADHD diagnosis, 7.8 percent of those under eighteen in North America had received the ADHD label. By 2014, the percentage under eighteen had jumped to 13 percent—a 60 percent increase. Among the overall adult population, the number has nearly tripled, from 1.5 percent of all adults in 2003 to more than 4 percent in 2015. Stretching it back to the early 1980s, when the terms ADD and ADHD began entering the mainstream, the diagnostic rate was 1 percent. All of this dwarfs the mere 13 percent increase in the North American population during this time.[15]

These increases are mind-boggling. Why are they happening? Are we really becoming that much more scattered, inattentive, fidgety, and unable to focus? Are we growing so dependent on the meds that we accept the diagnosis at face value, rather than diving deeper into what troubles and concerns us and our kids? Is our world bombarding us with too much external stimulation? Are devices scattering our attention span? Are societal and academic expectations crushing us with their pressures and causing us to act out impulsively or shut down completely? Does the loss of outlets such as recess and free time make it impossible for our neurological systems to handle it anymore? Could this be what the ADHD diagnostic checklist really reflects?

Yes, it could be, but we're not going to find that out from the in-and-out diagnostic exams that are becoming far more common when it comes to ADHD. "Too many diagnoses are made during a 15-minute appointment in the pediatrician's office," says Dr. Stephen Hinshaw, a University of California professor and leading international expert on ADHD, and coauthor of *ADHD: What Everyone Needs to Know*. "These quick-and-dirty evaluations are a leading factor in overdiagnosis and overtreatment."[16]

As Hinshaw and many others note, and to which I can attest, ADHD cannot be diagnosed by a blood test or brain scan, which rings true for all other mental health disorders except autism, which can now be seen in advanced brain imagery. Diagnostically, that leaves us with taking a thorough medical history, discussing symptoms with the patient, and getting 360-degree feedback from those who play a significant role in that patient's world. For adults, it means talking to loved ones and co-workers; for children, it means interviewing parents, teachers, school nurses, and even coaches. What's going on at home? What's going on at school? What outside factors are possibly causing uneasiness or unrest?

Had I been fortunate enough to sit in a doctor's office when I was a kid, they would have taken my family history and been able to diagnose anything from childhood trauma to anxiety disorder to impulsive behavior—all of which can be misconstrued as ADHD, but none of which, by themselves, would have categorically concluded that I *had* ADHD.

How much of this can a doctor find out and determine in fifteen minutes—or even an hour? The answer is simple: very little. Yet, in this climate of overdiagnosis, they are being rushed to diagnose by a variety of well-intentioned (for the most part) interested parties that include, but are not limited to, school district officials, teachers and/or school nurses, parents, pharmaceutical sales reps proffering the latest ADHD prescriptions, and employers. All have a stake in seeing Madison and Jim focus and perform at school or work, behave without disruption in the classroom or workplace, and channel their energy into school lessons or the client.

Along with those expectations come punitive measures for failure that are becoming quite harsh, in my opinion. If you fail at school, you fall behind, get held back, maybe miss out on a scholarship—or, worse, get passed over or pushed ahead, as schools only receive state funding for a student if that student passes into another grade. They have a vested financial interest in passing students. ADHD diagnoses and prescriptions solve many of those situations. "Teachers and other school personnel are often the first to suggest the diagnosis of ADHD in children," note Leonard Sax and Kathleen Kautz in an article titled "Who First Suggests the Diagnosis of Attention Deficit/Hyperactivity Disorder?"[17]

Not only that, but ADHD has been an eligible condition for the U.S. Individuals with Disabilities Act (IDEA) since 1991.[18] Under IDEA, a federal statute, diagnosed schoolchildren can receive special educational services, such as outside tutoring and special teaching assistants, that relieve the burden on overstretched teachers already contending with full classrooms. Translation: an ADHD diagnosis makes it easier on the classroom teacher, and more money is sent to the school for the additional services.

At work, it's pretty simple: if you don't perform, you don't keep your job. Losing a job in today's expensive world not only causes personal and financial difficulty—it can also be a soul crusher. So the overdiagnosis climate helps the workplace in many ways, too.

The United States diagnoses kids with ADHD at a far greater rate than other countries—and not because of advanced medical or diagnostic procedures. A study from the University of Exeter in the United Kingdom took a sample of fifty-three English schoolchildren and ran them through the DSM-V criteria for ADHD. It concluded that five would have been diagnosed with ADHD in the United States. English doctors then used their own criteria to test the same kids with the same symptoms. According to the study, one student would have been diagnosed under that protocol. One of the differences, according to the study? *Time spent evaluating the patient.* When you have more than fifteen minutes, you can probe beyond the nine-point checklist and a school or work referral—or, on a sinister note, a patient's ability to fake the symptoms and snow the doctor into diagnosing and prescribing stimulant drugs.

Sadly, overdiagnosing is increasing in this way, too, particularly among teens and adults. A very small but growing part of the stimulant addiction epidemic in the United States, particularly with Class II controlled substances like ADHD drugs, is being attributed to patients playing "rope-a-dope" with doctors in the office. They've read the ADHD diagnostic checklists and can readily mimic the characteristics. While DSM-V's relaxation of the diagnosis to more thoroughly include teens and adults has much to say about overdiagnosis, the hunger to stimulate and stay stimulated is creating more false diagnoses (as opposed to misdiagnoses)—and, I might add, a dangerous situation, particularly in the United States. Remember: the effects of methamphetamine are indistinguishable from the effects of the top ADHD drugs, according to Columbia University neuropsychopharmacolist Dr. Carl Hart.[19] According to Ilina Singh in her article "ADHD, Culture and Education," in a country that consumes 80 percent of the world's methylphenidate[20] (the active ingredient in Ritalin), that is scary business that will only get scarier until we rein in the rush to diagnosis.

But the biggest push to overdiagnosis comes from a simple statement at the heart of the marketing of ADHD: no matter how frightened we might be of the power of ADHD meds, what will happen if our child or our loved one *doesn't* use it? This leads to the number one reason for overdiagnosis: the fear factor.

We live in an epidemic of fear. It seems we're afraid of everything these days—the fear of being hurt, the fear of not hydrating, the fear of getting sick, the fear of others, the fear that your child will hate you if you don't do everything they want right now to appease them. We fear that our child will become a social outcast or academic failure and lose out on a normal life if we don't run them to a doctor's office and immediately put them on ADHD medications so they can focus better at school. It's as if that diagnosis and those stimulants are the solution to everything bothering the kid.

While overdiagnosis is truly frightening, there is another aspect that we need to wrap our arms around and get beyond—misdiagnosis.

6

WHY PERSONAL HISTORY MATTERS IN DIAGNOSING

One of my biggest gripes about the way ADHD is diagnosed and prescribed is a lack of depth in learning about individual patients. The looming question is one that begs to be picked apart: how do we diagnose and then prescribe powerful drugs for what could be a lifetime from a single doctor's visit in which very little patient history is taken? Whenever a diagnosis is rendered that involves long-term care and long-term prescriptions—two things built into the typical ADHD protocol—we owe it to the children and adults diagnosed to study their entire histories.

BACK TO THE BEGINNING

We need to go back to the beginning, to our personal and family histories. While the reasons for us arriving at an ADHD diagnosis vary greatly (cause in itself for longer diagnostic evaluation periods), I can assure you of this: somewhere in our backstories, we will find family members and/or dynamics that offer compelling clues as to why we can't sit still, pay attention, stop being nervous and hypertensive, or avoid being disruptive. Reviewing and pointing to family relationships and dynamics—especially with our parents—can be painful. However, I feel we owe it to ourselves to know and own our place in the events, traumas, and relationships that might have contributed to our unsteady walk in this

world—especially where life-altering labels and powerful pharmaceuticals are concerned! Even if we can no longer talk with family members
or make amends (or have amends made to us), we can at least better
understand ourselves through exploring these roots. We can take a huge
step forward in our own healing and our own ability to overcome the
characteristics associated with ADHD. And we can better know how to
relate to our kids, loved ones, jobs, society, and world.

For me, "back to the beginning" means exactly that: my early family
life, and its nuclear center, my mother. Like so many others, I can find
plenty of good memories and bad in my childhood and adolescence.
More importantly, though, I can see patterns forming, patterns that
played out in a number of troubling ways in my adult life—until I got on
top of them and turned them into a desire to inform and help others.
The big question is, do these patterns of behavior and characteristics
add up to ADHD? Doctors thought so in 2010. Others, like Dr. Tim
Royer, now think maybe not. The point is, without diving into my deepest personal history, how can anyone diagnose for sure?

Back to my life: my mom was a bit of a heartbreaker. She has always
been a determined and well-meaning person; she would try to help out
her children in whatever way she could. However, she possessed a more
intense side that sometimes possessed her; my sister and I feared it and
tried to avoid it whenever possible. When things were going well,
though, we couldn't complain.

Mom had a very tough upbringing, with a domineering mother and
passive father who would simply leave to get away from her intensity.
This domineering nature was passed down the line. My grandmother
believed her children *must* go to university to be held at the same
esteem as their neighborhood "counterparts." In her mind, school was
the ideal route to take. The way Nan drilled that into Mom's head was
intense to say the least. Mom was constantly pressured to live up to a
certain set of expectations; the punishment was frightening if she didn't.
Even worse, Nan's verbal weaponry would make the strongest of people
question their self-worth over time. Mom gradually became rebellious
and standoffish, acting out in her own self-defeating ways. She fell into
the wrong types of groups and eventually became pregnant with my
sister and later myself by a man who had nothing of any worth to offer.
He was an alleged con man of questionable mind and character. I've
spoken to him one time on the phone. I never had the desire to speak to

him again. So right away, my mother carried an inherent instability; she never felt totally solid on the outer or inner ground on which she stood. That type of anxiety passes right down to the next generation. I know. It's something I deal with every day.

When I was eight weeks old, my mom met Ken, whose parents were of far different dispositions. His mother was a kind, warm woman who worked in the retail sector for many years before living the remainder of her life enjoying her grandchildren and eventually great-grandchildren. She was always a joy to be around before her passing in 2007. Ken's dad (my "step-grandfather"), Albert, was a hard-working man until passing in 1985. However, he was cut from the cloth of his generation, a man who rarely, if ever, expressed his feelings. I still remember Dad telling me that he never got to say "I love you" to his father.

Notice how I call Ken "Dad." There's a reason for that: he's been Dad to me since he and Mom met. He has influenced me in a big way and cultivated my ability to get through many of life's challenges. Along the way, we built a magical friendship and bond. I've never met a more loving, caring, unselfish, and supportive person. I hold immense and eternal gratitude for his love and friendship, which helped make it possible for me to get through the tough times in my past. He did what he felt was right for the family he legally adopted, something many men wouldn't have done. Through all the days, nights, arguments, lessons, hopes, fears, stubbornness, and tears, Dad never wavered in his commitment to see me through my situation. I'm grateful to the end of the universe and beyond for his unconditional love, guidance, and above all, patience. Sadly, Mom and Dad couldn't make their marriage last, which leads us back to the beginning.

I see my early childhood as one of love and mischief, hope, mistakes, and plenty of great moments. My mother did the best she could, and I was surely worshipped by my family, as my baby photos show. Though my earliest memories start at around five, and become less sweet as my childhood progresses, I'm fortunate that I was surrounded by so much love early on—but we had our moments.

Mom and Dad argued for more nights than I can remember, the drama downright crazy at times. Mom would also physically chase after my sister, who bore the brunt of our mother's frustrations for whatever had happened. Sometimes, there didn't seem to be a cause or reason. My grandmother had subjected Mom to emotional abuse while growing up, and Mom ratcheted it up a notch—sadly, a common pattern. Dad saved both of us from probably more major beatings than I know. I still remember the hole in my sister's mouth from when Mom punched her. But she had it out for me, too. She was absolutely terrifying as she chased after me with an aluminum baseball bat. One time, she swung and connected; fortunately, it only caught my hand. I now think she never actually intended to use it but only wanted to threaten us, though I grew to fear that bat as if it were a club in the hands of a medieval warrior. However, when she became crazed with anger, all bets were off. Those were some crazy years, to say the least.

I have since learned that, when faced with such explosive behavior from one or both parents, children tend to veer in one of three directions: mimic their parents' behavior and become temperamental and even abusive themselves; act out in other counterproductive ways; or turn inward and look for the mouse holes within their psyches for physical, emotional, and mental sanctuary. Few children from such households truly emerge normal and well adjusted. Given that millions of households operate in some sort of dysfunction, you can do the math. The figures are fairly similar to the numbers of those diagnosed with ADHD, ADD, OCD, childhood or adolescent PTSD—a virtual alphabet soup of DSM-V diagnostics.

I fell primarily into the second behavioral pattern, though I carried (and carry) elements of all three. (It becomes clear as I look back.) At times, I was a little devil, but I didn't start out that way. One time in kindergarten, I held a seed in a plastic cup filled with soil, hoping it would grow in the windowsill of the classroom. I have no idea how it turned out, how it grew; the memory has faded. Was it a good one? I hope so. I get the feeling that I may have "blacked out," or that it was erased by the negative childhood experiences that ran alongside my happier moments. Unfortunately, I can rattle off quite a few of these incomplete stories, the endings blocked by the conditions surrounding me.

I was shy and guarded during the first few grades. My lack of self-worth and esteem made me easily anxious, although I obviously didn't know the meaning of either term until years later. I was already somewhat "fight or flight." I was quick to anger if provoked, and I lost my temper on a few occasions, hurting other children once or twice. I also felt extremely unworthy of friendship. Perhaps some of that is natural at age six or seven, but I was a very sensitive boy by nature, so who knows? Plus, my parents were fighting and my mom had a tendency to fly off the handle, which amounted to very shaky footing for a young, sensitive boy.

CONTRIBUTING FACTORS

There was basic encouragement from Mom and Dad, but in looking further back into my past, I can see quite a few contributing factors to my struggles in life, the characteristics of which were diagnosed as ADHD:

- Mom was a violent and emotionally sadistic woman who suffered from severe, rapid mood changes when she got angry. I know them well because I learned her behaviors growing up and witnessed them in myself at times into adulthood.
- Dad did his best to protect my sister and me from being attacked, screamed at, or beaten (he saved my sister from a few horrible attacks triggered when Mom didn't get her way), but he wasn't the strong, sensitive role model that (in a perfect world) would have been needed. Then again, Mom would never have been with him if he were that type of man—she had to be the "boss," that was her personality. I learned to despise those types of women—the flighty, "boss"-style personalities.
- I didn't learn ways to process the intense feelings I was experiencing while living through Mom's moods, her abuse of my sister and me, and her violent arguments with my dad. I loved her because she was my mom, but deep inside, I wanted to kill her at those moments. I wanted to get so big and strong that I could absolutely annihilate her from this very earth. It's a very hard thing to admit, but if we're not brutally honest when combing through our histories, then we will never get to the true bottom of whatever we're working on. As I cried in my bed listening to the fights, rage, despair, anxiety, and sadness festered within me. There were so many days and nights like this. I've blocked a lot of them out, but the *feeling* remains, and reemerges in instinctual ways during certain conflict or stressful situations.

- I had vision issues—that weren't discovered until grade three, when my teacher said that I "tilted my head a lot to one side in class when reading." We went to the local university optometry center, where I had a full vision exam. We were told I had "Aniseikonia"; my left eye was weaker than my right. I also had a "plus prescription," so my first set of eyeglasses magnified my eyes to an embarrassing degree—enter the "coke bottle glasses" remarks and taunts from classmates. (Quick update: in 2015, one of Canada's finest and most highly regarded optometrists, Dr. Patrick Quaid, did a basic vision therapy prognosis assessment on me. He discovered I have another condition: "moderate left eye amblyopia, convergence insufficiency and impaired depth perception." In other words, the way in which my eyes team to perceive objects and read is, in Dr. Quaid's words, "Significantly unstable." He told me, "Jeff, I'm surprised you made it past grade three with this condition.")
- I should add that, according to Dr. Quaid, a routine eye exam includes some basic testing. However, in children or adults with learning, attentional, or concussion-related issues, "a full and thorough visual skills assessment (i.e., detailed oculomotor and detailed visual processing exam) is required," he added.[1]

STRUCTURE, DISCIPLINE—HOCKEY

When I was five, I found something that combined structure, discipline, focus, effort, achievement, and all the other things we like our kids to learn: organized ice hockey. I embarked on what would become a ten-year indulgence. I wanted to be a goaltender and convinced my coach of it, my persuasive abilities already showing themselves. However, I couldn't see that well. It was so awkward (and noticeable) to wear eyeglasses and play hockey. On top of that, I sweated profusely, and the fog didn't help me see the puck. Needless to say, those glasses later stayed home on hockey days and nights, and I worked my way up to the highest level for my age for several years running. We won several championships, which was amazing.

Since hockey is to Canada what soccer is to Latin America and football to the United States, we didn't limit ourselves to playing in rinks. The neighborhood boys and I would play road hockey endlessly in the winter months, and stick ball in the warmer part of the year. We felt totally free, at least until my Mom would yell out, "Jeff, it's time to come in," to which I'd almost always reply, "Just a little more time, please." We would do anything to stay out there and pushed it all the way. It never seemed to end. We would play in bitter cold until we couldn't walk anymore, and then we'd play some more! It stung like hell when I'd catch a slap shot right between the legs and collapse like a ton of bricks—and then endure my friends laughing at my being "squared" by a slap shot.

We also were prone to mischief. On another winter day, we got together in my friend's backyard and threw snowballs at cars driving down the street. One time we hit a car—and it stopped! We took off running out of the yard, but I slipped on the ice and fell. Oh, man, I'm lucky that I regained my footing quickly! Oh, the urgency and excitement from those days. We were a rare breed!

My most important and special experiences came from the camaraderie and bonds we forged through playing together for years. Our core group stayed mainly intact, with the odd teammate moving away or being cut. Those times were so invaluable in teaching me lessons in teamwork, sportsmanship, and achieving goals—something hard to come by in a household where the drama, tension, and instability continued to grow, to the point where I could never be sure of what the next day would bring or where I stood—one day a beloved son, the next day the enemy or target of fearsome punishment. What I *could* count on was heading to the rink, strapping on my goalie pads for either practicing or playing, and spending hours with my teammates and coaches. To this day, I am a huge sports fan. Now you know why.

Those days of road hockey are frozen in time like the ice that would gather under the cozy layer of soft snow overnight. Those were truly my days of innocence.

ERRANT BEHAVIORS

Off the ice, my troubles began manifesting into errant behaviors. When I was six, I stole a twenty-dollar bill from my mother, and went to the local variety store to spend as much as I could on chips, candy, and gum. I then went to a green electrical box across the street from my house and tried to eat all of my purchased snacks, but the good memory fades from there—something about suddenly having to ditch my stash and race home. I don't know if my mom caught me, but something deep inside says she did. Perhaps I "blacked out" the memory of my punishment.

Not surprisingly, Mom sent me to a local two-week Bible camp for the next few summers, an interesting and unusual experience for a six- or seven-year-old. (Aren't little kids supposed to be home with their parents, and not shipped off to anything beyond day camp?) During my last Bible vacation, which lasted a bit longer, I grew several inches. I still remember the excitement of my new appearance, and jokingly thinking that time away from family was the best thing for me. Look how I grew! There were other benefits, too. I can still smell the butter and cinnamon from the cinnamon toast that the cooks would make for breakfast.

The camp was standard fare, as summer camps go: a lake, wooded areas, cabins with bunk beds, and plenty of daily activities. I rarely received any mail, perhaps once during my stay. Though filled with inner turmoil and concern about my family life back home, being away for so long at that young age was pretty traumatic for me, so mail was a very welcome thing.

I wish I could say camp left a great lasting memory for me, like it does for so many others. However, my parents didn't send me there for my enjoyment. I know that Mom wanted me out of her hair, so this was a way to make it happen that likely didn't cost very much, while offering her a break to live the life she really wanted.

When I got home, my mother hoped for the best: that the Lord, the Bible, and some good guidance counselors had steered me onto a path of more direct obedience and activities that didn't run against the grain of society. Well, it didn't work. Shortly thereafter, my sister took me out to a school several blocks away and decided to light a cigarette while telling me, "Don't you tell Mom!"

Naturally, I told Mom as soon as we got home. I was the stereotypi- cal little brother in that way. I could sure be mean to my big sister, who was six years my senior. I'm told I once threw a mustard jar at her while camping one summer. (Sorry, Kim!) I would also sit on top of the bar downstairs while my mother would watch her soap opera of choice, and we would talk at times. I later would sneak the odd sip of whatever bottle I could get my hands on from the rear of that bar. However, it tasted so bad and strong that it was an excellent deterrent.

There was one time every year when all the chaos, arguments, unsettled feelings, and trouble came to a screeching halt for me: Christmas. It was a wonderful time when several members of my natural and extended families would come to visit. As the youngest, I was typically fussed over, which I didn't mind a bit. I still have photos of my grandfather watching me play with my new train set. My uncle is there, as well as my grandmother, sister, Mom and Dad, and others. With its large fireplace and stone foundation, the downstairs area transformed into a great place to gather and enjoy Christmas Eve. Once, while twirling around with my sister, I cracked my head open after losing my grip. I still remember the bloody towels from that one; I must've scared my family half to death. I can still feel the two-inch scar. In this day and age, I would certainly have been diagnosed with a major concussion, something I've thought about from time to time. It is one of those little roots from the past that can take on present meaning.

Those highly positive, loving experiences grew few and far between. Mom and Dad's marriage was slowly but surely deteriorating before my very eyes. I still remember the screaming during the many fights they'd have on the main floor while I was upstairs (only a few stairs separated the top and main floor). Mom was on the offensive, the aggressive one, breaking Dad's ceramic plates and frames from his side business. He constantly pleaded with Mom not to break any more pieces, but when she reached a certain point, the pieces were going to be thrown about and broken. Like her own mother, she was the more assertive partner, and she quickly overwhelmed Dad's protests or counterpoints.

Mom also chased my sister Kim and me, truly frightful, and left me very panicky about everything. Had I been bigger, I probably would have *ended* Mom by force to protect my sister. Dad did save her from numerous beatings, but he was often not around to help us. I still remember the clumps of hair missing from Kim's head after Mom chased and caught her. I would sneak into Kim's bedroom at night quite often to talk with her. During times when Dad didn't catch me and send me back to my room, Kim and I played "I spy with my little eye," a game where she would look at something in her room and I would have to guess what it was based on the color. That was how we found a brief respite from the daily fear and terror, by comforting one another. I'll always remember her room as an escape from fear, even though some of her worst beatings from Mom took place there as well. Thank God my sister Kim left home at sixteen!

When I relive the sound of Mom slapping and punching Kim in the face and head, I literally have to take deep breaths. I didn't actually internalize how severe those days damaged us, how viciously serious they were—because I simply couldn't. Abuse is so insidious. Mom got away with so much more than she should have. In 2016, we would have been taken out of the home and placed with a foster family, or sent to Nan's to live with her.

When Mom and Dad separated in 1985, I was virtually catatonic at school for the rest of that year, except when I was stealing from classmates and getting into fights. I acted out at times, goofing off in class and having my grade 4 teacher Mr. Weaver (who impressed me with his professional, wholesome appearance) give me endless "times tables" to complete as homework for the next day. I rarely did, so my name ended up on the board in the "shamed" area for everyone else to see, with a ridiculous number of times tables still outstanding, sixty-eight if I remember correctly. There was a direct parallel between what I was dealing with at home and how I was behaving in school. The act of shaming a child without digging deeper into what that child is going through at home is like filling a jet with fuel based on guesses as to how much it will need for the next flight—just a tad dangerous, to put it mildly.

Dad moved from home shortly thereafter, leaving me in shambles. I completely withdrew socially and emotionally, and failed grade 4 miserably. I sat at my desk, listless, withdrawn, depressed, and lifeless. I'd entered my darkest time as a child.

The school administration was so concerned that they introduced me to "David," a Big Brother. They called him a "friend." We had regular appointments in which he'd show up at class time and take me away so we could spend some time together bonding. I idolized David, along with the smell of his cologne, his spiked "hockey-style haircut," and his stories of who he'd met. Sadly, however, on several occasions he would be a no-show for whatever reason. It crushed me when he couldn't show up.

THE AFTERMATH

One afternoon not long after Dad moved out, Mom met me on the front lawn as I walked home from school. She was energized, happy, and excited for us to "go out to dinner." At first, I loved the idea—what child wouldn't?—only to discover it was her way of introducing us to her "waiting in the wings" boyfriend, Michael. I mean, seriously! A sensitive boy is left without his Dad, is failing school, feels like a bag of shit, his sister is moving out, and he's left to deal with a violent mom with no protection. Into the house comes a new man who I perceived to be trying to "fill the role" of my Dad (even though he said otherwise). Then I become a bargaining chip whenever Mom and Dad speak on the phone and she grows angry—"Jeff's going to get it—I hope you're happy," or "We'll see what happens to Jeff over this." Then she hangs up on my dad.

I instantly and permanently viewed Michael with utter contempt, as well as Mom in association with Michael—how dare she! I had no idea as a child how to express my feelings, so they percolated inside me. If you drew a picture of me then, you could probably just skip the facial features and draw a tightly capped but boiling hot kettle.

In hindsight, I'm lucky I never decided to harm my mother. I was so sensitive and seeking of her approval that I think it held me back, along with the realization that something very bad would result if I harmed her. That intense, daily rage from childhood still lingers deep within me, although I've brought it to a standstill with considerable therapy. I have made my peace, but even now, I confess that writing this makes my blood boil at the injustice. I also realize that my mom was messed up, and I've got my own moments as a young man that weren't much better.

However, she and I both know that the past cannot be fully erased—especially when it leads to moods, behaviors, and characteristics that impact life moving forward. The point is, my experiences with her, and what grew from them, are examples of the traumas, tough relationships, bruises, and scars that leave indelible marks on our psyches, our outlooks on life, and how we feel in the world. These are the types of things every doctor should learn about every patient before making such a profound diagnosis as ADHD, which usually involves a powerful, potentially lifelong prescription. It matters—a lot.

7

THE LARGER PROBLEM OF MISDIAGNOSIS

Law enforcement investigators abide by a simple rule of thumb: follow the evidence wherever it leads. The same is true for the vast majority of medical cases and conditions. Doctors carefully test, and assess symptoms, traits, behaviors, and circumstances before rendering diagnoses that, in many cases, change the life of the patient—for better or worse. There is another principle that law enforcement and medicine rely on—ruling out all other possibilities before forming a final diagnosis or conclusion. Because of this, the number of falsely accused or misdiagnosed people stands at a very low percentage overall.

Then we have ADHD. Why are we rushing to diagnose at such an alarming rate when we're misdiagnosing more and more people every day (up to 50 percent, as many in the field believe)? Why aren't we approaching and treating the diagnosis and treatment of ADHD as carefully as we do heart attacks, diabetes, cancer, or other chronic diseases that utilize long-term medication, such as atherosclerosis or arthritis? And why aren't we taking the time to roll out someone's personal history when diagnosing something so consequential?

OVERDIAGNOSING AND MISDIAGNOSING

To the first question: are we really misdiagnosing and overdiagnosing, or forcing ourselves to believe that because we can't grasp the increas-

ingly high numbers of people living with ADHD? Consider this response from Dr. Susannah-Joy Schuilenberg:

> I don't "fear" that ADHD is being over/misdiagnosed; I *know* it is. I
> first encountered the behaviors of ADHD when I was tutoring in the
> early '80s. Throughout my professional life, I have stayed abreast of
> the developments in this area. I have seen the trend of labeling
> children (and adults) with the ADHD diagnosis after just a few mo-
> ments of observation, because of a description of a child's behavior,
> or because someone completed a checklist of symptoms. There are
> many, many other factors which contribute to both attention difficul-
> ties and hyperactivity, but certainly for about 10 years or more, the
> "go-to" diagnosis has been ADHD.[1]

I'm part of that history. I look at my own diagnostic record, with the
advantage of having Dr. Tim Royer unravel and explain it to me in
detail, and I wonder, how the hell did a doctor come up with ADHD in
just a few short minutes?

"I agree that if I sat down with the DSM-5 and went through those
behaviors, Jeff would completely check off those behaviors," Dr. Royer
said.

> If all I had was the DSM and that's what I was using, could Jeff
> identify six out of nine things, or even nine out of nine? Absolutely.
> And he'd be diagnosed with ADHD—as he was. The bigger question
> is, how accurate is that at assessing what's really going on with Jeff's
> brain?
>
> What we want to see is to get off of this whole lazy, short-sighted
> approach to diagnosing something going on in the brain. A lot of
> times, people sit in the lobby filling in a checklist, and then they're
> coming into the doctor and spending under fifteen minutes with the
> doctor and walking out with a diagnosis. Yet, nobody's ever looked at
> anything. But what if you see your brain wave activity on the [MRI]
> screen? You're able to watch (and evaluate), "when I think this way,
> this is what happens and when I think that way, this is what hap-
> pens," and you actually see it. It's like seeing your heart on an EKG,
> or an MRI of your brain. Now you're actually seeing something, and
> I'm able to point out your behaviors and the consequences of them.
> The bigger point is this: how do we effectively treat you in relation to
> what's causing these behaviors?[2]

As Dr. Royer said, you won't be having a discussion or examination at this level during a typical quick visit and diagnosis. Most stressed-out, overworked doctors can't see beyond the checklist when the four-year-old they're examining shows disruptive, excessive age-inappropriate behavior, enough to quickly merit an ADHD diagnosis. But what if that kid is acting out because of boredom, poor teaching, too little or too much discipline at home, troubles between the parents, tiredness, or a physical illness? What if the kid is expressing the spontaneous behavior normal to his age—getting excited, mad, impatient, aggressive, fearful, or happy, depending on the moment? And, honestly, what are four- , five- , and six-year-old kids getting diagnosed for, anyway? Being kids?

Add to that the findings of pediatrician Nicole Brown, who analyzed a national study of sixty-five thousand children for *The Atlantic* and found that most diagnosed with ADHD also experienced high levels of poverty, divorce, violence, and family substance abuse.[3] Seems to me, as it did to Dr. Brown, that these kids are suffering from something else, such as childhood trauma syndrome (absolutely as devastating as PTSD), anxiety disorders, depression, or undue stress. I can vouch for this firsthand—a childhood in a chaotic, abusive household creates a lot of fear, stress, anxiety, and impulsiveness that you won't find in a well-adjusted home.

That doesn't even include the countless children diagnosed with ADHD for what really turned out to be a learning disorder or uncorrected vision. Harvard Medical School professor Dr. Nancy Rappoport told the Child Mind Institute that fully 50 percent of kids with learning disabilities have inattention[4] —one of the two core types of ADHD. Is that inattention due to ADHD or to learning issues? Flip a coin. That's not what one wants to hear when trying to get a diagnosis right. In a blunt 2011 statement, psychiatrist Peter R. Breggin noted in the *New York Times*, "By making an ADHD diagnosis, we ignore and stop looking for what is really going on with the child. ADHD is almost always either Teacher Attention Disorder or Parent Attention Disorder."[5]

A few other quick figures to show how our ADHD diagnostic trends are following societal lines, rather than following the medical evidence that would lead to more careful diagnosing:

- According to an article in Romper.com, a highly respected website for children's health issues, many psychologists and health experts believe that up to 1 million children are being mislabeled or misdiagnosed with ADHD.[6]

- In the CDC's 2014 statistics, 13 percent of boys have been diagnosed with ADHD, and "only" 5 percent of girls.[7] Why the stark difference between boys and girls? Is it diagnosable objectively and medically? Or a more subjective question of behavior?
- 50 percent of kids who have learning disabilities are wholly or partially inattentive.
- According to a study of more than four thousand fifth graders of different races and ethnicities released in *Pediatrics* magazine, 7 percent of caucasian fifth-graders were taking ADHD medications, compared to 4 percent of African American children, and 3 percent of Latino children. Here's the rub: *none were diagnosed positively for ADHD!* Rather, they were diagnosed with "ADHD-like" symptoms and given ADHD meds largely at the request of their parents.[8] I find this a very dangerous trip down the road of misdiagnosis or incomplete diagnosis.

REASONS FOR MISDIAGNOSES

There are a variety of reasons why we are increasingly misdiagnosing ADHD. It is not because of lack of knowledge—we have plenty of knowledge—nor is it willful negligence by doctors. Let's start with simple math. As I've pointed out, with comments from the field verifying it, the all-important doctor's exam for ADHD takes as little as fifteen minutes. Heck, you can even go online on certain websites, such as ADDitudeMag.com or adhdandyou.com (a website produced by Shire Pharmaceuticals, the largest ADHD medicine provider), type in your "symptoms," and prequalify yourself for an ADHD diagnosis.[9]

Now to the generally accepted "symptoms" or characteristics of ADHD. Due to case overload on one hand and ease-of-use on the other, the majority of doctors diagnose strictly off the DSM-V checklist, whether patients walk in on their own or arrive with referrals from school administration and nursing offices. The latter are often encouraged to seek ADHD diagnoses for a variety of reasons (more later). It all begins with the DSM-V protocol: if the child tests positive on six of the nine items on the checklist, then as far as the APA is concerned, he or she has ADHD. Don't get me wrong: these DSM-V guidelines resulted from exhaustive work by a team of esteemed practitioners, researchers, and APA oversight committee members. However, what if some of those same symptoms, or traits, really indicate other conditions:

- Hypoglycemia
- Allergies
- Learning disabilities
- Hypo- or hyperthyroid
- Hearing and vision problems
- Lead poisoning
- Spinal problems
- Toxin exposure
- Carbon monoxide poisoning
- Seizure disorders
- Metabolic disorders
- Genetic defects
- Sleeping disorders
- PTSD
- High mercury levels
- High manganese levels
- Iron deficiency
- Vitamin deficiencies
- Excessive vitamins
- B-vitamin deficiencies
- Tourette's syndrome
- Sensory integration dysfunction
- Early-onset diabetes
- Heart disease
- Other cardiac conditions
- Bipolar disorder
- Central auditory processing disorder
- Worms (really!)
- Viral or bacterial infections
- Malnutrition
- Head injuries
- Dietary factors
- Anemia

- Inhaling toxic materials
- Some drugs
- Strep throat
- Lack of exercise
- Emotional problems
- Spoiled, undisciplined child
- Spirited children
- Lack of understanding, communication skills
- Early-stage brain tumors
- Brain cysts
- Temporal lobe seizures
- Klinefelter syndrome
- Extra "Y" chromosome
- Enzyme-deficiency disease
- Candida albicans (yeast infection)
- Intestinal parasites
- Gifted child

All of these conditions have at least one major trait or "symptom" in common with the ADHD diagnosis.[10] Most doctors I know, if given the time, would refrain from ruling it ADHD because of that common trait—but they don't have time. They are often pressured by concerned parents or educators to go with the ADHD diagnosis that they've already predetermined for the child. Common characteristics alone should lead to another round of testing or further inquiry into the patient's medical history. That would slow down the rate of diagnosis and make more and more ADHD diagnoses irrefutable. Most mimicking or similar symptoms can be ruled out with simple blood or lab tests, higher-level vision and hearing examinations, or further study into possible childhood trauma, anxiety, or stress-related causes. ADHD cannot be diagnosed with a brain scan or blood test, so if something shows up in a blood test, it would indicate another medical issue. Shouldn't we rule out these other possible diagnoses before coming to rest on an ADHD diagnosis? Shouldn't we follow the chain of evidence and rule out all other possibilities?

"The average GP [general practitioner] does not have the training required to accurately diagnose neurological and/or psychological disorders," Dr. Schuilenberg says.

Even such "simple" things as depression require rather more attention than what a GP might give in a standard office visit. In North America, pharmaceutical companies have direct access to doctors and thus to patients, and the practice of offering incentives for prescribing has led to a situation in health care which does *not* best serve the individuals seeking answers. Any disorder without a standardized medical test [i.e., a blood test] logically should be a "rule out" situation, eliminating *all* other possibilities before labeling. Sadly, this isn't the case, or it's the rare doctor who follows this practice."[11]

In September 2015, British medical journalist Jordan Raine stirred up the medical version of a North Sea frozen hurricane, and further fortified Dr. Schuilenberg's concerns, when he addressed the ADHD diagnostic world in his article, "Big Pharma and ADHD: Stop the Overprescription of Harmful Medication." Among other things, Raine wrote, "There is no doubt that, for at least some sufferers, ADHD is a neurological disorder with genetic roots and one characterized by clear functional impairments in the brain. But this avalanche-like rise in diagnosis comes despite there still being no clear utilizable biological markers, although EEG research is currently being done that may shed further light on a biomarker related to ADHD."[12]

Meanwhile, we continue to watch the diagnostic rate accelerate. "There are many medical and psychiatric conditions that can mimic ADD symptoms or are comorbid," Dr. Hirschfield warned. "We must recognize this when addressing various possible therapeutic interventions and when choosing appropriate medications. For instance, anxiety is a very common comorbid psychiatric condition that we see in children, but its treatment is much different from that of ADD. As healthcare professionals, we must all use standard of care practices and should expect that our mental health care providers exercise these standard procedures in all cases."[13]

Complicating the issue is that we display some of these common symptoms or traits as a result of external stimuli or sources. When I look at the food supply, the stimulant content is off the charts; add in food coloring, MSG, high-fructose corn syrup, and other chemical ingredients of processed and packaged goods, and we careen head-on into complications capable of throwing anyone's body and brain chemistry askew. This is something explored in depth in functional medicine, which, as we will explore later, is becoming a great step forward in addressing ADHD by non-pharmaceutical means.

How about sleep? Studies have concluded that, since 1900, our average sleep time each night has decreased from 8.5 hours to 6.8 hours. In the United States, 44 percent of all employed people are sleep-deprived on a regular basis, getting less than six hours per night. Lack of sleep triggers moodiness, irritability, impatience, incomplete thoughts, a fuzzy or racing mind, anxiety, and reduced productivity and creativity. Anxiety and depression create emotional pandemics of their own. Depression can easily be misdiagnosed as ADHD, depending on emotion-cycling patterns, as evidenced in my own diagnostic history.

Sadly, we don't get that far in the doctor's office. When many doctors see a fidgety, irritable, inattentive, hyperactive kid having trouble controlling his impulses or following simple instructions, and they receive confirmation of this behavior from schools or parents, they all too often default to the DSM-V checklist. The DSM-V checklist, however, combines elements of neurology, psychiatry, internal medicine, pharmacology, and even opthalmology in some cases—all beyond the range of the family doctor who often diagnoses without further examination. The doctor recalls the discussions with sales reps who visited the office or addressed the last mental health disorders seminar they attended, and they have a waiting room full of other patients to attend to.

WHERE DO WE DRAW THE LINE?

Where do we draw the line to diagnosing *conservatively*, based on medical and scientific proof that we've got it right and we've ruled out parallel or mitigating conditions? The answers lie in carefully following the progression of a person's symptoms, behaviors, and traits, how his or her daily physical, mental, behavioral, dietary, and social routines feed those symptoms and traits, and fully testing biochemistry and brain chemistry. We need all of this information. We need a world filled with the level of testing that thoughtful clinics such as Dr. Royer and his Neurocore team provide. We cannot solely rely on a single doctor and a checklist that could indicate one of fifty-plus disorders or other root causes.

According to Dr. Hirschfield, we need a more accurate, comprehensive feel for what's actually happening, with all involved parties in a child's life included.

"Checklists are only one part in the overall assessment of these mental health disorders," he explained.

> Remember, it is a team effort with the school system, families, and the mental health care professionals involved. Granted, there is subjectivity in patients, parents, educators, school, and others but it is just one part of the overall assessment. It is simple to conclude that a patient has hypercholesterolemia after obtaining repeated fasting blood specimens. For ADD, we do not have this ability. There are no validated blood markers to prove ADD. In the end, an ADD diagnosis should only be made upon satisfactory exclusion of all other medical or psychiatric conditions (i.e., depression, anxiety, obsessive compulsive disorder, and autism) that can mimic or complicate the diagnosis.[14]

Sadly, this leaves massive room for error. And plenty of errors are being made.

Dr. Marianne Kuzujanakis is among the growing number of medical pioneers baffled and frustrated by current protocols. A coauthor of the 2016 book *Misdiagnosis & Dual Diagnosis of Gifted Children & Adults [2nd Edition],* Dr. Kuzujanakis' work focuses on gifted individuals, especially those misunderstood by the educational and medical systems. She is also co-founder of the SENG Misdiagnosis Initiative, which offers support, guidance, and tools for the public and medical profession.

"Gifted children's developmental growth is complex," she said. "In some gifted children, gifted asynchrony may be erroneously labeled with a mental health diagnosis. In other gifted children, giftedness may be missed in a child with significant learning and/or mental health issues. Some other gifted children may be able to overcompensate in the short term for a learning disability or mental health disorder, thus possibly hiding both the disability and the giftedness. Without significant improvements in medical knowledge of giftedness and twice exceptionality, gifted children will inappropriately continue to be both overdiagnosed and underdiagnosed with mental health and learning issues, while their giftedness may be at risk of being entirely overlooked."[15]

MISDIAGNOSIS AND LABELING: THE ISSUE

The personal, professional, societal, and medical issues attached to an ADHD misdiagnosis are profound—and rarely discussed. We now have two generations of kids who have moved through school systems on medications, with a third being diagnosed at continually increasing rates today. But how often do we think of how this will impact their adult lives?

We live in a world where everything seems to carry a label or brand—and a ramification. If I own a machine shop, and I learn you have ADHD, do you think I will assign you to a complex project that requires high concentration? Let's say flying is your life's passion, and you want a pilot's license. If you're a sincere, honest person who points out on your medical questionnaire that you were (or are being) treated for ADHD, what do you think will happen to your dream? What if you want to serve on a police force or in the military? (Hint: *Do not* mention ADHD or ADD.) While these scenarios are less frequent than in the past, they certainly still exist.

At this point, the diagnosis can affect our identity as a person and, in many cases, seriously impair it. A diagnosis is often lifelong, and a child or adult's sense of identity can be ruined by it, depending on one's perspective, support structures, and self-esteem. This comment from Dr. Kuzujanakis paints a striking picture: "Too often, children of trauma, poverty, hunger and other diagnosable conditions are given the ADHD label."[16]

An ADHD diagnosis and self-esteem do not travel well together. We only make it worse by misdiagnosing or oversimplifying a diagnosis to rush the patient into an ADHD treatment protocol. We mean well, but generally, society will not view the person in a positive light. That will not help self-esteem or aid the development of a sense of higher purpose.

I have been more thoroughly assessed than most. I can firmly say that the "smoke" comes as a result of not taking time to separate the individual and his or her symptoms from the overall problem.

What they see is a new big picture for ADHD.

When I shared my history of diagnoses, assessments, and prescriptions in an online conversation with Dr. Kuzujanakis, she understood me in a way my general practitioner in Ontario did not. She also shared this bit pertaining to the prescribing of methylphenidate (Ritalin), the most famous of ADD/ADHD prescriptions:

> I think it's been clear that Ritalin worldwide is being prescribed in not infrequent haphazard and excessive ways. Do some kids have true ADHD? Sure. But how many really? The symptoms of ADHD can indicate so many other conditions and differences (the list is long). The want for a Ritalin prescription can also indicate so many other end-goals (many not for ADHD treatment). Barriers to proper identification are many. When Ritalin—and now shockingly even antipsychotic medications like Seroquel—are used in increasingly younger developing brains, we may not know all the measurable outcomes for sometime to come. Enough is enough. Time to do a full re-set."[17]

So what qualifies as a "right" diagnosis? How much time is enough time to evaluate? When can we decide, without question, that someone has ADHD? Dr. Schuilenberg's reasoned response presents a compelling case for slowing everything down—now—and adopting more thorough assessment and consideration: "A 'proper' assessment should be as long as it takes to be *certain* there is little or no ambiguity or question regarding the outcome," she says.

> Currently, ADHD is "diagnosed" by everyone from aunties to yoga teachers. Medical and psychology professionals may offer a checklist, and a computer-based test of focus, but they forget, don't know, or don't acknowledge that the computer test, while an objective measure, can only indicate that focus is a problem, but not *why*. That's the crucial question that needs answering.
>
> Just as an example, my specialty is trauma. Research shows that adverse childhood experiences [ACEs] may account for a staggeringly high percentage of the children diagnosed with ADHD. In other words, the stress and anxiety, and safety-making behaviors of a child traumatized by life, can look *exactly* like ADHD. And yet, when properly assessed, the child does not meet the DSM-5 criteria for this disorder. So, this means there are a huge number of children taking medication for ADHD, when in fact, they may have a burned out nervous system from trauma, or an undiagnosed learning disability, or sensory processing disorder, or anxiety, or . . . or . . . or—this is not cool.[18]

CONCLUSION

Makes your head spin, doesn't it? This is a clinical doctor's unvarnished account of misdiagnosis in action. When 80 percent of clinic referrals point to ADHD, most of those 80 percent will be clinically diagnosed with it, and only 5 to 7 percent of the patients actually *have* ADHD, we've got ourselves an epidemic of misdiagnosis. "As a mental health clinician, I find it fascinating the complexities of genetics, environment and stressors that contribute to mental illness," Australian practitioner Erica Dametto says. "ADHD is certainly blanketed to cover up many underlying trauma disorders. We always hear about that kid in school with ADHD and less of the kid who is experiencing abuse in the home and seeking emotional validation."[19]

I address mislabeling in chapter 17—and how we can hopefully rise above it.

Consequently, I'm afraid we're creating a new population of misdiagnosed kids and adults living on addictive prescription stimulants while never looking further to see what is really wrong with them—if anything is wrong at all. What if, instead, we've all been led to believe that ADHD is a huge medical and mental health problem by outside sources intent on selling ADHD to as many people as possible, for reasons that fall short of helping people heal, adopt healthier lifestyles, and make the most of their lives?

8

PRESCRIBING IN AN OPEN OCEAN

Whenever I try to wrap my head around the way we diagnose and prescribe for ADHD, I feel like I'm sailing in an open ocean of surprises, dangers, and faulty navigation. First of all, the territory surrounding this diagnosis is immense. Along with that, the ADHD diagnostic basket sometimes feels to me (as well as plenty of concerned medical and behavioral professionals) like a gyre, that Texas-sized mass of the world's plastic trash that spins like a whirlpool in the Pacific. The diagnosis draws from such a catch basin of behaviors. Then there's bouncing from doctor to doctor, desperately trying to find the therapeutic key to settle the mind into a better life. In my experience, a treacherous voyage across a storm-tossed sea is a fair comparison, for sure, but this voyage can last forever.

When we're talking about a condition like ADHD, in which 75 percent of prescribed therapy for young children is pharmaceutical, according to the Centers for Disease Control and Prevention[1] (which, incidentally, recommends behavior therapy over meds as a first treatment resort), shouldn't our diagnostic parameters be small and precise, rather than sprawling as an ocean? And shouldn't we be even more diligent in prescribing to young children, especially when dealing with powerful drugs that, according to a 2016 *JAMA Psychiatry* study, "have a distinct effect on children that may lead to lasting neurological changes"?[2]

A QUICK MEDICAL HISTORY

I had the advantage (or disadvantage, depending on how you look at it) of being a thirty-five-year-old adult when my difficulties in life prompted my walk of discovery and better health that led me to the fateful crossroads of ADHD. A quick review of my recent medical history points out just how hard it was to pinpoint an accurate diagnosis—yet how quickly I was prescribed powerful medications:

2010—I awoke in a cold sweat, locked inside my first-ever (that I know of) panic attack. Aimee and I decided that I needed to see a doctor about my increasing anxiety, which we both considered severe. It began after starting a new job in our new home city, one that required me to take several buses from the house. I was frozen with fear, in the midst of a full-fledged panic attack, one of the more frightening episodes for anyone, sometimes leading to dangerous, self-sabotaging behaviors. At the doctor's office, the physician put me on Zoloft, an antidepressant that did nothing for my root issues. My diagnosing/treatment journey was underway.

2011—After burning out and dropping out of university, I hit the darkest point of my life and tried to hang myself—like my brother Ryan did three years earlier. Unlike Ryan, I survived, and then I spiraled into a severe, acute depression. After the pain hurt too much and I couldn't "seal the deal" (end my life), I walked upstairs and told my wife to rush me to the emergency room. A team of specialists diagnosed me with ADHD and acute depression. They prescribed amphetamine and dextroamphetamine. I felt no difference in my moods, attention span, or energy level, and I quit the medication after two months. We tried different doses and gave the stimulant ample time to have some sort of effect, but as we're learning, stimulants "working" does *not* mean ADHD necessarily. There's a lot more to the biology of the brain and body/nervous system that requires a look at what's going on "under the hood." I was already racing so fast in my autonomic nervous system from the impacts of early trauma (and adult trauma as a result of my behavior and thought patterns) that the stimulants did nothing for me. Stimulants take effect immediately, as is scientifically known, and it may take up to two weeks to find a correct dosage amount for cases that actually need it (as a last resort, always). I needed much different help, I now realize.

I still had trouble with despair, anxiety, focusing issues, and anger. If anything, stimulants made it all worse. When you add to that the fact that I was already on blood pressure medication, it gets even scarier. Thank God I got off the amphetamine and dextroamphetamine and dug deeper into myself. There was way more going on than what a pill could help fix, and it wasn't even the right pill to begin with, nor was the diagnosis. In hindsight, I'm outraged by how haphazardly many are diagnosed with ADHD these days. I'm far from alone in this view.

At this point I started to wonder whether ADHD was the right diagnosis for me. I began to passionately research all sides of the condition, which proved to be the germination point for this book.

2012—While questioning the roots of my symptoms, issues, and erratic behavior, I drifted from job to job and from antidepressant to antidepressant, over a half dozen prescriptions in all. One medicine in particular, escitalopram, given for depression and anxiety, helped to a degree. I also received cognitive behavioral and compassion-focused therapy to work on my thought patterns and to learn better coping and management skills, and to work out the rage issues toward my mother for the childhood trauma I recounted in chapter 6. The only bright spots in life were my wife, our pets, and the hope of helping others find an easier way through these difficulties in their own lives.

January 2013—Suicidal ideation returned, penetrating my heart and mind as intensely as in 2011. With heavy hearts, Aimee and I walked into the outpatient clinic to commit me under a legal "form." Security escorted me to the locked mental health unit, where I stayed for two weeks. I was officially diagnosed with a "mood disorder" and put on quetiapine, an antipsychotic that helped me sleep but eventually led to horrible mood swings. I had to stop taking it for my own safety (as well as my wife's). Aimee and I remember my emotions becoming so intense that I smashed my fist into our solid oak dining room table one day. I tried to cry out of sheer frustration over my severe mood swings, but only came up with a scream. The doctor was very understanding as I questioned the medication, and she helped me taper off.

Therapy was really what I needed. I needed support from someone in my community as I faced an identity and career crisis (one the result of the other), with the root causes deeply linked to early trauma and resulting in my behavior toward women. My former criminal record also set my life on a viciously intense path toward an obsession to right those past wrongs—but other mistakes piled on. It became too much, and I tried to kill myself—out of sheer exhaustion, I now realize. I lacked the patience and work ethic to make it, but that was because I was desperately clinging to my armored-car goal deep inside. (I still burned within whenever I saw one of the trucks in the city.) I had fused my identity *to* that job, *to* that uniform. It became everything to me—a metaphor for "making it" in life, as fucked up as that may sound.

Now, with a suicide attempt and ADHD diagnosis on my permanent record, good luck getting hired by such a company! I reeled from that reality, struggling to come to terms as the clock kept moving around me; life went on, and bills had to be paid. I was just trying to hang on. I was clinging to hope.

July 2014—While working a night security job in downtown Calgary, which involved sitting in a skyscraper under construction, I suffered a horrible panic attack about sitting still, wasting my life away, and making a terrible wage with no prospects for a better future. I walked home and told Aimee how I felt, despairing yet again over my lack of career achievement and shortcomings as a husband. We marched to the emergency clinic in Calgary and saw a psychiatrist, who casually described the episode as a case of cyclothymia, a rare mood disorder. "Just go work in the oil fields and make your wife happy with good money," he told me. That left a bad impression, to say the least. More alarmingly, this particular psychiatrist was also a professor at a nearby medical school, teaching young, aspiring psychiatrists.

March 2015—I visited my new general practitioner after moving back to Ontario, Canada. I had just been admitted to the emergency room to see a psychiatrist due to rapid mood swings. Unless I committed myself to the psych ward, I was told, I would be put on a waiting list to see a psychiatrist; the wait was eight months. This doctor put me on strong mood stabilizers generally prescribed for severe cases of bipolar disorder and depression. The result? I felt worse. Eventually, we argued over what I considered her inability to listen to my frustration. Unless I committed myself, though, my hands were tied. I knew it wasn't the right course of action—proper assessment and treatment *were*—which led me to Dr. Royer.

THE PROLIFERATION OF PRESCRIPTIONS

The flipside of a standard ADHD diagnosis is the prescription, now one of the most talked about and controversial subjects in our society and the medical profession. As the Centers for Disease Control and Prevention (CDC) noted, 75 percent of prescribed therapy for ADHD is pharmaceutical, and those pharmaceuticals fall in the order of strength between mild stimulants and powerful, Class II drugs. While meds have been prescribed for ADD and ADHD for several decades, never have we seen the numbers or percentages prescribed as today—nor the concerns. Dr. Royer spells out another problem, which I'll elaborate on in the next chapter—where's the exit strategy?

"If my kid is now on a lifetime use of a stimulant, I mean there's no exit strategy for this, right?" he asks.

> Once you start it, you're on it, and there's [often] no way out. Now, all of a sudden, I found out, "Hey, one in three of these [diagnoses] are even accurate . . . and now it's my kid?" In 1990, one in forty kids were diagnosed with ADHD. Now, it's one in eight. If you are a low-income minority, it's one in three.
>
> It shouldn't matter if you're black, white, or orange. Something is going on here that isn't based on science. It's based on (1) a market for stimulants and (2) a lazy diagnostic process.[3]

Since we've addressed the issue of how ADHD is diagnosed today, let's look at the other half of this equation. We're in a white-hot prescription market for ADHD medication, led by the stimulants most often prescribed—Vyvanase, Adderall, Concerta, Metadate, Focalin, Daytrana, and Ritalin.[4] This "white-hot market" description alone should bring us to full attention, since there should never be a "hot" or "cold" market for these all-powerful prescription drugs. It should be an "as-needed" market. Any doctor who diagnoses carefully and treats his or her patients, including the vast majority of those we interviewed for this book, writes prescriptions only as warranted and needed.

"Any disorder which requires medication should be a diagnosis of last resort. Every other possibility needs to be eliminated first, before prescribing any medication," says Dr. Susannah-Joy Schuilenberg.

We end up creating a whole host of *other* issues by rushing to diagnosis. And even if ADHD is supported by a robust assessment process, behavioral interventions are just as effective as medication without the side effects.

Medication is a life-saving intervention for some children diagnosed with ADHD, but only a very small percentage of those who are actually taking these drugs. If ADHD is best a diagnosis of last resort, then medication needs to be the intervention of last resort.[5]

Yet, here we are—in a white-hot $12.9 billion market, according to market research firm IBISWorld,[6] driven by pharmaceutical companies, their advertising and media coverage, and fueled by the rush to diagnose. When 75 percent of diagnosed cases are given prescriptions as an immediate course of treatment, we are not dispensing medication as a last resort. Rather, it's the first resort. We're feeding the bear. Dr. Schuilenberg has another term for this approach: "the fast-food mentality in medicine."[7]

The numbers tell an incredible story that I find deeply troubling, enough to devote my life to finding ways to help us get out of this climate and approach:

- According to IMS Health, a drug market research firm, more than 87 million prescriptions were written for ADHD medication in 2015.[8] That's up from 67 million in 2010.
- Sales for ADHD medications nearly tripled from $4.7 billion in 2006 to $12.9 billion in 2015, according to a report from market research firm IBISWorld.[9] The same IBISWorld report projects sales in 2020 at $17.5 billion.
- According to the January 2016 issue of *Pediatrics* magazine, an estimated 5.8 million schoolchildren in the United States hold prescriptions for ADHD. Many of those were diagnosed between the ages of *two and five*, according to the CDC.[10]
- Kimberly Holland and Elsbeth Riley, in their medically reviewed article "ADHD by the Numbers: Facts, Statistics, and You," 6.1 percent of all American children were being treated for ADHD with medication in 2014. The states reporting highest medical treatment of children were Louisiana, at 10.4 percent, and Kentucky, at 10.1 percent. On the other side of the fifty-state spectrum, Nevada reported just 2 percent of its kids receiving medi-

cine for ADHD, with Hawaii and California coming in at 3.3 percent.[11]

- For children and adolescents in the United States, antipsychotics (the category under which ADHD meds fall) are now the third largest drug category being prescribed, according to Steven Francesco, author of the well-received 2015 book *Overmedicated and Undertreated: How I Lost My Only Son to Today's Toxic Children's Mental Health Industry*. Francesco, citing industry statistics, noted that such prescriptions increased by *600 percent* between 1998 and 2014.[12]

- Children in the United States are four times as likely to receive a diagnosis and prescription for ADHD as those in the United Kingdom presenting similar behaviors and traits, according to a 2016 study by the University of Exeter.[13]

- Nearly 20 percent of all boys have been diagnosed for ADHD and are on medication when they reach high school.[14] This is alarming: we are talking about the future movers and shakers of our society.

- From 2008 to 2012, prescriptions of ADHD drugs to adults jumped by 53 percent, according to Express Scripts, a national prescription benefit plan provider.[15]

- The American Psychiatric Association (APA), publisher of DSM-V, receives 28 percent of its funding from pharmaceutical companies, according to a statement the APA provided in 2008 to inquiring U.S. senator Charles Grassley (R-IA).[16]

- An estimated 75 percent of patients are receiving drugs as the first choice of therapy for ADHD, according to the CDC—even though behavioral and compassion-centered therapy is being advocated more and more by psychiatrists and behavioral scientists.

- In 2014, the year after DSM-V's new, streamlined ADHD checklist was published, a study in the *Journal of the American Academy of Child and Adolescent Psychiatry* estimated total spending on ADHD ranged from $143 billion (United States and Canada) to $266 billion (worldwide), with direct costs (doctor's visit plus prescription) of $1,574 per person.[17]

- *Bloomberg News* reported on June 22, 2015, that adults surpassed children as the leading recipients of ADHD medication in the United States—just nine years after Harvard Medical School psychiatrist Dr. Joseph Biederman's controversial and landmark 2006 study that sharply increased the estimate of prevalence among adults and one year after DSM-V relaxed its diagnostic requirement of adult ADHD from six of the nine "checklist" symptoms to five. According to *Bloomberg News*, citing data from pharmaceutical company Shire PLC, adults accounted for 53 percent of ADHD prescriptions issued in the United States in 2014, up from 39 percent in 2007. Conversely, in Europe, children account for 74 percent of ADHD prescriptions issued that same year.[18]

"Use of ADHD drugs by adults in the United States is growing at nearly twice the rate of the overall market," Shire CEO Flemming Ornskov told Bloomberg.[19] Shire, based in Ireland, manufactures Vyvanase, which reported fourth-quarter 2015 sales of $453 million, up 18 percent in one year—despite the fact that Shire's overall net income dropped sharply in the same time period.[20]

How the hell did we get here? How did this bell curve develop slowly for six decades—and then explode? While diagnoses of "hyperactivity" or "inattentiveness" have been in medical journals since the 1880s—and earlier, according to some—the first known medication to combat it was presented in 1929, when American chemist Gordon Alles experimented with beta-phenylisopropylamine, soon to be called "amphetamine." He reported a feeling of well-being in test patients within twenty minutes of administering. In 1937, Rhode Island psychiatrist Charles Bradley reported a positive effect with this amphetamine, just introduced by Smith, Kline, and French. Dr. Bradley administered it to kids diagnosed with ADHD-like behavioral problems. The so-called arithmetic pills helped many calm down and focus on their schoolwork (interesting how stimulants were seen as school performance aides almost eighty years ago!). According to the book *On Speed,* by Nicolas Rasmussen,[21] by 1939, sales of Benzedrine jumped from $95,000 to $330,000. Three other types of methamphetamine and mood enhancers hit the market shortly thereafter: Dexedrine in 1945, Methedrine in 1949, and Desoxyn, also in 1949. (The latter two are currently approved to treat ADHD in children six and older.)

Production and use of methamphetamines grew during the 1950s and 1960s, becoming a national epidemic by 1970, when an estimated 8

billion such pills were taken. It also became a more prominently prescribed drug for kids in 1968, when the APA's DSM manual first incor-
porated the concept of hyperactivity, calling it "hyperkinetic reaction of
childhood." By 1971, the Food and Drug Administration (FDA) cut
production limits on methamphetamines by more than 80 percent.

The next big turn came in 1980, when the DSM added attention
deficit order, or ADD, as an official diagnosis "with or without hyperactivity." That year, about five hundred thousand children in the United
States were so diagnosed. In 1987, the condition was renamed attention
deficit hyperactivity disorder, or ADHD. While many use the terms
interchangeably, or even as separate conditions, ADD and ADHD became the same condition in the eyes of the medical community. By
1990, the number of childhood ADHD diagnoses reached 1 million, for
which prescriptions were issued.[22]

That was the first news heralding the dawn of the 1990s. The second
was even more profound: in 1989, thanks to relaxed regulations, pharmaceutical companies in the United States were permitted to advertise
their products direct-to-consumer (DTC) after a decade of manufacturers trying to crack through the FDA's carefully placed ban on it.

The result? Game on for prescription dispensing. Since that time,
the market has been fueled like a California brushfire by three communication sources that, taken together, create a perfect storm of exposure. The first is rampant media coverage, thanks in part to aggressive
public relations efforts by pharmaceutical companies and those advocating ADHD as a growing problem in our schools and workplaces. The
other part is a 24/7 media cycle hungrier than ever for reader-grabbing
headlines and ratings-grabbing stories. Along with that has come millions of dollars of direct advertising, the results of sweeping reforms
enacted in 1989 by the FCC (Federal Communications Commission)
and FDA that make direct advertising to the public permissible for
pharmaceutical companies. Prior to that, Big Pharma had to advertise
through professional journals, doctor's offices, and hospitals.

Let's look quickly at a few numbers and other facts:

- According to Nielsen, drugmakers spent $5.2 billion on direct-to-
  consumer advertising in 2015, resulting in $457 billion in total
  sales (of which $12.5 billion is for ADHD and ADD meds). That's
  up from $2.5 billion in 2000 and $360 *million* in 1995, the latter

figure provided by the National Institutes of Health.[23] About $3.7 billion went to TV ads (with CBS leading the way, with $511 in Big Pharma ad revenue), followed by $1.3 billion for magazine ads. The remaining $200 million is split between print and online newspaper advertising.[24] Figures for social media and digital ads were not available, which would certainly drive up the figure by several hundred million dollars. I should add that the United States is one of only two countries in the world (New Zealand being the other) that allows such open-ended direct-to-consumer pharmaceutical advertising.

- Even though the 250,000-member-strong American Medical Association reversed its stance in November 2015 and recommended that pharmaceutical companies halt direct-to-consumer advertising immediately (citing an escalating abuse problem that I detail in chapter 8), it continues unabated. The reason? The ban must be enacted by U.S. Congress. That's not likely, since nearly all of its 535 Republican and Democratic members are supported by these companies and their lobbyists. We can already see the side effects: the astronomical prices of meds, a huge bone of contention that isn't going away soon.

- Drilling that down, a study by MapLight, which studies money's influence on politics, showed that for all senate and congressional campaigns from 2009 to 2015, *two people* received no contribution from Big Pharma: John Yarmuth (D-KY) and Jared Polis (D-CO). Only fifteen others received contributions of less than $1,000, including one U.S. senator—2016 Democratic presidential candidate Bernie Sanders. Among those atop the list, Senate Majority Leader Mitch McConnell (R-KY) was second among senators with $286,060 in campaign contributions from 2009 through 2015; and Speaker of the House Paul Ryan (R-WI) was second in Congress with $130,300 received. And that was before Ryan's 2016 reelection campaign.[25] Furthermore, according to STAT, the respected website that reports on health and medicine trends, 30 percent of senators and 20 percent of congressmen are shareholders in pharmaceutical companies.[26]

This is the nuts and bolts of the pharmaceutical climate for ADHD today. Sadly, the fix is in at the highest levels of governance. Media coverage—thanks in no small part to tremendous public relations efforts by Big Pharma and the associations it helps to subsidize, such as the American Psychiatric Association—has been far more of a proponent of diagnose-and-prescribe than a neutral journalistic party should be, although that is certainly changing with the rampant problems of overdiagnosed kids and stimulant drug abuse in the United States, which we discuss in chapter 8. Nothing short of a massive revolt by consumers is going to change things.

"In my opinion, the media should not be in this business," Dr. Jeffrey Hirschfield says. "If they are allowed to have the microphone, people will listen and internalize this information as inherently credible and scientifically proven. I am of the opinion that experienced healthcare providers would be in the best position to educate their patients and provide the necessary standard of care. I also maintain that no physician should ever be excused from following standard of care practices when diagnosing or managing patients. If a physician is pressured by external forces to provide an ADD diagnosis, they need to confront that situation."[27]

When it comes to prescriptions, another situation needs to be confronted. The principal reason for an ADD or ADHD prescription is to improve one's overall concentration and focus with the hopes of improving workplace performance and/or improving attentiveness in the classroom. Everyone agrees on that. This is fair enough for adults making their own decisions about their own lives, but what about the one in eight children (or one in seven, depending on your source) who are diagnosed and prescribed? What if I were to tell you that Shire, the maker of Adderall, is now openly marketing lesson plans and comic books directed at ADHD students and their teachers?

That brings up a shadowy undercurrent beneath another reason given for ADHD meds: *to help kids become better students.* It's heavily backed by many state governments and school districts, as I'm about to point out. What does the sole goal of improved grades have to do with a medical condition worthy of a long-term prescription to a powerful stimulant?

Not much—unless you're in the business of selling ADHD. This leads to some very serious unintended consequences that threaten our social fabric more and more, especially among boys and men.

9

WHAT WE'RE UP AGAINST

"This is your brain. This is your brain on drugs. Any questions?"
—Partnership for a Drug Free America public service announcement series, 1987–1997

As I hopped from doctor's office to emergency room to psychiatric facility, I asked myself the same question over and over again: "These doctors know what's going on inside my brain? What can they do to stop it? Anything?" Sometimes, I even asked my doctors these questions, especially when they prescribed me very different but equally powerful medications. No one gave me a full response—or at least one good enough to justify subjecting my brain to the chemical forces of these drugs. I can't tell you how many times I've thought to myself, "What is this shit doing to my brain?"

That possibility has only recently surfaced in media and public discussion after years of being blotted out by the rush to diagnosis and prescription for ADHD, bipolar, obsessive-compulsive disorder, anxiety issues, and other fast-rising neurological and behavioral disorders with biochemical connections. These connections are linked to our high-speed, high-pressure, high-expectation society like a giant and very uptight nervous system. To paraphrase former U.S. vice president Al Gore, it's an inconvenient truth, because it requires us to know more about how our brains work, and requires doctors to spend more time testing for that crucial knowledge. This slow pace runs counter to the diagnostic world in this "fast food" prescription market, to use Dr. Schuilenberg's term.

"The average general practitioner [GP] does not have the training required to accurately diagnose neurological and/or psychological disorders," she says.

> Even such "simple" things as depression require rather more attention than what a GP might give in a standard office visit. Any disorder without a standardized medical test [i.e., a blood test] logically should be a 'rule out' situation, eliminating *all* other possibilities before labeling. Sadly, this isn't the case or it's the rare doctor who follows this practice.
>
> To be fair, the pressure on our medical system is tremendous, and most GPs have very little control of the process of seeing patients. This leads to a 'fast food' mentality in medicine, which creates and perpetuates the pill-popping habit we all seem to have.[1]

Not only does it feel like a fast-food mentality, but it's beginning to look like a fast-food mentality as well. Take the May 23, 2016, announcement on STAT of Adzenys, a chewable, fruity candy that dissolves in your mouth. It also happens to be an extended-release amphetamine that equals Adderall in strength. Its mid-May market release by Neos Therapeutics, and ensuing in-clinic ground campaign by 125 sales reps, stirred up a small frenzy among doctors. Neos CEO Vipin-Garg, who sees the benefit of dissolving tabs because it is a more pleasant way to take medications and supplements, told STAT that his company is having "no problem" getting appointments with doctors who want to prescribe it, stating that it "will help harried mothers get their kids medicated faster before school." As for the adult ADHD population, "If they forget to take their pill with breakfast, they could just pop a tablet on the way to work."[2]

I don't know about you, but I have a serious problem with the overmedicating of children and adults with ADHD stimulants, and I'm not alone. University of California, San Diego psychiatrist Dr. Alexander Papp tells STAT, "This sanctions an orally disintegrating amphetamine for kids. What's next? Gummy bears?" Dr. Mukund Gnanadesikan, a child and adolescent psychiatrist, says, "I'm not a big fan of controlled substances that come in forms that can be easily abused—and certainly a chewable drug falls into that category."[3]

Overmedicating for ADHD has become a larger public concern, too. The questions are truly troubling: How do you distinguish between an energetic preschooler and one with ADHD? How do you know that a stressed-out teen that acts out has ADHD or simply is a stressed-out teen acting out? And how do doctors, those poor, overwhelmed souls caught in the middle between parents and Big Pharma, their Hippocratic Oaths and prevailing social or school demands, know whether they are seeing a kid truly in need of medicine to function properly—or one with parents obsessed with having the perfect child? What about the kid that's simply having trouble concentrating on a couple of school subjects? If this sounds like an outrageous list of "symptoms," think again: this is not an uncommon daily story in clinics across the land. More ominously, doctors have been urged to diagnose by not only some overwrought parents, but also by schoolteachers—whose monies, in the case of public schools, are tied to student test performance and attendance.

In late 2015, Cherokee County, Georgia, pediatrician Dr. Michael Anderson raised eyebrows when he told the *New York Times* that "we've decided as a society it's too expensive to modify the kid's environment. So we have to modify the kid." Dr. Anderson was speaking specifically to medicating low-income kids who get bad grades in order to improve their concentration and impulse control abilities. He added a caveat that, for me, takes this conversation right out of a discussion of ADHD and into the realm of "What the hell are we doing to our kids?": "People who are getting As and Bs, I won't give it to them."[4]

Weren't we supposed to be medicating (as a last resort) for ADHD? That's what I thought. However, many schools have shown little concern with substantial percentages of their student bodies being medicated. If those student bodies crank out grades, test scores, and attendance records that keep the all-important state and federal tax dollars and private contributions coming their way, then what's the problem, right? I'll get more into that, but this framework of thought puts enormous pressure on administrators, school nurses, doctors, parents, and even sports and extracurricular activity coaches to wonder about ADHD—and act—if a kid shows any difficulty paying attention, concentrating, getting good grades, or keeping up with ever-accelerating expectations. But here's the thing: I described *everyday high school campus life* in 2017.

Some pediatricians, psychiatrists, and neurologists see this growing situation of medication not as the solution to all school- or work-related issues, but as a train wreck gathering steam in a hurry. The heart of the argument: what is happening to the normal development of our brains, whether or not we meet the DSM-V criteria for ADHD? Dr. William Graf, a Connecticut pediatrician, told the *New York Times* that he feels parents, doctors, and teachers are obligated to respect what he terms "the authenticity of development," but he questions whether they are doing so—especially with the quick-fix potential of prescribed stimulants.[5]

Dr. Anderson was even more cynical, noting that behavioral therapies and other ideas to work with students were costly in terms of money and resources—and medications offer a quick fix that costs the schools nothing, since parents and/or insurance providers pay for them.[6]

Looking at the flip side of the doctor's office, Dr. Schuilenberg took a quick panoramic view of the situation that surrounds ADHD medication every day in every community: "Parents are under pressure to deal with the teacher's concerns in the classroom; teachers are under pressure to meet specific educational goals; schools are under pressure to do well on standardized tests; and the whole system makes the child the problem," she explained. "Teachers see medication as a way to make the classroom work, and parents see medication as a way to keep the school happy, and to minimize the chaos and conflict that has produced the label of ADHD in the first place."[7]

We have a big problem here. Isn't it time we stop overmedicating, overdiagnosing, and kowtowing to outside pressures, and start thinking about the *patients* by looking at what these medications can do to our brains?

CHANGING THE FOCUS FROM MEDS TO OUR BRAINS

This is the world in which we find ourselves. We should be learning more about what these drugs are doing to our brains—and what our brains are doing differently in this overstimulated society. But we're only getting there in fits and spurts. Why? Well, I can speak to one possible answer: we usually need to take hard, painful journeys that last years before we receive answers that make our lives better—or at least lead us in the right direction, which is how I ended up in Dr. Royer's office. There I received an explanation that changed my world and opened my eyes to what we are facing today. I also learned that we are not often given the *right* kind of information about our brains, information that could help us take charge of our situations. To do so, we need to find doctors with the strength to stand up to the rush-to-prescription sentiment, as Dr. Schuilenberg noted. (The American Medical Association's late 2015 call for Big Pharma to halt direct-to-consumer advertising suggests the tides are beginning to turn.)

Consider this, from Dr. Royer:

> Your brain's ability to learn things is far superior than any chemical, but we throw that to the side and just alter the electrical current with a chemical. We don't try to teach the brain how it should focus or how it should sleep, and use the available technology to actually restructure the speed at which the brain is going. On the treatment side, you can either take a painkiller for your bum knee your entire life, or you can go to physical therapy and get the thing fixed. We have so many people that think the only way out is to take this pill, and many times it's the wrong pill.
>
> I'm not opposed to medicines; I am opposed to misdiagnosis. I constantly see [misdiagnoses] time and time again like in Jeff's case, but I'll also see four- and five-year-old children on two to three times the dose of a medicine they should be on—and it's not even the right diagnosis. We're taking this four-and five-year-old brain, which is just in the midst of stabilizing itself, and we're overmedicating it in the absolute wrong direction.[8]

This brings me to my biggest pet peeve, along with overdiagnosis— the way we prescribe for it, especially knowing the impacts of these powerful stimulants. Yes, they do assist in focusing short-term productivity and getting jobs or assignments done for those having trouble functioning due to inattentiveness or lack of concentration. Without such medical intervention, many would spend a lifetime in deep struggle with their imbalanced brain chemistries—and do. However, *many* does not equal the tens of millions currently prescribed. My question is, what are we *really* doing to them?

HOW ADHD MEDS INTERACT WITH OUR BRAINS

ADHD meds are powerful stimulants. Many are methamphetamines with brand names like Adderall, Vyvanase, Concerta, Metadate, Focalin, Daytrana, and Ritalin. All can easily be habit-forming. The Drug Enforcement Administration (DEA) classifies them as Schedule II Controlled Substances—the same classification as meperidine, fentanyl, oxycodone, morphine, opium, and codeine—because of their strength and addictive properties. When they interact with a brain of abnormal biochemistry—a lack of dopamine or adrenalin—they fill the gap by offering stimulation that often reduces disruptive behavior while improving attentiveness, performance, ability to follow and act on instruction, and overall concentration. The longer meds fill the gap, the longer they are necessary. This can create a physiological and psychological dependence, making them more difficult to put aside. Given the tight relationship between ADHD diagnoses and meds, prevailing clinical wisdom leans toward prescribing for the long term more often than not.

These meds can produce troubling and dangerous side effects, which have presented in patients young and old: irregular heartbeat, growth suppression, increased blood pressure, hyperventilation when excited, and in rare cases, psychotic episodes (not as rare as manufacturers would have you believe).[9] A study in the January 2016 issue of *Pediatrics* cited a project conducted by Dr. Rudolf Uher from Dalhousie University in Nova Scotia, Canada. Dr. Uher studied 141 children and adolescents in the Families Overcoming Risks and Building Opportunities for Wellbeing program, which studies the children of parents diagnosed with severe mental disorders. (The American Psychiatric Association [APA] notes that children in such circumstances are four times as likely to develop ADHD or other mental issues as those in more stable homes.[10]) Dr. Uher and his associates found that 24 of the 141 had taken prescribed stimulants, and 33 had been diagnosed with ADHD. What he learned next shocked him: 15 of those 24 kids reported psychotic symptoms or episodes. Of the 117 kids not diagnosed with ADHD, a relatively few 33 reported psychotic experiences. Furthermore, the research showed that the psychotic experiences *did not appear to be related to the diagnosis of the parent or family history.*[11]

It seems to me we should be spending more time funding and listening to studies like these and the others finally seeing the light of day. From them we can gain a fuller understanding of these medications before prescribing them on a socially sweeping scale like Soma in Huxley's *Brave New World*, which, if you think about it, feels a lot like what we're doing, with schools, clinics, and workplaces right in the middle.

Now for the follow-up question, the one keeping myself and a lot of physicians, psychiatrists, behavioral experts, and even educators up at night: how do these same powerful Class II drugs work on the brains of children under twelve—or, to jump to the most-diagnosed demographic group, children under eight? For years, we've heard pharmaceutical representatives, physicians, and other proponents of a medical ADHD solution contend that the impact on a child's brain is inconsequential, or small, compared to the greater benefit of sharpening their attention spans, calming them down, and improving their schoolwork. This argument lacks one key ingredient: conclusive findings on the biochemical and developmental impact on preadolescent brains. Little research has been done on the developing brain. Prior to 2015, nearly all such research was studied only in animals, according to the official JAMA Network. [12]

However, we now have a study that has stopped some of the rush to prescribe among physicians aware of it. This double-blind, randomized, placebo-controlled study, first published in late 2015 in *JAMA Psychiatry*, investigated the effect of ADHD drugs on children and young adults. [13] The bottom line: the top substance used in ADHD drugs, methylphenidate (the active ingredient in Ritalin), can lead to lasting neurological changes in children. The University of Amsterdam physicians and researchers who conducted the research write, "Because maturation of several brain regions is not complete until adolescence, drugs given during the sensitive early phases of life may affect neurodevelopmental trajectories that can have more profound effects later in life." They add, "The adolescent brain is a rapidly developing system that maintains high levels of plasticity. As such, the brain may be particularly vulnerable to drugs that interfere with these processes or modify the specific transmitter systems involved."

Researchers began with "The Effects of Psychotropic Drugs on Developing Brain (ePOD) Study," [14] which they created. They randomly assigned ninety-nine male adults and children diagnosed with ADHD to be treated in one of two ways—with a placebo or with methylphenidate. After sixteen weeks, the researchers observed and recorded dopamine-related (dopaminergic) activity in children and adults using MRI technology. They found significant changes in the brains of children, specifically their neurodevelopmental trajectories. They did not see the same in adults. Rather than the changes having a positive effect on ADHD symptoms, they found adverse effects that can alter the brain's development over the long term. They even called further attention to another study, the Multimodal Treatment Study of Children with ADHD (MTSCA), the most comprehensive trial on long-term effects of ADHD and funded by the National Institute of Mental Health, to show what happens once medication-induced neurodevelopmental changes occur in young subjects. "Six years after enrollment [in MTSCA], medication management was associated with a transient increase in the prevalence of anxiety and depression," researchers wrote.[15]

The JAMA study is the latest piece of conclusive evidence that our decision to medicate first in ADHD diagnoses is steering us down a slippery path. We are altering the brain chemistries of children and adolescents with stimulants. We're also shepherding in a new generation of artificially stimulated young people who think a thirty-second movie or TV scene is long and rely on outside stimulation to feel "normal."

As alarming as I find this, my red flags fly even higher when I consider that the ADHD diagnosis has two directions in which it can go, hypoactive and hyperactive (which we rarely hear about)—and yet, we prescribe the same stimulants to each variation.

Dr. Tim Royer blames the rush to prescribe in large part on those changed FDA and FCC regulations. "In 1989 and earlier, you couldn't market these meds to people on the street; you could only introduce those to doctors," he says.

> But after '89, we started being able to market these things to teachers, to parents, and now everybody is asking their doctor for the next best, greatest med.
>
> In 1989, when we got Prozac, we thought we would eradicate depression in ten years. Well, now we have three to four times more depression than we've ever had on the planet. So this stuff isn't working as nicely as we like to think it is.

I think of that today, when we're putting people on these power-ful stimulants that can be—and often are—habit-forming. You say, okay, now if I take you off your medicine today, where are you twenty years later? They're right back where they started. We haven't leveraged the greatest potential, which is the brain's ability to learn.[16]

WHY STIMULANTS DON'T WORK THE SAME IN *ALL* ADHD PATIENTS

A friend of mine made an interesting observation while his physical education students learned dynamic stretches from a visiting physical therapist. They stood in the bleachers, following her direction on new hamstring, quadriceps, and other exercises. My friend noticed one of the students talking endlessly and aimlessly about a half-dozen subjects, his delivery rapid-fire, his arms flying about, his focus both frenetic and sharp. Next to him, another student stared into space, completely disso-ciated from the entire moment. His eyes looked like he was de-fogging a dream. It took several attempts to gain his attention.

Both of these individuals have been diagnosed with ADHD and have taken the same prescribed meds for years. Yet, one couldn't stop talking at warp speed, and the other was as inattentive as a statue. How could they need the same meds?

That question drives many medical professionals, neurologists, and neuroscientists crazy, not the least of which is Dr. Royer. He points out something that seems to get lost in the hard push to diagnose and prescribe: there are *three* different types of ADHD in the DSM-V diagnostic manual. When Dr. Royer was asked about the distinction, he provided a bottom-line description of how the brain waves work for those diagnosed with ADHD—a description you may not hear at your doctor's office but one that shows just how much we need to learn about our loved ones and their brains, or our own brains, before sub-jecting them to these medications.

"There is the inattentive type and there's a hyperactive type (of ADHD)," Dr. Royer says.

Then there's the combined type. All types are prescribed the same medicine. There's the child who's staring out the window in class and gets diagnosed with ADHD inattentive type, meaning they're just not paying attention. They're not causing a problem; they're just staring out the window. He'll get put on the same medicine as a child who has ADHD hyperactive type. This the child bouncing off the walls you typically think of when you think of ADHD.

So the question is, why do both of these kids respond similarly to a stimulant medicine? Why do they both start focusing? If you look at the behaviors, it makes no sense, because one looks almost lethargic and the other looks overactive. However, we're in a culture that only wants to look at the behavior. They're not looking at the neurological activity. When you look at the neurological activity, if it truly is ADHD, what you'll find is in both of those kids, the brain is not getting in gear correctly.

The brain can't stay in gear correctly. The brake pedal keeps activating. The brain is releasing too much of a theta wave, a slow action in the brain. The one child that matches these behaviors zones out, but the other child reacts in a way that happens at times when our brain starts to get out of gear, or not be in a stable spot. Imagine a little child that can't go to sleep at night. It's getting close to bedtime, and the next thing you know, this child is running on an engine, all over the place. You're thinking, "I thought he was tired." Well, he *is* tired, but he's trying to keep his brain awake, so he's activating his environment constantly. It's a constant "startle" effect.

That's what happens with these hyperactive kids. Their brain keeps shutting down, but they're always trying to reorient to their environment. It creates this constant interaction where they're touching everything and darting from one thing to another, because they can't keep that brain in the right speed.

So you give them an amphetamine, which doesn't seem to make any sense. Why would I give them speed, a Class II substance? Yet the next thing you know, this child who's been bouncing all over the place is able to sit there, still, relaxed, and focused. That's because you've sped up these brain waves that were actually disabling him from staying focused, and his behavioral reaction was to be constantly moving to try and keep his brain awake. And then once you gave him a stimulant, he didn't need to do that anymore. Stimulants work because they're increasing the electrical activity in the brain, which then puts the brain in gear for these individuals. But at what cost to their brain's natural development?[17]

Lately, we've been hearing more about what happens when these medications either end up in the wrong hands, or the people taking them legitimately (per doctor's prescription) overdose. To the first point, we've all been mortified to watch substance abuse rates skyrocket in North America for stimulants of all types this decade, along with heroin and opioid painkillers. Our communities are being ravaged by pill dealers, the loss of life of some of our brightest young people, and teenagers smart enough to figure out how to present for ADHD on the DSM-V checklist, receive prescriptions for Class II controlled substances, and then abuse them. Or, they use them to perk up their minds, according to an April 2014 CNN special report, which estimated that up to 30 percent of students use stimulants non-medically.[18] In my book that's a "misuse of substance" problem—and a big one.

This is why we should prescribe as a last resort, not a first. "Any disorder which requires medication should be a diagnosis of last resort," Dr. Schuilenberg says.

> Every other possibility needs to be eliminated first, before prescribing any medication. We end up creating a whole host of *other* issues by rushing to diagnosis. And even if ADHD is supported by a robust assessment process, behavioral interventions are just as effective as medication without the side effects.
>
> Medication is a life saving intervention for some children diagnosed with ADHD, but only a very, very small percentage of those who are actually taking these drugs. If ADHD is at best a diagnosis of last resort, then medication needs to be the intervention of last resort.[19]

I couldn't agree more. Never should a pharmaceutical on the order of powerful ADHD medications be prescribed until we've ruled out other contributing factors, conditions, disorders, or mitigating symptoms. This is even more so with behavioral, mood, or neurological disorders—*especially* when that drug affects brain chemistry (serotonin and norepinephrine levels, in this case). We're talking about the function of the brain, the most important organ in our bodies besides our hearts and lungs! Many leading-edge doctors and neurological experts, including those mentioned in this book, would advise getting another opinion—or heading for the hills.

I can speak from personal experience to another thread of overmedication—trying different medicines until one seems to work. There are eight primary medications for ADHD, which I've mentioned, but what about those for obsessive-compulsive disorder, hypertension, anxiety, bipolar, insomnia, depression, or other disorders that have traits and characteristics in common with ADHD? I know the answer to this question firsthand: it ain't good.

Here's a quick look from my own life. We tried different medicines, starting with antidepressants, escitalopram (which briefly helped my acute depression before "wearing off"), bupropion, sertraline, and aripiprazole. These made me feel like a "zombie" at times; two of them temporarily curtailed my sex drive. The antipsychotics that followed drove me to horrible mood swings and added weight to my already large body (I was 5-foot-9 inches and 240 pounds from all the years of bodybuilding and eating well.)

Then I was put on lithium, in combination with lurasidone, an antipsychotic. It drove me to intense anger and sadness, making me feel like I had bipolar disorder. Then it mercifully ended when I visited Dr. Royer. For his part, he is characteristically blunt when describing the impact of all these medications.

"Health is not a deal here. This is all just putting a Band-Aid over something and people are realizing it's making things worse," he explained. "Most of the people I see plan on starting on one medicine and they end up giving their kids two or three or four meds. They bring their kid into me and we have a lot of undoing to do, because the first medicine was wrong, and consequently the next three are wrong."

How do we begin to get it right? Let's take a look.

10

THE ADHD BUY-IN

I was "sick and tired of feeling sick and tired," as they say in substance-related recovery programs. My problem wasn't addiction, though: it was getting answers for my suicide attempt.

This is why I found myself in an appointment with an outpatient team shortly after my suicide attempt and emergency room visit in 2011. Soon after I arrived, I was given a diagnosis of ADHD by the lead psychiatrist. It was like a massive weight had been lifted—finally, everything in my past made sense.

That is how I felt then. I feel a little differently now.

LOOKING BACK

Looking back on that experience is both concerning and disheartening. Rather than await the psychiatrist's treatment suggestion, I suggested to him that I try Adderall as a "magic pill" to help me focus more, to somehow stay on track with goals, and to be more stable in general. In what medical world does the patient call the shots on what he wants to be prescribed, unless he's a doctor himself? The world of ADHD, as it turns out.

Without batting an eye, the psychiatrist said, "Sure," and wrote me a prescription on the spot. There was no discussion of behavioral, creative, or compassion-based therapy, and no ruling out of anything to do with my traumatic past. I don't even remember an official checklist being used, though I was given tests (checklists) by my own general practioner (GP) during the process to rule out bipolar and bipolar-II, as well as hypomania. So at least there was some "ruling out," a vital step. Yet, we only had a rudimentary discussion that, I realized over time, glossed over the issues with which I was dealing.

Right now, as I write this and think about that period of time, I feel myself becoming physically and emotionally angry. I've already shared the prescription part of it. Here's the rest of the story.

I now believe my doctors in 2010 and 2011 were at a loss to figure out the causes or contributing factors to my issues. I was one of very few to even have access to an entire team in the first place, and they *still* stuck to surface features. That pisses me off. They left a ton of things on the table that could have been ruled out, but instead they were not discussed at all. They proceeded with the checklist-ADHD diagnosis, and left it at that.

In my case, so much was missed that would have benefited me beyond a prescription. My deep fear is that millions are in this exact same boat. Furthermore, unlike me, most don't have access to a team, and/or they can't afford it. Even with access to a team, you can see just how easily childhood trauma and the resulting self-esteem issues can blossom into full-blown anxiety, as it did for me. The identity crisis that followed as a result of having a criminal record all but destroyed my career ambitions, followed by my subsequent suicide attempt.

When I truly hit my bottom, my crisis point, when I was more open than ever to finding out what was wrong and to work toward healing it, what did my team of specialists offer up? ADHD—with a prescription.

Today, my diagnosis and the reasons for it make some sense. This is why I speak out like I do, to make people realize that we must dig deeper into the inconvenient truth behind mental health "diagnosing," such as the driving force behind this rush-to-ADHD environment in which we live.

It took me some time to realize something odd: if the doctor had never seen me before, or spent much time looking at my record, how was he able to funnel lifelong behaviors and tendencies into a spot-on diagnosis in just a few minutes? And to do it without other specialists joining in, at least while diagnosing me?

I thought of other diseases and disorders that result in long-term treatment or prescriptions, like diabetes, arthritis, and heart disease, or bipolar disorder and autism. All of these develop or make themselves apparent over time, like ADHD, but their diagnosis protocols are far different. Patients spend weeks, months, and even years going through batteries of tests, evaluations, and exams before the diagnosis is given. Several physicians consult on the diagnosis, some specialists in their fields. They rule out other causes or possible diagnoses before ruling in the diagnosis that gives a name and treatment options—and often changes a life.

PUSHING TO DIAGNOSE

So how is it that, in a few minutes, I received a diagnosis and a prescription for a powerful stimulant? Was my doctor an absolute wizard at diagnosing ADHD from the dozens of other conditions I could have had? Or was he specifically looking for ADHD—and why?

I don't want to sound like a conspiracy theorist—and I'm sure as hell not one. However, when I started sharing my experience online, and my hundreds of thousands of followers started sharing theirs, I realized something very disturbing was going on: doctors were pushing to diagnose ADHD for a reason. *Were they being pushed to do so?* And if so, by whom?

This question dominates much of the discussion about the alarming diagnosis and prescription rates of ADHD today. In my opinion, it's a fair question, too, one that should always be asked when a medical/behavioral disorder is routinely measured in the media and within the medical field by how many millions have been diagnosed, how many billions of dollars of prescription drugs have been sold, and how much the diagnosis rate has increased in general and in specific age groups. This question has been asked by many in the past few years, including the *New York Times*, which in December 2013 ran an eye-opening article by Alan Schwarz, who later wrote the 2016 best-selling book *Overselling ADHD*. A few important points I drew from the article:

- ADHD diagnostic pioneer Dr. Keith Connors, who has advanced the cause to validate ADHD for a half-century, calls today's rates of diagnosis "a national disaster of dangerous proportions." Hardly what you'd expect to hear from a man with his central role in ADHD's rise to awareness and relevance.[1]

- The current levels of diagnosis and prescription reflect a concerted twenty-five-year effort by pharmaceutical companies to publicize, market, and sell the disorder and pills to doctors, educators, and parents.

- In 2013, the DSM-V task force expanded the diagnostic age range for ADHD from six to twelve years, to four to eighteen years—effectively bringing preschoolers and adolescents "into the market."[2]

- Pharmaceutical companies have advertised in consumer and lifestyle publications. Ads in magazines like *People* and *Good Housekeeping* sell common childhood forgetfulness, poor grades, and occasional acting out as just cause to diagnose and medicate.[3]

- Shire PLC, the largest ADHD medicine manufacturer, financed a comic book, of which more than 100,000 have been distributed to schools since 2012. Among the messages delivered by superheroes (note the tie-in to the type of Hollywood movies kids and adolescents watch more than any other) is this: "Medicines may make it easier to pay attention and control your behavior!" It is even available on Amazon.com.[4]

- The FDA has cited every major ADHD drug numerous times for false and misleading advertising since 2000.[5]

- Manufacturers send sales reps to doctors' offices to present and pitch their products. For instance, in 2016, Neos Therapuetics sent 125 sales reps into the field to promote its new candy-flavored ADHD stimulant, Adzenys. CEO Vipin Garg told STAT that the company is having "no problem" getting appointments with doctors.[6]

- How about the name "Adderall"? Know what it means? "ADD-for-All". The phrase was coined by Roger Griggs, the pharmaceutical executive who brought Adderall onto the market in 1994.[7]

- In its 2000 and 2001 guidelines, the American Academy of Pediatrics (AAP) advised parents to choose between drugs and behavioral therapy to treat their ADHD kids. In 2011, the AAP revised its guidelines to say that parents should "preferably" be using both at the same time. Why the change?[8]

I could spend the rest of this chapter—and the next—writing bullet points of the ways in which ADHD is attached to the profit wheel of medicine, with current and future patients looked upon as "market growth" as zealously as they should be viewed as patients. Mr. Schwarz's book covers this topic exhaustively.

The people who rightfully have ADHD and are receiving the proper treatment are being dwarfed by cases influenced, in whole or in part, by the efforts of external businesses and organizations to stoke the ADHD fires. These fires, I will reiterate, began to burn with the advent of Ritalin, when a conscious decision was made to market ADHD directly to clinicians and consumers in the 1990s.

SELLING ADHD

I see a lot of problems associated with this full-court ADHD press. First, we have pharmaceutical companies doing what companies in the for-profit market do in a market-based economy—market, promote, and sell their products to as many people as possible. Are they selling ADHD? You bet. Why? It's a proven profit maker, and they are in the business to make money. Understood—that's the point of being in for-profit business. So, no matter how upset you or I are with their intentions, claims, or ways of conducting their business, or how ethical or unethical we might find them, they are operating as businesses operate. They participate in everything from the diagnostic process (Shire, on its adhdandyou.com website, provides pre-diagnosis checklists)[9] to creating ADHD activity books aimed at schoolchildren to sending fleets of sales reps to doctors' offices. In North America, this is high-penetration business marketing.

Of course, we consumers have a simple choice: to use the product or not. Even when a doctor prescribes it, we carry that choice for ourselves and our kids.

Then there are doctors and clinicians, psychologists, and psychiatrists, all hopelessly overstretched by demands of the public, school systems, and insurance companies. More and more, doctors are stepping out and insisting that ADHD diagnoses be done collaboratively, between primary care physicians, a psychiatrist, behavioral experts, and even neurologists. (I cover this extensively in chapter 14.) Yet every day they walk into their offices and are bombarded by appointments from well-meaning parents and others who are convinced their fidgety children have ADHD and must be diagnosed and prescribed; or their kids are falling behind in school, and they need to focus better to keep up.

Whatever the case, doctors take (or, in most cases, only have) an average of fifteen minutes to evaluate, click off likely "symptoms" from the DSM-5 checklist, and diagnose. The parents have "sold" the doctors on their kids' situations. When you have fifteen minutes to evaluate something, no matter the endeavor, you rely heavily on all outside information presented. When ADHD is one of the most publicized medical labels by the media, and heavily promoted in our society, the mind can easily track back to the label that "seems to stick out." But what about childhood trauma? Anxiety? Stress? Learning disabilities? Vision issues? Congenital or biological factors? When you have fifteen minutes, these possible causes will be given short shrift.

"I constantly worry about health care providers who succumb to external pressures from parents or teachers or provide a quick diagnosis of AD(H)D from superficial symptoms alone," Dr. Jeffrey Hirschfield says. "This worry is then compounded when one considers the fact that many of these health care professionals go on to wrongly prescribe stimulant medications under this false guise of AD(H)D."[10]

Do I feel doctors can put on the brakes more, reassess their positions, and create a more thorough diagnosing process by involving specialists and spending more time with their patients? Absolutely. In fact, the American Association of Psychiatrists has advocated this very shift for its physician members, while also recommending that doctors de-emphasize prescription drugs as a first course of treatment. The Centers for Disease Control and Prevention agree.[11] This recommendation stands in opposition to—and hopefully not in the way of—a sharply inverted bell curve of the ADHD market that is expected to vault from $14 billion in sales in 2015 to $25 billion in 2024, according to Persistence Market Research and reported in *The Pharma Letter*, a newsletter for the pharmaceutical and biotechnology industries.[12]

I've spoken and exchanged correspondence with doctors who are trying to put on the brakes and take a different route to treating ADHD. However, doctors are locked in the bull's-eye of the marketplace. It pulls them in separate directions, with one voice seeming to rise above the others: get little Mark and Mary, or adult employees

Mark and Mary, to settle down, focus, and do better—by medication. Again, this isn't illegal or against the grain of a market-based society. It's a stark example of the market-based economy working at its best, whether that "best" is something we can live with or not.

> Perhaps unfortunately, society has allowed the direct advertising of pharmaceutical products via television, print magazines, and newspapers, and through the Internet. The confusion then arises whereby the public may misinterpret advertising/sales for the needed education. Physicians also are at risk of developing trust with pharmaceutical representatives who visit their offices, provide samples of medications, and offer enticements at conferences for other monetary prizes.[13]

THE SCHOOL SYSTEM

This leads to what I feel is the most critical "boots on the ground" part of the ADHD equation—our school system. Neither doctors' offices nor pharmacies would be dealing with overwhelming appointments or orders if schools did not actively engage in the diagnosing and promoting of ADHD—not that they're supposed to. Furthermore, in the United States, it is technically illegal for educators to mention ADHD to a student, or to imply that the student has the disorder to his/her family. Educators can express their concerns with school doctors, nurses, or high-level administrators, who can then notify the parents. Is this the actual protocol being followed?

That's a loaded question. Here's how it works in the U.S. public school system. A school receives state and federal money based on two principal criteria—student performance and student attendance. The higher the percentage of kids graduating, or advancing, the more money received. The higher the standardized test scores, the more money the school gets. In a climate of slashed school budgets and fewer, narrower classes, a world that did not exist when I was in grade school, schools rely heavily on standardized test scores, performance, and attendance. Students learn basic core subjects, such as math, science, and language arts, and they practice for the tests that determine their schools' future funding. Isn't education supposed to benefit *the student*, and not the school system?

The pressure is on like never before for high school kids to excel. College costs are through the roof, competition to get into desired schools is more difficult than ever, and advanced placement (AP) classes, far tougher than standard freshman-through-senior high school fare, become a necessary means to get coveted academic scholarships.

School kids today must be prepared for these tests. Their brains must be razor-sharp forces that can memorize and recall numbers, statistics, facts, and vocabulary. They must become proficient critical thinkers by the time they're sixteen. They must be prepared to focus at levels no generation of children before them had to experience, at least not on the same subject matter. They must be attentive, concentrate like champions, and be as self-disciplined and organized as executive assistants.

This is where well-meaning educators, school administrators, school doctors and nurses, and parents come in. When they see kids fidgeting, not paying attention, disrupting the class, or not focusing on the day's lessons, they often come to one conclusion: ADHD. Why? Because with an ADHD diagnosis comes a required IEP (Individual Education Plan) and, in the United States, enactment of the 504, part of the Students with Disabilities Act that incorporates ADHD. Something else comes with that diagnosis, too: the stimulant medication that enables jumpy minds to sharpen their focus.

If ADHD is an epidemic, then the school is the beachhead of that epidemic. Parents worried about performance, behavior, college, and their kid simply "keeping up," might look online at ADHD self-quizzes or checklists, decide their kids have enough characteristics to qualify, and notify the school or family doctor. Or, a teacher might say something to a vice principal or nurse, who then examines the kid and concurs. Sometimes older children will prediagnose themselves, convince their parents that they fit the DSM-V criteria, and take a ride to the doctor's office and pharmacy. Meanwhile, the powers that be marketing ADHD are providing more tools, more materials, and more resources to grow this relationship between hawk-eyed parents, concerned educators, and caring but overwhelmed doctors.

"The alleged cases of ADD diagnosis stemming from teachers, parents, and children/adolescents continue to rise dramatically," Dr. Hirschfield says. "ADD, like any diagnosis, deserves accurate solutions, allowing for improvements in a patient's emotional, social, and academic well-being. I believe that many of the modern diagnoses of ADD do not accurately represent genuine medical diagnoses, largely due to a current medical trend to treat ADD as an excuse for many varied symptoms of inattention."[14]

Dr. Hirschfield then elaborated on how an ADHD diagnosis can make its way from a classroom to a doctor's office. "There are many people that work with children daily and who discuss a children's symptoms with parents. Many times these symptoms exhibited are developmentally normal but are described to the parents by teachers or other caregivers as results of 'poor attention,' 'hyperactivity,' 'misbehavior,' or 'an inability to complete tasks,' just to name a few," he says.

> I am not discussing this to place blame, but rather to focus on physicians' diagnostic evaluations. Unfortunately, many diagnoses are driven by non-physicians [i.e., educators and parents], and this is never acceptable.
>
> I absolutely believe that some physicians are succumbing to external pressures for ADD diagnoses, resulting in subsequent overprescription of stimulant medications.[15]

I'm not quite sure that's how we want to view our classrooms. I'd rather see them as places where our geniuses and future leaders are learning all they can. Maybe when we begin to rebuff the beliefs and actions connected to the ADHD buy-in, we will again.

11

WHAT ABOUT OUR BOYS?

Recently, the American Psychiatric Association released an alarming statistic: one in five high school boys has been diagnosed with ADHD[1] or is sent to the doctor to evaluate for it. How is that possible? Why do we hear about it, often quite openly, through everyone from administrators to nurses, coaches, and teachers, like it's a trip to the drinking fountain? What about other problems potentially affecting the adolescent boy, such as depression, anxiety, abuse, childhood trauma, lack of self-esteem or self-worth, vision issues, or sleep deprivation? Notes Australian mental health clinician Erica Dametto, "We always hear about that kid in school with ADHD and less of the kid who is experiencing abuse in the home and seeking emotional validation."[2] How sad but true.

What alarms me even more is the ramification of what Florida International University psychiatry professor Dr. James Swanson told the *New York Times*: "If we start treating children who do not have the disorder with stimulants . . . some of them are going to end up with abuse and dependence."[3]

Dr. Swanson's comment might be one of the most significant in this book, because today's high school boys are tomorrow's men. They will go into the world and start families, work their jobs or create businesses, and build futures. Much will be put on their shoulders. The way they are perceived—or labeled—will impact their lives in many different ways. They will serve their various stations in society for the next forty to fifty years.

What will those stations and our world look like when these boys-to-men deal in a world with more distractions and divisions than anyone can remember, along with higher expectations and shorter attention spans? Behaviors that they themselves exhibit, and have been *labeled* for? Will they rise above the challenges of being diagnosed with ADHD and become model citizens? Struggle with addiction, crime, violence, lost opportunities, broken relationships? How will they handle the stigma that comes with the compromised view that others will have of them? (If you have an ADHD diagnosis known to those outside family, such as employers, I can tell you from firsthand experience that you are compromised.) Will these boys be able to focus in a society inundated with technology, media, and information flying from all four directions and 360 degrees? Or will they be a generation that spins out, bounces to and fro aimlessly, lives with their parents into their thirties and even forties, never lands in the right place—or stays there—and disrupts lives in the process?

I look at the question quite personally. Will these diagnosed and prescribed boys become the kind of man I've learned to be at age forty, or the younger me, who struggled so hard to get there?

Here is what bothers me and most professionals, doctors, therapists, and parents I talk to in person, through my YouTube channel, or on Twitter: because ADHD is as much a part of the daily vocabulary as "attitude problem," we don't bother to consider the other issues with which adolescent boys must deal. We see an adolescent being mildly disruptive or inattentive in class, perhaps to the point of slipping grades or other drops in functionality, so we send them to the nurse's office. From there, it's a quick call to the parents, an appointment with the doctor, a quick exam, an evaluation of their "symptoms" against the DSM-V checklist, a positive diagnosis of ADHD—and a trip to the pharmacy.

While some boys definitely have chemical imbalances and need proper medication, I'm describing an everyday occurrence at elementary, middle, and high schools throughout North America and, increasingly, the world. We're not talking about a 1 percent diagnosis rate as we were in the 1960s and 1970s; we're talking about *20 percent*, as Dr. Swanson cited in the *New York Times*. That number doesn't just impact individual lives or school dynamics; it can change the future of *societies*. A 20 percent shift in anything causes massive change.

The average adolescent boy is a walking pressure cooker of hormones, new and changing interests (girls are high on most lists), increased expectations from home and school, the increased stress of course loads (especially advanced placement tracks), thoughts of college and career, and getting jobs. They are trying to figure out who they are and the mark they'll make on the world, while getting benevolently pressured and pulled from all sides—teachers, coaches, parents, bosses, peers, girlfriends, other students (for rides, parties, etc.), colleges, and outside activities. Many are as big as men and making decisions as important to their futures as men, but they are not yet fully developed men, especially mentally and emotionally. In our current era, when more boys than ever are living without fathers at home, or with stepfathers or big brothers acting as step-in fathers, many do not have the role modeling advantages their fathers and grandfathers received.

This is what our high school–aged sons or the boys we know down the street or next door deal with every day. Yes, it is a normal part of growing into a man, but it's something we need to remember in ourselves and empathize with more deeply when our boys come home and say they "can't handle it" or "have more than I can deal with." Most boys will *internalize* such feelings of self-perceived weakness, keep to themselves. We need them to talk openly about it. What we don't need is to take this behavior, or isolated angry outbursts or lack of focus, as "proof" our kid has ADHD and needs to be medicated *right now.*

No matter how scattered we boys are, we always find something to occupy our minds and interest. It might not be what our parents, teachers, or doctors would prefer. In my case, it was a continued fascination with bodybuilding and weightlifting—to the point of obsession—just like I'd focused on hockey before that. Maybe I couldn't concentrate on school or behave a certain way in class, but get me into a weight room, and I was *in the zone.* Some said I was focusing on the wrong thing, causing my attention to waver in class—a sign of ADHD, right?—but here I am, twenty-five years later, recalling it fondly as my commitment to fitness stretches into my forties. Was this a distraction worthy of an exam, diagnosis, and prescription or the beginning of a lifelong passion for an adolescent boy searching for something to join, to belong to, to participate in? Hmmm . . .

Sometimes what our families, teachers, and other well-meaning people see in us, or "prescribe" for our life path, isn't the way it's going to end up. The reasons have less to do with medical or behavioral issues, and more to do with where our souls and passions take us. Not to mention life circumstances, which, in my case, involved my natural father being out of my life, my mother being emotionally erratic, my stepfather living elsewhere, and the time I spent living with my grandmother. Then I bounced like a basketball through adulthood until 2009, when Aimee and I met.

I became obsessed with weightlifting, at the expense of school at times. At the local YMCA, we admired a few "veteran" weightlifters/bodybuilders. One was very tall and large; and my closest friend, Greg, became a definite admirer; he was like a "big brother" to us. There were also a couple other people near our age who had already been working out for a year or so, and was I constantly jealous of them and their muscular physiques. I wanted bigger muscles overnight as most young men do, but those same young men often resort to anabolic steroids to get there. I was no exception, starting steroids at the age of sixteen on and off for about a year. We all became more muscular and didn't need to be asked twice to flex or pose, regardless of what was going on. I look back on those days fondly, as I learned all about healthy and unhealthy competition between friends.

One of those friends was Sean, who'd I met at a day camp at the same YMCA. Like me, Sean was somewhat hyper and liked to sneak around at night, which became fun to me as well. Even though I was lifting, I was thirsting for new forms of excitement. I wanted something fresh and novel, now that I wasn't going to be a professional hockey player—my dream for years. Sean moved in and out of the next decade, in a variety of ways. He was my soul brother, the brother of the girl who gave me my first kiss—we enjoyed quite a friendship.

My young life makes it clear I was, and in some ways still am, one of those searching, novelty-stricken, easily distracted, occasionally rebellious, and somewhat disruptive boys—all part of the *normal, common* adolescent experience, one that seems to be viewed as more and more aberrant today and a cause for concern among those charged with shepherding us into adulthood.

Let's return to today's high school classroom. By the time students show up for high school at 7 or 8 a.m., they've already checked their mobile devices, texted, scrolled or posted on Instagram or Snapchat, checked in with friends, and either accepted or repelled instructions from a parent or two. Some got up at 5 a.m. to finish homework or get in that 5:30 a.m. swim or cross-country practice. Maybe they ate something: cereal, a package of donuts, or some other quick-sugar fix—maybe not. They sit down, crack open their notebook, and watch the teacher break out the day's classwork. Nine times out of ten, something other than the contents of that notebook crosses their mind—practice, a project, fixing the used car they just bought, balancing three things on their schedule at the same time, an upcoming date, or what those morning texts said. Some might even be worrying about a test coming up and sneaking peeks on their devices or notebooks to cram.

Already, teachers operating in the "sit still, pay attention" mode are at a disadvantage. Maybe in those texts, or talking to friends, something new came up, something to check out for the first time—a novelty. Another distraction to join those marbling around in their brains. The boy shoots off a text while holding his smartphone beneath the desk, then flips open his laptop and checks a video game review instead of clicking onto his assignment file, or he jets through a half-dozen book-marked sites in a minute. Then he visualizes touching the wall first in his 400-meter freestyle race at the afternoon swim meet. Unless the kid is totally into that first-period writing, science, math, literature, or government class, then we might assume the chances of focused, atten-tive, productive learning aren't that high. Then again, young minds are pliable and able to spin on a dime—and they usually do. Not that I was one of them.

My obsession with bodybuilding spilled into my high school corri-dor, when I'd literally bring protein shakes to class, and plastic storage containers full of meals and muscle magazines to read. I would "tune-out" from classes that didn't impassion me. I was so fiercely driven and focused on working out and pursuing the goal of becoming a pro body-builder that I'm lucky my grandmother wasn't stricter, pushing me in the direction she wanted me to go. That would have gone very, very badly, no matter the amount of her loving, caring concern. I was already on a mission, and no one was going to tell me to take another path in life—no one. I had to learn for myself.

Sound farfetched? It's not. The school day I described, and my own method of tuning out, is not unusual for the 20 percent of diagnosed or evaluated boys—and, for that matter, the other 80 percent alongside them. Today's students are that mentally engaged. When it's time, most can switch gears and lock into attentive listening and learning. Some find it more difficult. That their parents and grandparents, and those their folks' age, can't figure out *how* they switch gears is part of the overprescribing problem.

Now to the other side of a boy's life: information overload. Since high school is a quantum leap into information and knowledge, requiring an equal leap from our minds, it's vital that we grasp what our kids and their brains are dealing with today. Our ADHD culture contains a "perfect storm" component: the amount of information that crosses our brains. It is a storm that, if you are over thirty-five, you never experienced as a kid or an adolescent. Right now, this second, there are 295 exabytes of information available to you and me—or 315 times the number of grains of sand on earth, according to University of California-San Diego researchers in their report "How Much Information?," noted in the journal *Science*).[4] This volume of information almost makes the universe look like a side-room collection of stars. Here are two other statistics that can bring on headaches—or a yearning for the "good old days":

1. According to University of California professor Dr. Martin Hilbert in a study with a University of Southern California team, we took in four and a half times as much information daily in 2011 than in 1986. He added that, in 2007, we absorbed the equivalent of the type on forty large newspapers. By 2012, that figure was 174 newspapers (and no, he didn't "shrink" newspaper size as online advertising has done!).[5] We're now in 2017. That number has certainly expanded, especially since mobile devices have become our primary information-receiving vehicle.

2. Every day, according to 2013 statistics from Cahn Communications Social Media Manager Shea Bennett in *Adweek*, a trade publication for the advertising industry, we digest 285 pieces of content online per day. That is spread over 100 to 1,000 emails or links. Our daily input is equivalent to a 54,000-word novel (or 100,000 words, if you cite the UC-San Diego study), or 443 minutes of video.[6]

3. To give these numbers some historical perspective, according to British linguist Geoffrey Nunberg in a 2011 *New York Times*

book review,[7] we absorb as much or more information every day than a seventeenth-century Englishman consumed in a *lifetime.* Keep in mind that printing presses, books, newspapers, pamphlets, and other print media were all the rage in the seventeenth century. What an incredible statement!

Our brains might be wonders of neuroplasticity and adaptability, qualities that allow us to take in new information and process it, but the amount we encounter is boggling. Is it any wonder that so many of our elementary, middle, and high school students alike have trouble focusing or paying attention? This alone would make me hit the "pause" button if I were a doctor and get a good workup of the other issues in a kid's life before diagnosing.

DISTRACTIONS

Along with information overload comes the other factor that, I believe, feeds into this spike in ADHD among adolescent boys: distractions. First of all, what boy isn't distracted from time to time? After twelve or thirteen somewhat sheltered years, when you hit puberty, the world starts to feel like your oyster—and it's time to check it out! Our senses of adventure, discovery, risk-taking, learning, entertaining, competing, and relating to others become focused. We want to see what this world has to offer, and our hormones are flying off the Richter scale to get us there! Paying attention no longer becomes something we do naturally; it becomes something we must *remember* to do amidst this new treasure trove of life.

Now for my question: Do we call this struggle of teens to focus their attention, with this degree of information overload and equal need for constant connection to others, clinical ADHD? This is where I feel we need to better understand distraction and novelty, and its value to our growth process—as well as its negatives. In his essay, "Addiction to Distraction," *New York Times* journalist Tony Schwartz cited an August 2015 Adobe Campaign survey that found adults spend an average of four to six hours per day on email.[8] That doesn't include other online time—website surfing, online shopping, and so on. He then mentions Nicholas Carr's book *The Shallows: What the Internet Is Doing to Our*

Brains, which among other things states that we accept the loss of concentration and focus willingly. We also allow our attention to divide and our thoughts to break apart in exchange for receiving compelling information—or information that distracts us from our mundane lives.[9] Put it all together, and we live in an era that is one big compulsion loop, where novelty, distraction, and instant gratification jump aboard and ride our brains—then ride some more.

This is unhealthy distraction and novelty. However, many of us battle with it daily. If that's the case for us, what about our kids, who grew up with the technology that creates this endless 24/7 compulsion loop? I look at the incredible things that make up high school students' loops today (which I listed earlier), and then look back at my own "compulsion loop" as a kid—bodybuilding, mischief, clowning around, bodybuilding, mischief, clowning around—and feel both the distraction and thrill of being pulled out of studies all over again. That's what novelties do.

What if we showed the *positive* side of distraction and novelty? What if we taught kids the great things that happen when we brainstorm, dream, visualize, and follow the trails of our imaginations? What if we assure them that creative, out-of-the-box "monkey mind" brainstorming and thinking is a *good, positive* thing? We even have lofty names for the people who emerge from school with these instinctive skills intact— "innovators," "change agents," and "disrupters" (in the most positive sense). I don't know about you, but no one ever talked to me about this, or anything close. As it turns out, I've been practicing this mind-set for many years, though horribly unfocused during my long journey to hell and back. My self-taught ability to free my mind to dream, imagine, and brainstorm saved me from destroying myself. I feel every schoolteacher in the world should be celebrating creativity, imagination, and brainstorming. My guess is you'd see a sharp drop in ADHD diagnoses and a sharp increase in classroom attention and focus levels. You'd also see a very, very happy teaching community, thrilled to be freed of the standardized testing shackles to present wholesome educations!

Here's an example that lasted a generation. In the 1960s and early 1970s, those of us who were alive looked to the heavens as the Americans and Russians raced for the moon with technology less powerful than your mobile device. Imagination and brainstorming thrived in classrooms and became part of everyday lessons. Science classes became experiments in building rocketry or studying effects in space; that led to the current program, where a student experiment (or more) is taken on every space flight involving a NASA astronaut. In literature classes, along with a few required texts, you could read whatever lit you up, short of porn. Today's strictly prescribed, government, or school board–mandated reading lists and their unspoken censorships would've been ridiculed. Young people sought to expand their consciousness and possibilities, and they would try a variety of approaches. It was a culture of "Why do you think you can do it?" And the answer: "Because I can."

What did the Space Race and its presence in the classroom (right down to watching Mercury, Gemini, and Apollo flight launches on TV in class) do for the popularity of science and math? It pushed it through the roof. How many standardized tests were there per year? One, maybe two—not one *every six weeks*. What did it do for language arts classes? It created a fleet of imaginative storytellers, maybe the last generation to write science fiction en masse. Distraction and novelty were celebrated as vital to learning; they were not muted with drugs. If you had a wild idea, you were encouraged to see where it went. If something distracted you, you were urged to see if it benefited you— but also to cut it loose if it did not. Novelties? If they could grow into something that fed a kid, then great!

The 1960s and 1970s were times of wild distraction and shifts in the way we viewed the world, taught, and learned. It was a time when our technology was being driven forward big-time by the spoils of the Space Age. And the prescription rate for "hyperactivity disorder," or ADHD, during that time? It was just *1 percent*.

What about novelty? Isn't novelty a good thing? Novelty and change compel us to seek out new solutions and to innovate. It's been that way since survival was the first, middle, and last item on the daily to-do list. Novelty is hard-wired into us *genetically*. As adults, we might fend off that natural urge to innovate and seek out the new when the status quo doesn't suit us—for better or worse—but why expect that of a high school kid? I was always looking for new things. I absolutely loved smooth 1990s R&B music (I still love it!), television shows like *New York Undercover*, the O.J. Simpson trial (which my grandmother and I watched religiously, inspiring my interest in the law), bodybuilding, going to the odd dance or an all-ages nightclub, and hanging out with awesome friends like Sean and Greg. Those were a few of my hobbies during high school, where some of my finest early memories were made, ones I still hold sacred. They all began with a novelty, something new, something I checked out.

Since the constant seeking of new things is currently considered part of ADHD behavior, I have a question: what if it's not a disorder at all, but our brains having a hard time coming to grips with this world we live in? Did you feel that way in high school a few times? Many of us wanted to change the status quo, right? What happened when you *did* find something that interested you? Most likely, your attention grew laser-like, and you spent endless hours on that activity alone. So much for being unfocused and inattentive! As Richard Friedman wrote in a November 2, 2014, *New York Times* article, "the more novel and unpredictable the experience, the greater the activity in your reward center."[10] Or, in other words, we're learning something new and we crave it.

For these reasons, every time I think of the one in five diagnostic statistic for boys and ADHD, a fire alarm blasts inside my head. What this straight-line diagnosing is doing is just what fearsome straight-line winds do when they blow through your neighborhood—change the look of the neighborhood. In this case, it's the course of adolescent boys and young men, and the society they create from here.

I feel that when clinicians write ADHD scripts, some forget how they arrived at where they now sit. They dreamed. They tried and explored new things. They disrupted lives (including their own) at some point. Things distracted them—and they followed one or more wayward trails wherever it led, only to learn something about themselves or discover a hidden potential. Maybe one of them became a physician in open defiance of the parent who was hell-bent on making them an engineer! They probably enjoyed "monkey brain" mode, cutting loose and letting their brains fire in its fullest 360-degree range. As for extra energy, when you work years of sixty- to one-hundred-hour weeks, as most medical practitioners do, then you have a lot of energy. Some camps might call it "hyperactivity." Maybe some take off their smocks, go home, and play music or paint stunning silhouettes. Maybe they shoot hoops while ignoring their wives' calls for dinner, briefly disrupting suppertime.

What would happen if prescribing physicians overlaid their own experiences onto the nine-point checklist? I bet they would find a few matches.

We are genetically built to seek, to discover, to fall down and get up again, to sometimes disrupt the moment or be distracted, to move around, and to try many different things to see what works for us. This is *who we are*. There's a lot of wisdom to the saying *boys will be boys*.

Part II

Getting Beyond ADHD

12

WHAT IS WITH MY BRAIN?

Fascinated. Amazed. Enthralled. Enlightened. How else to describe The Day When Everything Made Sense?

Whenever I return to those first sessions with Dr. Tim Royer, my body and mind still feel a thrill. He took me to a place the majority of doctors never take their patients when making diagnoses—and lo and behold, he found out I may not be as deeply afflicted with ADHD as my previous doctors believed and diagnosed.

In fact, he questioned the diagnosis entirely. "I agree that if I sat down with the DSM-V and I went through those behaviors, Jeff would completely check off those behaviors," he said later. "If all I had was the DSM and that's what I was using, could Jeff match nine out of ten things, or six out of nine? Absolutely. The bigger question is, how accurate is that at really assessing what's going on with Jeff's brain? And what drives his behaviors? The nervous system does. What am I actually going to infiltrate and change with a medicine? Nothing. Instead, I'm going to infiltrate the nervous system and try to change the electrical current in the nervous system."[1]

Dr. Royer explained the full battery of tests. "We're all about looking at not just the behaviors, but trying to look at the brain," he said.

> There can be a lot of reasons why people have different behaviors, but if you don't look at the organ that you're trying to treat, many times you can be inaccurate and in some cases harm the organ you're trying to treat, which would be the brain.

For most people, the general rule of thumb is that, just because the first case of ADHD was diagnosed in the early 1900s based on behaviors, that we can still diagnose basically off behavioral check-lists. We [Neurocore associates and Royer] do not do it that way, because we found that we can be much more accurate if we measure the brain and different other systems within the body.[2]

The medical world's current preference to diagnose ADHD without automatically incorporating brain scans and other neurological testing grates at Dr. Royer. He finds it astonishing that a condition with such a profound first-resort treatment (at least in North America)—powerful stimulants—does not come with an addendum to the DSM-V guide-lines: *Administer an EEG.* "Nobody's looking at the brain," he says.

I've been division chief of psychology and psychiatry at one of the largest children's hospitals in Michigan, and I've been doing neuro-science for twenty-some years, and people come up to me at a lec-ture and say, "Hey doc, what'd'ya think? Do you think my kid has ADHD?" Nineteen years ago, I would have scratched my head, rubbed my chin a little bit, have a contemplative look and say, "Yes, of course I think your child has ADHD, look at him, right?"

Now I say, "I have no idea whether your child has ADHD. Do you know why I don't have an idea? Because I'm not looking at his brain." I can tell you based on his brain whether he has ADHD, but without looking at it, that's like you walking up to me and saying my chest hurts, and me diagnosing a cardiovascular disease.

What we want to see happen to get off of this lazy, short-sighted approach to diagnosing something going on in the brain. When you see your brain wave activity on the screen, and actually start to see, "when I think this way, this is what happens and when I think that way, this is what happens," it's like seeing your heart on an EKG, or an MRI. Now you're actually seeing something."[3]

Well, I know one brain getting examined directly for ADHD—mine. I wanted to see those pictures and start to make sense of my life.

Dr. Royer put me through several in-depth brain and body tests/scans, including auditory and visual recognition (speed) testing, cardio/respiratory system scans, and blood pressure and heart rate reviews. I also took a survey on overall health that was inputted into a computer database, which helped to further explain some of the test results. I took a sophisticated IQ test, which revealed an IQ of 115. "You will likely be in a gifted IQ range once your brain use is optimized," Dr. Royer told me.

When we got to my EEG work and Dr. Royer received the data, a funny thing happened. He realized that, according to his baseline drawn from more than ten thousand brain scans he and his Neurocore colleagues analyzed, my readings did not fit the theta wave range associated with ADHD. My focus levels were too high, he said, and other measurements pointed to the same conclusion. My prior auditory and visual processing tests also indicated something apart from ADHD.

The issue, Dr. Royer noted, lay in how I processed and utilized input to the brain. The EEG showed that while the center of my brain was working at the 58th percentile (per a baseline of approximately ten thousand scans), the right (creative) hemisphere was at the 29th percentile and my left (logical) hemisphere was at the 33rd percentile. Both numbers were too low, especially when the ultimate goal is 100 percent function in all three areas.

Dr. Royer reviewed my brain's frequencies; they were haywire. "Your brain's ability to learn things is far superior to any chemical," he explained,

> but in the way we're treating ADHD, we throw that to the side and just alter the electrical current with a chemical and don't try to teach the brain how it should focus or how it should sleep. We don't use the available technology to actually restructure the speed at which the brain is going.
>
> The brain is an electrical device that uses neurotransmitters. It works on electricity. An EEG is an electrical distribution of brain wave activity. That's what keeps you alive. If the electricity stops, you're dead. But that electricity can run at about thirty-five different frequencies.[4]

There are three key frequencies, which most of us have heard about in one form or another; they all have catchy Greek alphabet names. The lower range is comprised of *theta* waves, associated with sleep and deep meditative states, as well as the beginning of deeply creative thinking. They run at 3 to 8 hertz. *Alpha* waves, at 8 to 12 hertz, are most active in daydreaming, basic meditation, and resting. Then there are *beta* waves, which operate at 12 to 30 hertz. They bring along the fruits of waking consciousness—alertness, reasoning ability, and logical and crit-ical thinking. The well-balanced brain switches back and forth between the three states, never spending too much time in one, always regulat-ing itself.

"The ideal frequency is 12 to 20 hertz, where the brain is able to accomplish tons of work at very little energy expenditure," Dr. Royer explains.

> It's the sweet spot. I do a lot of work with professional sports teams, quarterbacks, and basketball players. When we see that iconic ath-lete, their brain is running at that perfect speed of 12 to 20 hertz. Really high functioning executives who are very calm under pressure also run at that bandwidth. When you get above 20 hertz, you have all the fast waves. We all have those in case we ever run into a life-and-death situation, a fight-or-flight response. It's what activates our HPA [hypothalamic-pituitary-adrenal] access, which kicks out adren-aline for us. ADHD runs at a lower set of frequencies, so when you give that brain a little bit of stimulant, it tends to focus a little bit better. That's the point of prescribing stimulants. [5]

When we reviewed my scans, my brain waves were not properly balanced between *theta, alpha,* and *beta.* No surprise there! I expected him to confirm that my levels were too far in the *theta* and *alpha* wave range, below 12 hertz. "We expected to see with his history of ADHD slower speeds, more theta activity, which would benefit from a stimu-lant," Dr. Royer concurred.

> The FDA has approved a measurement for diagnosing ADHD that measures *theta* above a marker of 3.0 hertz. What you'd expect to see if people truly have ADHD is high volumes of theta greater than 3.0. However, no area of Jeff's brain was even close to 3.0; actually, they were in the opposite direction, suggesting that his brain wasn't rest-ing enough, not over resting, like typically happens in ADHD. It suggested more of an underlying sleep issue.
>
> In Jeff's case, when we look at the high frequencies, those were dominating the brain. There were too much fast frequencies, which makes it really hard for the brain to rest at night, which then creates a negative thought pattern over time. [6]

My friends and family know that I can sometimes take a troubling thought, fear, or concern to very dark places once my brain wraps around it, loses some sleep, and hits the launch sequence.

Dr. Royer elaborated:

> The fast brain waves inhibit the sleeping brain waves, and then there's more fast brain waves the next day. This grows over time, and so when we were looking at Jeff's brain, the brain waves related to sleep were disruptive, but they were reacting to the brain running faster. When we started with him in training, we were measuring the high beta waves, those fast waves, and over time, those high beta waves would get lower. As they did, his sleep brain waves started to become more predominant and the brain started to balance out. [7]

I don't recall hearing any of that when I was diagnosed with ADHD. I don't recall hearing anything about how my brain functioned, only that I had a series of behaviors and characteristics that could be remedied with medicine and cognitive behavioral therapy.

Dr. Royer proceeded to show me "spikes of creativity" on the screen. He noted how my brain wasn't nearly as calm as it could be during my output of creative energy, but that I could be trained in that area. Specifically, he gave me mindfulness breathing exercises and other relaxation-inducing breathing techniques. This also got my heart rate variability scans improving toward the desired range. I fell in love with diaphragmatic breathing right away, since it calmed me down, pumped optimal levels of oxygen to my brain, and slowed my heart and nervous system down. I wasn't in "fight or flight" mode nearly as much.

These simple exercises proved so effective that, two months after first seeing Dr. Royer, my mother-in-law asked Aimee if I'd found a new medication that worked. "Actually, Jeff is off of medication completely (other than a blood-pressure pill)," Aimee replied much to her surprise.

Wait a second. Isn't ADHD a potentially lifelong condition to be treated for the rest of one's life, or at least well into adulthood? According to the American Psychiatric Association, 60 percent of people diagnosed with ADHD as children carry those symptoms and behaviors into adulthood. That is on top of the 5 percent of adults diagnosed with ADHD after their childhoods. [8]

In this moment, while evaluating my brain scan with Dr. Royer, I found out the true answer to that question: *Not. At. All.* In fact, the umbrella of behaviors and traits associated with ADHD pertain far more to how the neural centers in our brain fire, and why they fire as they do. We have 80 billion to 100 billion neurons in our brain, with one quadrillion connections—and up to 83 percent of those neurons are situated in the cerebral cortex.[9] In his book *Burning Out Rembrandt*, Dr. Royer describes this as "the body's equivalent of a Central Processing Unit on your computer."[10] In that case, wouldn't it be wise to put everyone through EEGs, at the very least, during an examination before diagnosing and prescribing?

Dr. Royer puts the importance of examining the brain into perspective in *Burning Out Rembrandt*:

> It can not only catch a ball in the air, it can decide whether to catch it or not. In fact, it can invent and construct the ball, make up the rules of a game, and convince other brains to play with it. It can speak, sing, compose music, make instruments to perform, and sell tickets to listen. It can not only read, but it can write a novel, and judge a good novel from a bad one. It can not only tell us how to mate, but also choose to love.
>
> Our body is made up of fourteen systems. Our skeletal system keeps us from lying on the ground as gelatinous blobs. Our circulatory system transports blood, which contains oxygen, nutrients, and wastes, to wherever they need to go in the body. Our endocrine system releases just the right chemicals at just the right times in just the right places to prompt our organs to perform various functions. And our nervous system connects the brain to the rest of the body.[11]

Next we switched to my autonomic nervous system (ANS), the trigger for the "fight-or-flight" response. Dr. Royer explained that the ANS regulates the electrical currents our bodies are continuously generating. We make body electricity for food, water, and oxygen, and the ANS regulates how we utilize that current. Moods, emotion, and affect are all regulated by the ANS. When it goes haywire, you may experience enormous amounts of stress, anxiety, fear, heart rate spikes, shortness of breath, bad thinking and decision making, and the fight-or-flight response—a downside I know all too well.

Dr. William Dodson, whose Missouri-based clinic specializes in teen and adult ADHD, claimed in the October 2013 issue of *ADDitude* magazine that those with ADHD actually have a unique ANS with its own set of rules, borne by a higher IQ, internal hyperactivity, and ability to pay much greater attention to the world around them than those without ADHD. He added that the typical motivators to act—importance and reward/punishment—do not apply, but challenges and novelty do.[12] The person with ADHD bores easily, but when engaging the brain and ANS in a challenge that sweeps them up, they often won't stop until the challenge is solved—likely at a high rate of achievement.

Taking Dr. Dodson's logic a step further, if ADHD and other common brain disorders are disturbances or *different from normal relationships* between the neural circuits and brain, doesn't it make sense to check the ANS if you're examining for ADHD and preparing to put someone on powerful amphetamines that can (and do) alter the brain's chemistry? I sure as hell think so!

Dr. Royer, who cited the flight-or-fight response (the consequences of which I and many others fear like no other) to illustrate how his battery of tests present the inner neurological world of his patients, thinks so too.

> If I'm being chased by a lion, my autonomic nervous system is going to say, "Hey, you need to go really fast, your heart needs to beat faster, your breathing needs to go faster, you need to release adrenaline out of your endocrine system, and your nervous system and brain waves need to go faster." Any glimpse into what somebody's autonomic nervous system is doing gives us a good idea how to, why they're eliciting certain behaviors. . . .
>
> We also want to look at the cardiovascular system. The heart. In a resting state, what is their cardiovascular system doing? We're measuring heart rate variability, how the heart is working as an organ. Is it stressed? Relaxed? What speed is it in?
>
> The same idea applies when we're looking at respiration. When somebody's in a relaxed state, how are they breathing? Is it rhythmic? Is it deep breaths, or more shallow and sporadic, like when somebody's more anxious? From there, we'll measure the endocrine system via hormone testing to see if they're releasing adrenaline, if they have any odd variations in their testosterone for males, or progesterone and estrogen for females. We look at endocrine functioning.[13]

In *Burning Out Rembrandt,* Dr. Royer further describes the central purpose of our autonomic nervous system:

> [It] is the body's operating system, operating below the level of conscious thought. You don't tell your heart to beat, your stomach to digest your food, or your pores to sweat to cool your skin. Like a computer's operating system, it functions in the background. The brain and body are constantly communicating, electrical signals racing through your body, even while you sleep.
>
> The ANS is the answer to many mysterious and frustrating questions about why our body does what it does, when it does it, and how it does it—including the perplexing problem of ADHD. The ANS not only accounts for some of the symptoms we usually associate with this condition, but it is the key to either treating or mistreating them. . . . [O]ur children's behavior often has an underlying cause rooted in the ANS, which is easily misunderstood. Our attempts to address it often miss the point or make it worse. Sometimes our attempts to treat children we believe have ADHD irreparably damage their ANS and the marvelous brain that controls it.[14]

The results of these tests opened my eyes. I was breathing at approximately eleven breaths per minute, five more than the ideal range. "That's normal for an adult man under forty years of age," Dr. Royer explained. (I was thirty-nine at the time.) He added that, with actual physiological screening (cardio, respiratory, brain, adrenals, etc.) brought into the mix, doctors could increase their diagnostic accuracy of ADHD from the current 50 to 55 percent to a whopping 88 percent—and that, in all likelihood, I didn't have ADHD as classically defined, though I possessed many checklist behaviors and traits.

For the first time in my journey through doctor's offices, I had been examined at Level 4, as clinicians call it. By comparison, the typical ADHD exam and comparison to the DSM-V checklist is a Level 1 exam—very basic, as though being examined for a bruised knee. At Level 2, a more in-depth exam based on behaviors or obvious effects occurs. That's better, but still not to the place I feel we need to go before administering prescriptions of Class II stimulants. At that point, Level 3, neurological and psychological tests take place, such as those I had with Dr. Royer, in order to gauge IQ, processing speed, learning style, and visual/auditory testing. Level 4 rolls out the major physiological testing, such as heart rate variability, respiration, EEGs, blood work, endocrine and adrenal tests, and the others I underwent.

This gave me the first full picture into what triggers my impulses, depression, anxiety, and stress, as well as answers to the creative surges, sometimes boundless energy, love of novelties, and knack for working to the point of obsession over things that matter most to me. More importantly, it also opened a window into the neuroscience of ADHD, which led to the deeper factors that can sometimes *dismiss* it. Also within these deeper causes were the secrets of how to rise beyond it. The key, Dr. Royer said, lay in the *management* of my brain and autonomic nervous system, not the pharmaceutical *changing* of it. It's amazing what new tests, an EEG, and a specialist who thinks outside the box can deliver. In my case, it was the golden key that opened a far happier life.

Something else happened, too. Everything my wife and I ever thought about ADHD began to unravel in front of us, like forcibly fitted blocks suddenly tumbling and scattering in all directions. I realized that once we reassembled our perception, we would see a different picture altogether. We could dissect the current ADHD environment, look at each diagnosed person as a unique human being, and get to the bottom of what ailed them. It was time to start focusing on the deeper causes— wherever the evidence took us.

13

EXPLORING THE DEEPER CAUSES

During the twenty-first century, autism and ADHD have become almost *de rigueur* disorders. How else to describe two conditions with their own magazines, newsletters, support groups, organizations, educational toolkits, in-school specialists in the United States (via the Americans with Disabilities Act), specialized schools, and, of course, treatment regimens? Increased public awareness and greater comfort with the diagnoses, along with crafty diagnostic simplifying (folding Asperger syndrome into the autism spectrum in 2011 on the one hand, and the DSM-V checklist for ADHD on the other), has contributed to the huge upsurge in cases during the past decade.

From 2000 to 2015, the ratio of autism in North America has grown from 1 person in 512 to 1 in 68 (1 in 42 boys, 1 in 189 girls),[1] while ADHD had jumped from 1 child in 33 to 1 in 8.[2] Did that many more people suddenly exhibit the symptoms and characteristics? Or did more doctors feel comfortable diagnosing, based on greater knowledge, awareness, and kindly pushes from well-meaning parents, educators, and influencers within their fields? How can diagnoses that once took years to pin down be rendered "successful" and "accurate" in single visits?

Many people, myself included, stew over the ease with which one can be diagnosed with ADHD or autism spectrum disorder. Because of that, I work hard to help us elevate from this maddening "find something wrong/diagnose/prescribe" mentality. Our way out of this hot zone—and into a healthier, saner, and more realistic place—is not to keep diagnosing, prescribing, and labeling based on symptomatic checklists. Instead, we need to spend more time looking at, exploring, and coming to grips with the deeper causes behind an ADHD diagnosis. When I consider the difficulties one faces within hidden or deeper causes, four feelings grip me: frustration, anger, stress, and anxiety.

I'd like to run down a partial list of deeper or hidden causes beneath many an ADHD diagnosis. I'll also share the efforts that caring, dedicated professionals are making to create greater recognition of these causes—and, more importantly, to properly diagnose patients for *these* conditions and symptoms, rather than being lumped under the ADHD umbrella.

In the past five years, I'd have to say nearly half of my discourse on social media, both on YouTube and Twitter, has concerned these deeper causes. Why? Because, in my opinion, they tell us what is really wrong with the 50 percent of ADHD cases that Dr. Royer says are wrongly diagnosed—and, I'd suspect, a fairly high percentage of "accurate" ADHD diagnoses as well. When we find the root causes, we can pinpoint therapies, often drug-free, that greatly enhance health and the chance to lead normal, productive, creative, and inspired lives. I will withhold discussion of educational issues until chapter 15. For now, we'll stick strictly to medical concerns or behavioral/emotional issues.

ADVERSE CHILDHOOD EXPERIENCES/CHILDHOOD TRAUMA

During the past forty years, the dynamic and structure of the family has changed—a lot. Divorce is now a 50/50 proposition (at least in Canada and the United States), children are often raised by a single parent, one or both parents are stressed by long hours and difficulty paying the bills, and "blended families" are a daily reality in the twenty-first century like multiple-relative families were for the entire history of humankind prior to that. Some kids grow up with two loving parents who remain together; others live through one, two, or several stepparents, each with temperaments and expectations. As one of *those* kids, I can certainly vouch for this! Some kids grow up in mixed-parent or gay parent households; others become "second adults" as they help an aunt, uncle, grandparent, or older sibling carry a load that no child should ever have to carry.

On top of that, family members communicate with each other less than ever. If you're forty or over, you probably experienced everyday talk at the dinner table, random playtime with siblings and friends in neighborhoods or your own yard, and good one-on-one time with one or both parents. How many of us remember our mothers or fathers reading us to sleep or talking to us well past our bedtimes (even incurring the chiding of the other parent for taking part in the delicious little "conspiracy")?

Those days are disappearing as a social norm. They are becoming the exception. Instead, we spend our time online, on our mobile devices, glued to streaming video or video games, with no time to talk to our overworked, constantly hurried parents. Nor do kids want to—they're too entrenched in their devices. Families that can rise above this din of distractions, obligations, and the "Internet of Things" ("IoT," the technology industry moniker for our device-based virtual connectedness) are downright heroic. Right now, as I write this, tens of billions of devices are interconnected—from home appliances to security systems, your car, your smart watch, and personal and business devices. According to premier market research firm International Data Corporation, the worldwide market for IoT devices and this cyberspace connectedness is rising toward $7.1 trillion in 2020 from $1.9 trillion in 2013.[3] Unless you're living in a cave high in the Himalayas, you're somehow connected.

This leaves us with a society of kids who feel socially distant or disconnected, anxious, frustrated, angry, fragmented, scared, and stressed beyond belief, sometimes before they ever set foot in a classroom. Not surprisingly, these children of traumatic home environments are diagnosed more often for ADHD than kids raised in more stable environments, according to research provided by the Children's Hospital at Montefiore (CHAM) in its 2016 report "Associations between Adverse Childhood Experiences and ADHD." The report, which used a sample of 76,227 children (8.8 percent of which were diagnosed with ADHD, within the national figure), pinpoints both ends of the problem—childhood trauma/family stressors and hot-button diagnosing—in one telling sentence up front: "Current ADHD clinical practice guidelines recommend evaluating for other conditions that have similar symptoms to ADHD, such as disruptive behaviors, impulsivity, and issues with memory, organization and problem-solving, but few pediatricians routinely ask about psychosocial factors that could be effecting a child's health during ADHD assessment."[4]

This collection of experiences has a name, which I think is important to learn, memorize, and include in our evaluation of kids: adverse childhood experiences, or ACEs. These are the situations or events that cause childhood trauma. The CHAM report cites as ACEs all forms of child abuse and domestic violence, familial mental illness, neglect, divorce, death, substance abuse, incarceration of family members, neighborhood violence, socioeconomic hardship, forced or voluntary separation from one or both parents, living with no parents, and difficult adjustments to stepparents or parents who date frequently or engage in multiple relationships. Now, compare those causes to these effects, all in the DSM-V checklist: impulsivity, disruptive behaviors, issues with memory and problem solving, and lack of attention or focus.

It's not too hard to figure out why a child may be having difficulties, and it's not necessarily because the kid has a biochemical imbalance that can be remedied with an ADHD stimulant.

I wish behavioral therapists were around to pinpoint ACEs and provide proper treatment and therapy when I was a kid. I could have used it.

There's more. According to the report, these disruptions cause behaviors similar to ADHD, along with toxic levels of stress. Toxicity not only means "danger" or "poison" in this case but also an increased level of hormones associated with fear, fight or flight pumping into the brain—the hypothalamic-pituitary-adrenal (HPA) triad. The resulting chemical imbalance can impair normal brain development. Lead author Nicole M. Brown, attending pediatrician, Division of Academic General Pediatrics, CHAM, and assistant professor of pediatrics, Albert Einstein College of Medicine, noted that "[i]f clinicians aren't routinely discussing exposure to traumatic experiences and identifying ACEs, particularly among children with behavioral concerns such as ADHD, there may be a heightened risk of missing an underlying trauma history or misattributing some of the symptoms of traumatic stress as solely those of ADHD."[5]

Dr. Brown and the other authors conclude with a recommendation, which I fully endorse: try to drill down to find ACEs that are impacting a patient's life before assuming it's ADHD. Even if ADHD is diagnosed, they (and I) add, focus the therapy on trauma treatment versus stimulant medications or targeting certain behaviors. If we can just take this one step, in doctors' offices throughout North America, imagine how much we will do to heal a deep social wound *and* focus on what ails our loved ones.

SOCIAL COMMUNICATION DISORDER

We have a social communication problem. It's not good enough for two people to talk in person or on the phone anymore. Now, most of our communication takes place through emails, chat rooms, texts, Facebook pages, Instagram, Snapchat, or Twitter posts. Heck, connecting via FaceTime or Skype is considered progressive! Predictably, we have an entire generation that has entered adulthood with underserved and underdeveloped social skills. Many have trouble working in office teams, engaging socially, making physical in-the-flesh friends (despite thousands of online "friends"), and communicating face-to-face without a screen, mobile device, or cyberspace to cushion their angst at feeling emotionally vulnerable. Imagine how much more civil the American presidential dialogue could have been at the citizen level if people talked face-to-face rather than on social media, where it's easy to insult, demean, and criticize. Why? Because we don't have to *face* the person we're insulting, demeaning or criticizing!

This trend is growing among today's students and younger children. It amounts to, quite literally, disorder in social communication. We are out of alignment with our inherent nature to communicate, to commune, or to form a community. The days of neighbors talking over the fence, or two casual friends spending hours chewing the fat, are growing fewer. Now, we're as likely to be suspicious of our neighbor as to befriend them—which the powers that be, from governments to schools to businesses, are *aiding and abetting* with their constant warning of threats, risks, and "you can't be safe enough" messages. No wonder anxiety disorder is quickly becoming a state of being.

It doesn't take much to offer up a quick solution: visit a friend and talk to them! However, that is far easier said than done. When you're a kid or young person brought up to be wary of strangers, to suspect others before trusting them, and to hole up in your home or a small environment for safety's sake, well, what is going to happen to your natural social communication skills? They're going to atrophy, and slowly fade away. I can point to the prevalence of autism and ADHD, show when those curves started jacking skyward, and directly correlate it to the time when open neighborhood play was replaced by play dates, when school campuses started closing, and when alarmed parents started telling their kids to be far more selective in the friends they choose.

In today's label-conscious world, this set of circumstances and its resulting stresses and anxieties has a name: social communication disorder, or SCD (once known as pragmatic language impairment and, before that, semantic pragmatic disorder). We have trouble talking to each other, reading the subtext and nonverbal cues behind what people say (such as facial expressions and body language), and communicating with the right words in socially appropriate ways. Often, SCD is mistaken for ADHD, autism, or Asperger syndrome, according to the American Psychiatric Association (APA), which introduced the disorder and its diagnosis in DSM-V. However, those with SCD don't exhibit other trademark characteristics of the better-known disorders, such as repetitive behavior (autism) or inattentiveness (ADHD).[6]

Since many clinicians stick ADHD labels onto kids with SCD, often at the urging of stressed out, frustrated parents or teachers, it is important we know the key differences between the two:

1. Those with SCD often don't know how to start conversations, or the right words to use. They often won't speak or will use quick sentences conversations. Conversely, classic ADHD kids are more talkative than not.
2. SCD sufferers have trouble reading facial expressions, nonverbal cues, and the subtext of a conversation, similar to those with Asperger syndrome. They need to be trained. Those with ADHD can have that issue, too, but often a sharpening of focus alleviates it.
3. Living with SCD means a tendency to be overly literal and not understand jokes and sarcasm. This is not an ADHD behavioral characteristic.
4. Those with SCD tend to fall behind in reading and writing due to difficulty in understanding subtlety in social situations. The issue with ADHD is one of attention span, not lack of understanding;

in fact, when ADHD minds lock into specific situations, they often comprehend them more thoroughly than others.

The APA estimates up to one in two thousand schoolchildren have SCD, though the disorder is so newly named it will take a while to get more solid stats,[7] but that's enough for me. SCD is remedied with something far different than stimulant drugs, namely, speech and language therapy, with specific language and behavioral therapy for recognizing proper behaviors in social situations. The American Speech-Language-Hearing Association (ASHA) recommends having your loved one, or child, or you (if you suspect SCD) take tests like the Clinical Evaluation of Language Fundamentals, the Test of Language Competence, and Vineland Adaptive Behavior Scales. It also recommends the Children's Communication Checklist and Pragmatic Rating Scale.[8] That's a whole lot different than a trip to the doctor's office, a run through a checklist, and a prescription!

TOXINS

Here's one we don't often put in the same sentence as ADHD, but let's face it, nothing ruins a physically fit body or sound mind like toxins. Unless we live in pristine backwoods locales, far from a busybody civilization, we are exposed to more and stronger toxic agents in our daily lives than perhaps any generation that has preceded us. Toxins are prevalent in our food supply, drinking water, backyard lawns and gardens, the exhaust pipes of our vehicles, clothes we wear, pipes that carry our water, lakes and rivers, oceans in which we swim and fish, and so much more. Add to that the unprecedented noise and light pollution we experience, from honking horns to the screens on our TVs and devices and their unhealthy positive ions, and we're being bombarded in a way that leaves me, for one, in pure amazement at our resiliency. How do we manage to survive?

We manage, but not without a cost. Among other things, toxins compromise our bodies at the cellular level and weaken our immune systems. When these two things happen, we become less healthy, more stressed, less tolerant, more anxious, less focused, and more impulsive.

When you add those up at face value, what do you have? An ADHD diagnosis.

Except, it's not. At the very least, we're drilling down to deeper causes. In 2016, *The Lancet Diabetes and Endocrinology*, a medical journal, released a study that showed that exposure to everyday chemicals found in thousands of everyday products—laundry detergent, plastic and metal food containers, plastic bottles, toys and cosmetics—can increase the chances of ADHD, diabetes, autism, and cancer. The study added that endocrine depleting chemicals (EDCs) are partially or wholly responsible for $340 billion in annual health-care costs in the United States alone. Researchers said that more than 80 percent of the health impacts pertain to neurological damage and/or behavior problems, including ADHD and autism.

The part of our body taking the hit is the endocrine system, which regulates energy levels, hormone production, growth, development, *and our response to stress or injury.* I highlighted the last bit to underscore how easy it is to diagnose a toxic set of behaviors like ADHD, because a stressed body will lead to a stressed person, who will often act out in a way that matches the checklist. It seems to me that focusing more on flushing those toxins via a cleaner diet, purified water, and medications that lower toxicity answers the call more than diagnosing for ADHD and missing the deeper cause entirely.[9]

What about auto exhaust fumes and factory smoke surrounding us day in and day out? They impact us, too. A study by the medical psychology department at Columbia University Medical Center tracked 462 inner-city children, ages twelve to eighteen, from conception until present day. By taking blood samples from pregnant mothers, the umbilical cords, and the kids post-birth, researchers determined that kids most exposed to diesel fumes suffered some brain damage before they were born. This increased their impulsivity and aggressiveness, decreased their social competence, and triggered behaviors and traits consistent with depression, anxiety, and ADHD. The culprits, in this case, were diesel fuel chemicals known as polycyclic aromatic hydrocarbons (PAHs). They slow processing speeds and destroy white matter in the left hemisphere (the logical, critical thinking side) of the brain.[10]

When you throw in lead, polychlorinated biphenyls (PCBs), and pesticides, all prevalent in our society, the toxic pool only deepens. We have to better consider the things a person eats and exposes himself to when evaluating for ADHD, or any other behavioral disorder. This is where, in my opinion, a blood workup should be added as a pre-diagnosis requirement. We might find out there is something very bad eating at the person—quite literally.

DIGITAL TECHNOLOGY

In a highly praised *New York Times* article, "A Natural Fix for ADHD," Richard Friedman[11] made a connection that I feel speaks to most of our attention-deficit problems. He linked the regimented, demanding school environment to a focus on testing, math/science and achievement, and digital technology. We used to go to school, learn our (wider range of) subjects, go home, and play until dark. Now, we must hyperfocus to keep up in class, then go home—and study until we drop at some late hour. Chances are better than average that we wind down with video games or online posts. As I noted earlier, the average daily online time for teens is eight hours. Technology promises instant gratification, excitement, and fulfillment of that quest for novelty we have, while school can regiment us into sheer boredom. When we're bored, we lose attention and focus. We stop caring, and we start strategizing about that multilevel, multiplayer online video game we stopped on level 32.

I believe technology is a huge driving force in ADHD. We're totally hooked up, as are most of our kids. Rare is the preteen or teen who doesn't have a mobile phone, two or three social media accounts, email, freedom to text, a video game console, desktop, laptop or tablet computer, a GameBoy or similar handheld console, or other devices. The mobile device is the center of their universe, taking care of everything from music to math calculations, contact with the outside world, photos, video, and online inquiries. Young people (and many adults) are absorbed by a world where everything moves fast, responses are quick or instant, and the action (in video games) is colorful, rich, and multi-layered. Who wouldn't want to spend their every waking moment in this space, when the rest of your day is filled with obligations, classes, and parents chirping at you?

I'd like to invite you to try something. Spend the next ninety minutes immersed in technology—computer game, video game, social media,

FaceTime, or texting. When you're done, try to go outside and exercise, call a friend and visit a museum, or burrow into a good literary novel or well-written book. Not so easy, is it? This is the challenge your kid battles every day—and ninety minutes is not a long immersion time.

The American Academy of Pediatrics (AAP), among others, feels the technology problem is pervasive. The AAP also sees it as something else, according to the *Huffington Post*—a parent problem.[12] While adults must be responsible enough to monitor and limit their own technology time, and teens understand the concept, kids don't possess that facility, especially young kids. The AAP recommends no screen time before age two (do we really even have to *say* that? Why would anyone let their kid see a computer screen before age two?), daily limits of 30 minutes for non-education-related technology use for young kids, and 90 to 120 minutes for teens. I'd personally drop that latter number to 60 minutes, because when you go above it, the likelihood of getting up and doing something else falls. The reason? The brain can't reset itself that quickly to a normal beta wave state after all the electronic stimulation. The AAP also recommends spending three to five times as much time in conversation than in front of a screen. That's difficult for most. Also, call for "technology breaks," turning off all technology for 15 to 30 minutes at a time. Don't use technology at all in the hour prior to bedtime, so the brain has a chance to wind down before sleeping.

When you try to limit technology for the first time, your kids may freak out. Those tongue-in-cheek AT&T television commercials that ran in 2015 and 2016 and show the family going ballistic when their home Internet fails tell a not-so-funny story of dependence and addiction. The sixty-second commercials show it all: impulsive behavior, mood swings, lack of conversation, inattentiveness, frustration, inability to concentrate, and complete boredom when the grandfather tries to tell his daughter and grandkids a story from memory lane. I've kiddingly labeled these "the AD&D commercials."

We need to gain control of technology. It is leaching from our greater, more thoughtful, more deeply concentrating minds. Rather than rushing out for an ADHD diagnosis and stimulants—which can worsen the problem, since the stimulants can help us stay up longer for those all-night gaming sessions—doesn't it make sense to reduce our time on our devices and computers? That alone will increase focus, attention span, and engagement with the outside world, as well as calm our nervous systems and brighten our social lives.

VISION IMPAIRMENT ISSUES

When I recall how much I struggled in school from my childhood vision problems, I also remember the way it made me feel. Words like *frustrated*, *enraged*, *demoralized*, *worthless*, *stupid*, and *chastised* come to mind. Elementary and middle school playgrounds can be quite formidable jungles where meanness and bullying occur, especially among boys, and I experienced my fair share for my vision problems. Teachers also made it a point to call out my lack of comprehension of subjects and my inattentiveness in class. Half the time, I didn't pay attention *because I couldn't see*. To compensate for how awful I felt about myself, I pulled pranks and called attention to myself; I became the class clown.

Had ADHD been as commonplace then as it is now, I surely would have been diagnosed and prescribed in order to get my head back in the game. But doctors would have had it totally wrong. My problem wasn't misfiring neurotransmitters; it was the trauma at home combined with my difficulty in seeing.

I didn't really know about this correlation until 2014, when I began associating with optometrist Dr. Patrick Quaid, FCOVD, PhD. A down-to-earth, witty, tireless, and brilliant man whose work is making imprints in four places—Canada, the United States, the United Kingdom, and his native Ireland—Dr. Quaid is using advanced tools of optometry and neuroscience to unlock ADHD and other misdiagnoses that trace back to vision issues, correct those mistakes, and restore or correct their sight—along with their self-esteem and sense of purpose. A lifetime of poor vision and poor treatment can have that effect. So can being misdiagnosed because of vision issues that were overlooked.

When we first started talking, Dr. Quaid told me something startling: since 40 percent of the brain is primarily visual machinery, charged with how we see and perceive the world, according to the journal *Cerebral Cortex*, vision problems can lead directly to ADHD-like behaviors.[13] He cited the National Institute of Health's Trial of Treatments for Symptomatic Convergence Insufficiency[14] when stating that five of the nine core ADHD symptoms in DSM-V also present with a diagnosis of convergence insufficiency, a common vision problem in which the eyes and brain don't work together properly to merge what our left and right eyes see. When people have difficulty moving your eyes inward toward their nose, or lining up an image so it doesn't appear crisscrossed or existing on two different levels, they have convergence insufficiency.

It didn't surprise me that there would be a similar characteristic or two between convergence insufficiency and ADHD; I knew through my own myopia, or nearsightedness—a different condition—how hard it was to concentrate, pay attention, and sit still in a classroom when you couldn't see the chalkboard or read the assignments. Convergence insufficiency is estimated to affect between 2 and 4 percent of the general population, according to Dr. Quaid, "with this prevalence found to be dramatically higher—15.9 percent—in ADHD patients," he adds. "It's not ADHD, per se; that's their issue. It's convergence insufficiency, treatable with in-office vision therapy and at-home therapy. But it hasn't been diagnosed, so parents aren't aware of it." [15]

That's a huge difference. Dr. Quaid identified five parallel traits between convergence insufficiency and ADHD. Remember, the magic number that DSM-V cites to recommend an ADHD diagnosis is six checklist traits that, collectively, impair everyday function. How many overwhelmed doctors, I wondered, took in kids presenting five characteristics and diagnosed them? "Some of the symptoms with convergence insufficiency are rubbing of the eyes from reading, getting distracted and frustrated easily from near-point activities, resistance to near-point activities like reading, losing concentration or getting headaches from doing close work, and trouble remembering what you read," Dr. Quaid notes.

Now imagine you're a teacher in a crowded classroom, trained to look for ADHD-like symptoms, and you see children doing these things. What will be your first assumption? That's why we need to get vision thoroughly checked before assuming kids might have ADHD and marching them off to the doctor's office.

TRAUMATIC BRAIN INJURIES

The great neurological advances of the past decade have stemmed from one of today's great social and medical problems: concussions and traumatic brain injuries (TBIs), and the devastating impact they have on victims, families, workplaces, and friends. Between the wars in Iraq and Afghanistan; the mounting problems of head injuries in youth, scholastic, and professional sports (particularly the National Football League and National Hockey League); and the leading cause of TBIs—vehicle crashes—we have been inundated with a decade of studies, findings, verdicts, symptoms, heartbreaking stories, statistics, and treatments.

Every concussion is now considered a traumatic brain injury, no matter how "minor." It is a violent collision between your soft brain tissue and your hard skull, caused by an equally violent outside event—a hard hit, a roadside bomb, a collision with a vehicle or another person, and so on. Now that we've thankfully graduated from the machismo of "I got my bell rung; put me back out there," we see concussions for what they are: injuries that damage the brain. When something damages the brain, it also alters how neurotransmitters relate to one another, causing glitches in communication. Heavier damage can cause ongoing migraines, changed behaviors, memory loss, and in worst cases, eventual premature death.

It is in this mysterious place—mysterious only because we're just now fully studying it—that TBIs intersect with ADHD, especially in adults. A study of four thousand TBI patients aged eighteen years and older, conducted in 2011–2012 by the Centre for Addiction and Mental Health Monitor in Ontario, Canada, and published in August 2015 in both the *Journal of Psychiatric Research* and *Medical News Today*, showed that 6 percent reported being diagnosed for ADHD and another 6.6 percent tested positive for ADHD on a self-report basis when questioned by phone. Memory and attention impairment, deficits in planning and organization, and impulsive behavior were among the reported symptoms. One reason, researchers found, is that TBI contributes to psycho-neurological changes that can trigger the development of symptoms on the ADHD checklist.[16] Or could it be that they are the *same symptoms*, and that the "triggering development of symptoms" is really the lingering effects of damage caused by the TBI?

There is no question that the symptoms of TBI and ADHD parallel and intersect. If I didn't know any better, I might not be able to tell the two apart—forgetfulness, poor focus, inattentiveness, impulsive behavior, and mood shifts are part and parcel of both diagnoses. There's no question that someone with a significant TBI has impaired function, a principal determining factor in an ADHD diagnosis. The easy diagnosis is, in fact, ADHD, but if the person reports a TBI, shouldn't we be more concerned with treating that? As noted in a *Psychology Today* article, one is a serious physical brain injury, the other a developmental disorder.[17] One does not necessarily lead to, or indicate, the other—although as the Centre for Addiction and Mental Health Monitor study showed, it can and sometimes does. Researchers concluded that doctors should ask for history of TBIs from patients before rendering a diagnosis of ADHD.

These are the main deeper or "hidden" causes that can lead people to exhibit symptoms that also fall on the DSM-V checklist. We don't need to quickly resort to ADHD medications or treatment protocols; enough time should be spent with the person to get to these deeper causes. Then we can treat or adjust properly and not assume they have ADHD. Of course, if they do have ADHD, then we diagnose and begin appropriate therapy, hopefully with as few stimulants as possible. This type of deeper-level diagnosing is popping up more and more.

14

NEW WAYS OF WORKING WITH ADHD

I receive responses of all kinds to my posts on Twitter and YouTube channel about ADHD. Here is a typical letter:

> *Hi Jeff:*
> *My name is Brad Mecha, and I have an 8-year-old son named Connor who has been struggling with ADHD symptoms since he was 3. I recently discovered your fantastic content on Twitter, YouTube, etc.!*
>
> *I'm looking for better professional help near Milwaukee, WI, that could help with re-diagnosing and treating my son without the help of drugs like Vyvanse.*
>
> *If you can recommend anyone in the Wisconsin/Chicago area, or point me in the right direction of additional books, publications, dietary plans, or family coping strategies, that would be greatly appreciated!!!*
>
> *Keep up the great work!!!*
> */s/Brad Mecha*

Letters like this touch my heart and make me feel for men like Brad Mecha; what a tough situation! They also remind me of what drew me into this discussion, and of things that I feel we need to improve or transform if we are to leave the current ADHD mindset:

1. How do children exhibit ADHD symptoms that require strong prescriptions when they are *three years old*? Do doctors consider the changes to the brain that occur from taking these stimulants?

2. Do health-care providers consider the individual gifts, talents, quirks, and personality traits of people they diagnose—and other ways in which their energy can be channeled and attention better focused?

3. Are single practitioners experts in all areas represented by the ADHD diagnosis?

4. What therapies, life practices, and activities can replace prescriptions and create equal or better solutions and lives for those with ADHD symptoms?

Thankfully, I'm not the only one asking these questions. There is also a growing volume of published findings that show more and more doctors are not sold on how we currently do things—treating symptoms rather than causes, when finding the deeper cause is the only (or best) approach to take. Experts from all stripes, including the American Medical Association, are seeking answers beyond checklist diagnoses and ways of treating that add to or supersede prescriptions, though that still remains Door No. 1 in 75 percent of cases involving small children—the most vulnerable and sensitive to prescription drugs.[1]

The day will come, I hope, when prescribing goes from being the first to last option. What if a whole variety of drug-free treatment doors were to open? How would we treat the widening stream of kids and adults who think (or their parents, therapists, or educators think) they have ADHD?

I have good news for you: many of these other treatment options already exist. Some have always been there; we've simply forgotten about them. Not only do they exist, but they are also highly effective in treating ADHD behaviors, and, more importantly, in focusing on the whole person by pointing at the deeper causes. When you enact cause-based treatment and therapy, not only do you heal people, but you also change, inform, and help grow their lives. In many cases, such as my own, that's all it takes. This flies in the face of the pharmaceutical industry and its business model that relies on prescriptions to survive. However, my concern—and that of many health-care professionals, educators, and parents, some of whom you've met in this book—is to get above medications, restore and heal, answer questions, and redirect people toward attaining their highest potential.

Why keep asking and looking for other solutions? For starters, as Dr. Royer notes, we are still learning about the way the brain works—and with it, how brain function and behavior relate. "We're learning very complex things," he says.

> For example, I can drive a car full of people that weighs a couple thousand pounds at 70 miles an hour, listening to the radio and having a conversation, without even looking at my speedometer. How did you ever learn to drive 70 miles an hour to the point that if your speedometer breaks, you don't have to pull over to the side of the road? Well, you've learned what that speed is. It's second nature for you (to know) what 70 miles an hour is. Your brain learned of that speed.
>
> Just the same, your brain can learn its own speed if I show it to you. In Jeff's case, I wanted his brain going 70 miles an hour, and it was going 110 miles an hour. In the ADHD kid, it might be going 40 miles an hour. If I give him a stimulant, yes, he'll start focusing, but what if I can teach him to get his brain to start to run at 70 miles an hour naturally? Now it's a whole different game. Now I just haven't Band-Aided him and made him a person that needs to take this medicine the rest of his life, but I'm actually empowering him to use what his brain can do, which is to learn to go the right speed.
>
> As for the other type of ADHD person, who can't sleep at night because their brain is going 200 miles an hour, can I teach their brain to go 70? Absolutely. Do they need (a medicine) to slow them down when we're done? No. They now know how to slow themselves down.[2]

When I hear breakthrough comments that fall under that old biblical adage, "Physician, heal thyself," I just want to grab the giant lever of the way ADHD is treated today—and we're conditioned to "just do what the doctor says"—and shut it down. We can't do that, since most medical advice and treatment really helps us. What we *can* do is solve the deeper causes—and use approaches other than (but also including, as a last resort) conventional medicine to get there.

GETTING OUT OF THE BOX: NEW APPROACHES

In 2016, researchers at three Toronto-based locations—the Centre for Addiction and Mental Health (CAMH), the Hospital for Sick Children, and the Holland Bloorview Kids Rehabilitation Hospital—identified similarities in the white brain matter of children living with autism, ADHD, and OCD (obsessive-compulsive disorder). White matter connects cell bodies across the brain, affects behavior, and enables communication between different cerebral regions. It feeds the neurotransmitters—the central concern with all three disorders. (ADHD stimulants speed up, enhance, and somewhat balance faulty neurotransmitters.) Researchers focused on the corpus callosum, the first and largest white matter tract to develop—suggesting that white matter issues might start while babies are in the womb. In addition, researchers stated that the white matter problems are more serious for autism and ADHD kids than for OCD kids, which is why you sometimes hear a correlation between autism and prenatal development but not so much with ADHD and OCD. I would consider this solid medical evidence that, yes, there is something going on in the brain of a kid who might be diagnosed with ADHD.[3]

Likewise, the NEBA test began gaining traction within the first few years of its availability. Named for the Georgia-based company marketing the procedure, the NEBA test uses Neuropsychiatric Interpretive EEG-based Assessment Aids, or NIEAs, to measure brainwave activity directly attributable to ADHD.[4] This fifteen- to twenty-minute noninvasive test uses an EEG to assess electrical data in the front part of the brain, which delivers a biomarker. After combining those results with their own diagnostic impressions, doctors (usually psychiatrists) can arrive at one of four conclusions:

1. Positive confirmation of ADHD
2. Support for further testing—focus on ADHD
3. Support for further testing—focus on other conditions
4. No evidence of any conditions

According to the FDA, NEBA can help clinicians reduce misdiagnosis of ADHD to as low as 3 percent from its current 45 percent to 50 percent.[5] If this is true, and doctors will commit to ruling out other causes before ruling in ADHD—which would be a quantum shift from current practices—then the NEBA test could be a great medical advance. However, I must stress, as does the FDA, that the EEG is used only as an assessment aid, not a determining factor.[6]

Why do I mention these two developments? Because both involve deeper medical assessment—not eyeball determinations off the DSM-V checklist. Also, both involve spending time with patients, rather than in-and-out visits. The NEBA test presents four possible outcomes of the assessment, a welcome expansion from the "yes, he has ADHD" or less frequent "no, he doesn't" diagnostic reality of the past two decades. These developments point to why we need to slow down and be damned sure we know for sure that our kids, loved ones, or we have ADHD.

There are many other ways that people within and outside the sphere of pharmacological medicine are treating ADHD. They might be outliers to some degree now, but I find all of them very promising for treating the whole person and learning more about the deeper causes.

EEG Biofeedback

More and more, neurologists and neuroscientists are working with EEGs to better understand the relationship between brain wave patterns and ADHD (like the example above). This focuses on physical, biochemical signs of ADHD—an objective measure—rather than subjective observation, like the DSM-V checklist. With EEGs, we can better understand the theta-beta-alpha wave relationships that Dr. Royer discusses. Believe me, when you are armed with precise knowledge of how your brain is functioning, you can work wonders in both self-improvement and self-care—two critical components of ADHD that need to move from the fringes to the center of public discussion.

With EEG biofeedback, a child is given a full-engagement task, such as playing a video game in which his goal is to keep the ball in the air. If the ball starts to fall, the doctor will know he is distracted. The kid will be motivated to keep it off the ground, thus improving his focus. Once he understands how he can make the ball rise and fall, he will be able to better see in other parts of his life how to remain focused and steer away from distraction. By doing so, he begins to take charge of his life.

Spending Time Outside

I feel almost embarrassed having to say this, but if we simply spend more time outside and engage with nature on its own terms—taking a hike, swimming in the ocean, birding or studying stars, hopping along large river rocks, or jogging on a forest or meadow trail—we will sharpen our focus *and* improve our overall health. The activity will command full focus and attention, as well as our physical skills. Nature returns us to our more natural states, the 360-degree "hunter's mind" that we discussed earlier in the book. When the mind is fully engaged, we feel completely attentive and alive, and distraction slinks into the shadows. Thankfully, it is starting to happen again with the millennials, the generation most impacted by ADHD, as boldly stated on the cover of the October 2016 issue of *National Geographic* magazine: "The Selfie Generation Goes Outside."[7]

Exercise

The other half of spending time outside is exercising. We need to exercise more; even thirty minutes per day is good, though I'd recommend an hour. School campuses used to be filled with children running, jumping, playing tetherball or hopscotch, riding swings, or playing games like kick ball, dodge ball, or baseball. You could walk onto any playground and see a dozen or more different forms of exercise going on. Once the bell rang to bring everyone back to class, they sat in their chairs, felt good inside, and concentrated on their lessons.

We've largely lost this simple part of raising kids and teens, and I think it's directly reflected in disruptive behavior. A cooped-up kid—or man or woman, for that matter—will soon become stressed and tense; eventually, he or she will need to blow it out, which is where impulsive acting out or mindless daydreaming come in. We have and build up more energy than we release, and then the volcano erupts. Before we know it, we're wondering what's wrong with the person.

Let's focus on exercise—without devices and other distractions. Take out the earbuds on your next walk or run; listen and pay attention to the sounds around you. I feel we also need more *free-spirited exercise*, which doesn't involve heated competition, winners and losers, or even rules. Once in a while, run wild and free, and cut your kids loose the same way. I'll be the first to tell you the benefits of competition, since I spent most of my younger years playing high-level competitive hockey. However, when it comes to our mental health, and breaking this hold ADHD seems to have, let's focus on quality exercise that fully engages our mind and senses. Push for our schools, workplaces, and others in our house to increase emphasis on it, too.

More Engaging Activities

We waste a lot of time playing on our devices and consoles, and watching TV and videos. Its impact on our nervous system and brain is like feeding ourselves pure sugar—a momentary rush, then we're continually craving more. Whether this video stimulation invokes ADHD or vice versa isn't known, but ultimately ADHD, as Dr. Stephen Hinshaw wrote so succinctly in his book *ADHD: What Everyone Needs To Know*, can be seen as "a condition of underarousal with a need to satisfy that state of being."[8]

Why not find more engaging activities that utilize more of our minds and senses, and create less sugar-like neurotransmitter stimulation? For example, instead of playing a video game, why not power up a remote-controlled car or drone (or those "ancient" toys—kites and model airplanes)? Instead of playing video or device-based games, why not pull out board games and play with the entire family? How about interactive games, like tag or other friendly chase games that involve strategy, concentration, problem solving and cooperation? Instead of throwing your kid in front of the TV to while the hours away, why not have them color, draw, make crafts, or even try to write a video game? Engage the mind and attention in a positive way.

It's amazing how many of these simple little activities we throw aside in our crazy busy lives. Yet, they create active children and adults who feel comfortable in various situations and around different groups of people, which, I can tell you, is a major part of living with any kind of stress, anxiety, or behavior-based disorder.

Behavioral Therapy

The American Medical Association, American Association of Pediatrics, and American Psychiatric Association all finally begun to push back (somewhat) at the rush-to-prescribe mentality that has dominated ADHD treatment. They are starting to advocate behavioral therapy as a first course of treatment, rather than the supplement to a prescription. With 75 percent of young ADHD patients medicated, that leaves 25 percent of diagnosed cases currently working with drug-free therapy of some sort. We need to move that 25 percent figure toward 100 percent as rapidly as we can.

I liken behavioral therapy to driving a car. We can have others drive us, such as the medications that sharpen our concentration and focus, and reduce our hyperactivity and anxiety, or we can learn to drive our own lives and manage these behaviors and feelings without outside help. The therapist becomes the driver's education instructor who is in the car with you, highly involved with teaching you how to drive, yet loosening the wheel more and more as you get the hang of it. One day, you find you can drive yourself, and the instructor can step back. That is a wonderful, empowering moment—one that, I believe, almost every diagnosed ADHD patient can experience for the rest of their lives, starting now.

Let's spread the recommendation of these esteemed organizations across the board and relegate prescription drugs to the back burner, used only as a last resort. Therapy works much better to resolve specific problematical behavior by reviewing situations and working out solutions between therapist and client. Role playing, acting, and conversation all are effective. Good therapists set up goals for the client to achieve, and also provide tools, or coping devices, such as anger management, better communication, problem solving, conflict resolution, better interpersonal skills, and making and keeping friends.

Good therapists allow their clients to co-participate in the development of their own behavior modification, coping, or personal development tools. That's when great things can happen, especially when working with all three sets of tools together. First, the client is empowered to co-create a strategy that makes life an easier, happier, and less stressful existence. Engagement is everything. It motivates the client to modify impulsive and disruptive behavior, often eliminating it. Second, the client learns both sides of situations, as in conflict resolution; that results in less tense moments that not only have better outcomes, but keep the neurotransmitters and HPA (hypothalamus-pituitary-adrenal) hormones from going haywire. That diminishes the fight-or-flight re-

sponse and makes it easier to "hang in there" during the difficult moments. The result? More peace of mind and brainpower to focus on
finding out how resourceful, gifted, and great we can really become.
That's the personal development piece, which my co-writer calls the
"becoming a superbeing" step. Everyone around the child or adult in
therapy benefits enormously, but none more so than the child or adult
themselves.

Our ability to further dial into the behavior of individuals, and work
with that behavior, must grow as we move forward. Not only do we
often pass up behavioral therapy for prescription therapy, we often
misread the behavior that leads to the therapy and diagnosis. That
makes it a problem to work behavioral therapy and prescription therapy
together. As Dr. Kuzujanakis notes, one of the biggest blind spots in
ADHD diagnosing concerns another type of behavior—that exhibited
by gifted children. "Bright and talented children are at high risk for
medical misdiagnosis of ADHD (both under- and overdiagnosis) for
several reasons," she says.

> Their boredom in the classroom coming as a result of already master-
> ing the materials one to five years ahead of classmates places them in
> a position where, in many states, nothing is done to encourage their
> education. Gifted children are also complex and intense. The inten-
> sity can play out as high activity levels, talkativeness, impatience, et
> cetera, factors that can easily be confused with ADHD. Gifted chil-
> dren can also have comorbid conditions including ADHD, and their
> intelligence can mask the symptoms of ADHD, leaving it unsup-
> ported until later adolescence of college age when the complexity of
> time management for the first time leads such a twice-exceptional
> child to come crashing down.[9]

We'll get to her larger discussion about gifted children in chapter 17,
but this speaks to the necessity of using behavioral therapy to find those
deeper causes behind an ADHD diagnosis. We need to make it a top
priority—a first-resort treatment. To borrow a phrase from twelve-step
programs, "It works if you work it." This book is living proof of that.

Yoga, Tai Chi, and Qigong

These practices have histories dating back thousands of years. They provide physical exercise, and so much more. They are among the best developers of strong bodies, minds, and spirits that mankind has ever developed. Taken purely in their physical form, they provide great exercise that increases strength and flexibility, increases oxygen in the blood, improves blood flow, reduces stress, balances hormones, and builds stronger hearts and lungs. Endurance goes up as pulse rates and respirations (breathing rates) go down. When you add the "mind" component, they can take us to very deep, peaceful states, so deep that little from the outside world seems to bother us.

Practitioners of yoga, tai chi, and qigong enhance their concentration, focus, and ability to respond positively to any situation. Brain waves slow into that ultimate beta state where we operate at our quiet, concentrated best. Yoga, in particular, also sharpens the communication between neurotransmitters through the combination of *pranayama* (deep breathing) and quieter, deeper *asanas* (or postures).[10] Teens and children with ADHD who practice yoga twice (or more) per week are less anxious, less hyperactive, and less prone to distractions or daydreaming. Yoga classes are daily necessities for college students on virtually all campuses, for a very good reason.

My strong recommendation is to find someone who teaches any of these three great ancient traditions (studios and sessions are plentiful), explain the ADHD situation with you or your loved one, and start. Beginning practices may last fifteen to thirty minutes, but most find themselves quickly building to sixty to ninety minutes, and continuing forward for months or years. Some transform as their bodies become flexible, their minds sharper and more focused, and their stress levels far less.

There is a reason why an estimated 36.7 million people in North America practice yoga, according to *Yoga Journal* and the Yoga Alliance.[11] I feel it's time that we bring these practices directly to bear on the ADHD issue. If we do, we may see truly transformative results.

Ayurveda

Let's stick with Eastern approaches to look at a wonderful philosophy that has combined diet, self-care, and medical practices for more than five thousand years—Ayurveda.

Briefly, Ayurveda breaks foods, herbs, supplements, our energy, and body types into three principal categories: vata (light, changeable, cool, mobile), pitta (high-energy, highly concentrated, intense), and kapha (slow, low-energy, easy to relax or be lazy). One of these predominates in each of us, but we all possess combinations of the three *doshas*, as they're called. Those with ADHD either have too much vata (like myself, where my alpha brain waves can be off the hook), or too much kapha (the inattentive, daydreaming branch of the ADHD diagnostic tree, dominated by theta, or low brain waves). When vata is balanced in our systems, we lead balanced lives. With an ADHD patient, vata tends to be predominant, which leads to anxiety, inattention, restlessness, and sleep problems. It becomes further disturbed when we seek out more action, excitement, and distraction—the reaction we have when our energy is out of balance.

An Ayurvedic doctor will look at a situation like this and create a treatment plan of foods, supplements, spices, and personal life practices and activities that calm the patient's vata. That, in turn, helps control impulsive behavior, relaxes the mind, and relieves anxiety, tension, and stress. For activities, they might suggest more walking in the woods and less playing in crowds, or owning a pet (especially a cat) and learning how to operate within the cat's rhythm.

An Ayurvedic specialist will often begin with a full body relaxation done while lying still, which in Ayurveda and yoga they call *shavasana*. Parents can guide kids through this by telling them to imagine themselves as ice cream melting in the sun, or pretending they are absorbed by the sea. The goal is to use deep breathing and total relaxation to reach a parasympathetic nervous system state, which relaxes and restores. With ADHD, people often live in a constant sympathetic state, where everything is felt and we tend to react too harshly, kicking in those HPA hormones and the fight-or-flight response (as with childhood post-traumatic stress disorder or PTSD, hence the easy misdiagnosis).

Next up, at bedtime, is to give massages. Massage belongs on this list anyway, as I believe everyone in the ADHD or behavioral disorder boat should receive regular massages. They stimulate and clear energy blockages in the body; they relax our bodies and minds; and they slow down the energy in our nervous systems. They are deeply restorative and healing. One difference between a soothing general massage and an Ayurvedic massage is that the latter uses organic unrefined oil (almond, olive, and sesame oils are the best for grounding). Among other things, this is a great way to lead your child or loved one into sleep— and a restful, peaceful sleep at that.

Ayurveda also has a complete food, herbal, and supplement branch, one too thorough to break out completely in these pages. However, by quickly assigning certain foods to the *doshas*, you can see which foods work best to calm the mind and nervous system—root vegetables, leafy greens, grains, and herbal teas enhance vata; spicy and sugary foods, acidic, and hot caffeinated beverages feed pitta; and cheese, creams, pasta, white processed foods, and other heavy "comfort" items promote kapha. A good Ayurvedic food tip: the more natural colors in a meal (except white), the more nutritious and complete in vitamins, minerals, and amino acids. For instance, if you eat a salad with leafy greens, red and yellow vegetables, along with eggplant parmigiana (purple eggplant, red tomato sauce), you're eating a healthy meal that includes all three doshas (vata, pitta, kapha) and balances your biochemical system.

Along with Ayurveda, we would also do well to explore traditional Chinese medicine (TCM), acupressure, acupuncture, Thai yoga, and other practices that revolve around the union, or perfect balance, between mind, body, and spirit—for the purpose of harmony, health, and happiness. And, I might add, wonderfully balanced biochemistries and brain wave activity!

CONCLUSION

When dealing with our own ADHD, or working with adults or children, our main goals should be the same: alleviating or rising above situations that create more stress, more anxiety, or cause disruption; making sure the brain is fed properly to balance our neurotransmitters; and growing forward with tools, activities, and practices that bring out more of ourselves. Nothing beats continual improvement, where you look in the mirror every day and ask, "What can I improve on today?" and then set out to achieve that goal. It is amazing how life changes when sticking to that daily objective, and how far in the background those ADHD symptoms crawl when faced with the pure positive energy and intent of focused attention.

My feeling is that, while we can improve brain function for underperforming brain wave patterns with stimulants, we cannot take this next vital step of improving *ourselves*. Nor can we really find out the deeper truth of what ails us without getting a full assessment from a variety of specialists—especially when they work collaboratively.

15

TOWARD COLLABORATIVE DIAGNOSING AND CARE

What happens when a person suffers a serious injury or begins to present symptoms of a major chronic illness, such as cancer or diabetes? Their first stop is usually the hospital or doctor's office, where a point person (a nurse physician, nurse, or clinician) evaluates them. After establishing the type of injury, or symptoms, the point person will run tests and seek out specialists to examine further. Depending on the situation, condition, and type of health problem, the patient is seen by anywhere to a few to a half-dozen specialists, perhaps more. They take advantage of today's real-time communications technology to pass notes, files, CAT Scan, PET Scan, MRI, EEG and test results back and forth, sometimes across states, countries, and continents. Participants compare findings and add vital insights from their specific areas of specialty.

Both the diagnosis and treatment plan are of paramount importance. You're not going to treat a significant traumatic brain injury the same way you would a simple head contusion; you're not going to treat diabetes the same way as pancreatic cancer, though initial symptoms might be similar. The specialists are going to talk, and talk some more, until they get it right. Then they will outline the treatment plan that may or may not involve them, but will likely involve others on the treatment-therapy side.

This level of collaboration happens every day in hospitals, clinics, and doctors' and therapists' offices around the world. When lives and livelihoods are at stake, or you're looking at an intense acute illness or a long-term chronic prognosis, common sense dictates getting multiple opinions as your doctors collaborate on their findings. Even at the high school sports level, a busted leg or torn knee ligament suffered during a game or match brings in the emergency medical technicians (EMTs), emergency care physician, orthopedic specialists, a surgeon and his or her operating room team, and aftercare and rehabilitation specialists. This "it takes a village" approach is the cornerstone of twenty-first-century medicine.

If so, then why are we relying on individual clinicians to make critical ADHD diagnoses based on a checklist of behavioral traits that, if broken down, should involve a clinician, psychiatrist, behavioral psychologist, pediatrician, and neurologist or neuroscientist at the least? Why are we saddling overwhelmed primary care physicians and general practitioners with making diagnoses that can last for a lifetime? This raises my dander, partially because I have experienced it up close—with a series of misdiagnoses to show for it. Also, it upsets me that, in this era of increasingly collaborative medicine, we continue to rely on two points of contact for the vast majority of ADHD diagnoses: the observant, worried parent or educator, and the clinician.

"We have not changed our approach to diagnosing ADHD since 1903, when it began to be diagnosed medically," Dr. Tim Royer says. "It's been done the same way, off of behavioral checklists. We're not diagnosing any system in the body as we were in 1903, but for some reason, we're diagnosing brain and behavioral disorders the same way— off of [observed] behaviors. It makes no sense."[1]

It sure the hell doesn't. Unless your sole goal is to get yourself or your kid into a clinician's office to receive an ADHD prescription— whether for improved grades, greater focus, or because you really want to alleviate observed symptoms—then there is no reason to meekly accept a checklist diagnosis from a single doctor. Especially when the misdiagnosis rate hovers at or around 50 percent. Granted, the DSM-V checklist took years of work to sort out. However, we need to rise above checklists to know for sure if it's ADHD, or one of the up to one hundred comorbid conditions. The thing is, we can do that—right now.

As with other therapeutic approaches, which I outlined in chapter 13, collaborative medicine for ADHD does exist. It is highly effective not only at getting diagnoses right, but also in pointing the person exhibiting such behaviors *and* corresponding brain wave activity in the right therapeutic direction. In many cases, those directions never stop at a pharmacy, or if they do, not for very long.

One of the greatest benefits of collaboration is that it can rule out other causes before establishing a final diagnosis. A great example of this takes place at the Guelph Vision Therapy Center in Canada, co-founded by Dr. Patrick Quaid. Dr. Quaid works collaboratively on clinical cases and publishing papers with a number of noted vision experts, physiotherapists, audiologists and neuropsychologists, including Dr. Susan Barry, author of the popular vision therapy memoir *Fixing My Gaze*, John Hopkins University neuro-ophthalmologist Dr. Eric Singman, and hormone dysfunction specialist Dr. Lawrence Komer, MD, author of *A New Hope for Concussions*.[2] Dr. Quaid, a sought-after speaker at seminars and conferences in North America and Europe, has helped reverse hundreds of ADHD diagnoses (and their prescriptions), redirecting exams and diagnoses toward one of the many real causes: vision problems. He also points out, "The issue of an ADHD diagnosis and a vision issue co-existing is always managed in collaboration with all other health care professionals involved."

"Even though research shows overlap in the symptoms of ADHD and eye disorders, it is very surprising that little to no mention is made of vision in pediatric guidelines on managing ADHD," Dr. Quaid writes in his as-yet unpublished book *Seeing Is Believing*.

> One 2005 peer reviewed study looked at 266 children on ADHD medications and determined that these children had a three times higher incidence of eye co-ordination issues (specifically a condition called Convergence Insufficiency or CI). This CI condition happens to be the exact condition I had as a child. The really interesting part was a note by the authors that five out of the nine symptoms of CI overlapped with the symptoms of ADHD and there is clearly potential for diagnostic confusion between ADHD and CI. This was quite a statement from an ophthalmology journal. As an optometrist, my hat is off to the authors for highlighting this obvious overlap.
>
> It comes down to this: if your child's eyes cannot pull inwards (or converge) effortlessly, it stands to reason that they may have difficulty focusing on a task. They may also appear to have attention issues, or be resistant to reading.

"Although there is indeed research to back up the significant overlap between ADHD and eye teaming dysfunction symptomatology, as one of my colleagues said it, this falls under the category of "The University of My Eyeballs" (also known as common sense). Essentially, it is not rocket science to think that poor eye teaming skills will lead to poor attention. It is logical to connect the two!"[3]

In Michigan, Dr. Royer and his fellow neurologists, neuroscientists, and collaborative team at Neurocore find themselves reversing some ADHD diagnoses. It's not that they don't consider ADHD a disorder—Dr. Royer makes it very clear that it is—but that continuous overdiagnosis has prompted them into action. Not surprisingly, when a diagnosed child or adult receives a more strenuous battery of tests and exams by Dr. Royer and his team, the conclusion often changes. As an example of collaboration working well, he refers to the NEBA test, the FDA-approved combination of an EEG and diagnostic observation.

"Right now, our diagnosis accuracy rate is 55 percent; that's like flipping a coin," he says.

> To see the difference, a neurologist, a neuropsychologist, social worker, therapist, and two physicians got together and went off observation and the checklist. But these six observed from their own areas of specialty. Six people looked at a group of already diagnosed kids. They concluded some were not ADHD, and decided some were. What we learned is that their accuracy was very similar to what they used in EEG (the NEBA test protocol). Which is about 90 percent [author's note: the FDA claims 97 percent].[4] You have to remember that diagnosing from a checklist of observations is like surveying a spot on the ground from 300 feet up. You'll see a general pattern, but that's it. We need the specialists and tools that can take us right to the ground.
>
> With EEG involvement, measured brain waves and patterns, one doctor can match this panel of six people. But you take the EEG away, and it goes to 55 percent. So many times when the diagnosis made, it is just one doctor, one patient, and no EEG. But if you bring in a pool of experts and put them next to a physician, the (accuracy) rate goes from 55 percent to about 85 to 90 percent. My team and I see the same rates. That's why we need collaborative diagnosis.[5]

As Quaid and Royer make clear, we work best on the ADHD issue if we work *together*. We need to learn the full story within a kid or adult exhibiting ADHD symptoms, rule out all other possible causes, *and then* treat. The more I learn, the more I realize that no single person should ever diagnose ADHD on his or her own. We need an interdisciplinary diagnostic team. Out of all the suggestions or calls to actions I make in this book, interdisciplinary collaboration is one of the biggest.

This vital step revolves around checking our egos, credentials, and "territory" at the door, and then collaborating. Dr. Andres De Los Reyes, director of the Comprehensive Assessment and Intervention Program (CAIP) at the University of Maryland's department of psychology, is firm about this. "We are at a critical point in mental health research where we finally realized that to enact positive change, no one discipline needs to be involved. This is the work of nurses, teachers, epidemiologists, psychologists, social workers, neuroscientists, and those in medicine," he says. "No one can do it alone, but the problem is that the next generation of scientists need to learn how to work in teams of people from different scientific backgrounds, and basically learn the 'street smarts' of academic work."[6]

And, I would add to that, vision therapy experts, optometrists and parents.

COLLABORATIVE DIAGNOSES

Drs. Royer, Quaid, and De Los Reyes aren't the only health-care experts actively participating in or advocating collaborative diagnoses. Furthermore, everyone seems to want the same three outcomes: verification that it really *is* ADHD before diagnosing; re-testing for other conditions, disorders, or syndromes if it is not; and treatment options either in addition to or in place of stimulant prescriptions.

As these examples show, the types and degrees of collaboration are not only alive and well but reflective of the effort some in the health-care field are undertaking to get beyond the current protocol.

COLLABORATIVE CARE FOR CHILDREN WITH ADHD SYMPTOMS

In a 2015 study called "Collaborative Care for Children with ADHD Symptoms: A Randomized Comparative Effectiveness Trial," the American Academy of Pediatrics (AAP) studied two care management systems for six- to twelve-year-old children to determine the effectiveness of combining collaborative care with interventions (treatments). Besides medical experts from a variety of specialties, "care managers in the enhanced care arm also were trained in motivational and parent management techniques to help parents engage in their child's treatment, address their own mental health needs, and manage challenging child behaviors," the AAP abstract stated.[7]

The preparation of diagnoses, participants, and care managers was extensive, according to the main text of the study:

> If an ADHD diagnosis was confirmed by the primary care provider, the decision support team provided guideline-concordant pharmacological guidance, and advice on monitoring and treating to a target symptom score. Decision support was phrased in nonspecific terms: for example, if a suggestion was made to start a stimulant medication, a specific medication was not named. For those with ADHD–inconsistent presentations, the decision support team provided guidance about diagnostic next steps. The electronic health record provided the medium for communication.
>
> Enhanced care managers received additional training to address 3 common reasons for ADHD symptom persistence: ambivalence toward engagement with behavioral health care, parental mental health, and oppositional child behavior. To address the first 2, care managers were trained in motivational interviewing and followed a standardized script to resolve ambivalence toward treatment. Consistent with previous work, care managers used motivational interviewing principles to explore parents' stressors, and to offer referrals to adult behavioral health services if indicated.[8]

What they found was rather astonishing: only 40 percent of the kids being evaluated for ADHD actually presented consistent with ADHD. Forty percent! That's 10 percent less than Dr. Royer's own assessment. This number intrigued me, since earlier in 2016, on Twitter, I posted a pie-chart graphic from the Cedarbook Center, an organization that helps patients diagnosed with disorders such as ADHD, dementia, Alzheimer's, and others, that indicated only 43 percent of those prescribed stimulants for ADHD actually *have* ADHD.[9] Furthermore, of the 40 percent cited by the AAP abstract, collaborative care and behavior-based care management and therapy resulted in, to quote the abstract, "superior change scores for hyperactivity/impulsivity, oppositionality, and social skills." The word "prescription" is nowhere to be found.

What does that mean? It tells me that by replacing an individual clinician with a team, and a pharmaceutical solution with care and therapy from specialists representing some, or all, of the items on the DSM-V checklist, we can arrive at ADHD in a very healthy way. If they even *have* ADHD, which, as the study and other citings suggest, is a 50/50 proposition at best.

TORNADO PROGRAM

In the Netherlands, where the majority of general practitioners (GPs) are uncomfortable diagnosing for ADHD, the so-called Tornado program allows diagnoses to be made by second- and third-tier specialists, with the GP monitoring medication. According to the ADHD Institute website, also published in abbreviated abstract form by the AAP,

> "in this collaborative approach, children with suspected ADHD were referred by GPs (n=15) to a 1-day-to-diagnosis psychiatric service. Concurrently, the GPs received a 1-hour, online course during which they were educated about the characteristics of ADHD, use of the ADHD rating scales, initiation of pharmacotherapy and monitoring of side effects. Children with uncomplicated ADHD (without comorbidities and family problems) returned with medication advice to the GP, who assumed responsibility for treatment initiation and monitoring. A semi-structured phone interview was conducted by a trained medical student to collect information regarding GPs' satisfaction with the programme and the role they perceived for themselves in the diagnosis and treatment of ADHD.[10]

This study was far more focused on a prescription-based treatment than I'd prefer. The larger point, though, is that GPs, the diagnosers in North America, are not diagnosing in this study, experts on mental disorders are, which takes the percentage of ADHD diagnoses down, as they see other causes. When the Dutch GPs were asked why they did not see themselves, or wish to see themselves, as the primary diagnosing doctors, their answers offered insight into two big problems in North America: lack of collaborative care and imposing on GPs to make complex diagnoses that impact entire lives:

> Most of the 15 GPs did not see a role for themselves in the diagnosis of childhood ADHD and would prefer a specialist to diagnose ADHD. Barriers to diagnosis in the primary care setting included GPs' limited experience, GPs' time constraints precluding the collection of diagnosis-enabling information from parents and teachers, and the need for diagnostic accuracy to educate the GPs' prescription practices. All interviewed GPs saw a role for themselves in pharmacological treatment of children with uncomplicated ADHD, which they hoped would save time in secondary care and subsequently decrease waiting times. The shortened diagnostic procedure and the opportunity to confer with a specialist during treatment was deemed beneficial."[11]

DOING IT RIGHT: AN INTERDISCIPLINARY MODEL

The National Institutes of Health also put out a revealing study, "Doing it Right: An Interdisciplinary Model for the Diagnosis of ADHD."[12] It focuses on the work of the Colchester East Hants Attention-Deficit/Hyperactivity Disorder Clinic (ADHD Clinic) in Nova Scotia, Canada, which, according to the abstract, "uses a best practice, interdisciplinary service model to provide diagnostic assessment and treatment services for children suspected of having ADHD." The eight coauthors interviewed clinic service providers, along with parents/guardians, teachers, and family physicians. The clinic's diagnostic services are run by a team of pediatricians, clinical psychologists, and school psychologists. I'd like to see a neurologist or neuroscientist, a psychiatrist, and vision therapy expert added to the list, but it certainly qualifies as a collaborative team.

In the study, the Colchester East Hants ADHD Clinic's best practices objective is clearly stated, and I'd hold it up anywhere to show it as Exhibit A of strong collaborative care for the single purpose of diagnosing, treating, and healing a patient:

"Best practice involves a thorough evaluation to determine the origins of behavioural symptoms and requires expertise from professionals in health, mental health, and education," the study states.

> A complete evaluation for ADHD should include obtaining information about development and general health, conducting clinical interviews with parents, teachers, and perhaps the child to look for other mental and physical health difficulties, and completing a psycho-educational assessment to determine whether the child has a learning disability which frequently co-exists with ADHD or can present similarly to ADHD in the classroom setting. [13]

The study states two points that present themselves as the bugaboos of our currently predominant one-doctor, one-exam, one-diagnosis system: "Information from these multiple sources is necessary to enable professionals to eliminate other explanations for the symptoms of inattention, over-activity, and/or impulsivity. [Bugaboo #1: We often diagnose ADHD without eliminating other possibilities.] Although the utilization of interdisciplinary teams in mental health settings has become widely accepted as best practice, the reality is that current diagnostic practices often fall short of this." [Bugaboo #2: We don't collaborate enough.]

The study's goal was to deliver accurate diagnoses and ADHD-specific interventions. They studied 198 children suspected of having ADHD based on standard checklists. Only 112, or 58 percent, were actually diagnosed with ADHD. (There's that drift into the 50 percent accuracy range again!) Other diagnoses included Tourette's syndrome, autism spectrum disorders, learning disabilities, anxiety, and depression. (I'd also bet vision issues were either involved to some degree or might have disqualified a few more from having ADHD.)

After being deemed a major success, the study drew its conclusions. I'll stick to the highlights, again quoting directly from the National Institutes of Health published findings themselves:

> The overwhelming endorsement of the interdisciplinary, multi-system model used by the Colchester East Hants Attention-Deficit/ Hyperactivity Disorder Clinic has broad implications for clinical practice beyond the confines of this setting. Teams of professionals described as multi- or interdisciplinary are often not that in practice.

In terms of client contact, they work in parallel, not as a team. Recent research and the results of this evaluation of the ADHD Clinic have both emphasized the general importance of and the benefits for professionals and service consumers that can be derived from interdisciplinary cooperation.[14]

Pretty compelling case for collaboratively diagnosing ADHD, isn't it?

FUNCTIONAL MEDICINE

Now let's explore a health-care model gathering steam quickly in the United States: functional medicine. Functional medicine combines several worlds—traditional medicine, diet and nutrition, clinical advice to patient-clients, highly trained coaches helping those clients act on the findings and reorient their lives, and medical and therapeutic solutions that don't involve pharmaceuticals. Not only are prescriptions considered a last resort in functional medicine, but specialists steer patients and clients toward diet, nutrition, supplements, and healthy life choices. In other words, they work with people to take charge of their own health.

Functional medicine emphasizes locating and addressing the cause of a patient's health problem. It is predominantly practiced clinically by chiropractors, medical doctors, osteopathic doctors, naturopaths, homeopathic doctors, nurse practitioners, nutritionists, and coaches. Its starting point is the series of lifestyle, dietary, and medical choices we've made to get to where we are now. For most, that looks more like the tip of a very toxic iceberg, as our medical charts and ailments can verify. Functional medicine considers the toxicity of the environment, all of the pollution, poisons, existing toxins in our food supply (of which high fructose corn syrup, a staple in the U.S. food supply, is a perfect example), and the prescription drugs we've taken recently or are taking. The goal is to reverse the damage done to our bodies through administering proper nutrients "to bring the body back to life, and back into balance," according to "The Functional Medicine Niche," an official report offered to "chiropractors who want to take responsibility for the improved health of a new population of patients" by the Functional Medicine Institute.[15] Another, "About Functional Medicine?" is readily available online.[16]

While functional medicine practitioners can use lab testing such as blood, stool, saliva, or hair samples to determine the cause, they treat as naturally as possible—lifestyle changes, food, nutraceutical products, detox programs, and similar approaches. Their goal is to reestablish proper function for each of us, which includes bringing lab values to a "functionally normal" range where our food intake and lifestyle choices again support optimal body function.

FUNCTIONAL MEDICINE AND ATTENTION DEFICIT HYPERACTIVITY DISORDER

How do functional medicine specialists, coaches, and clients work together to reestablish proper function for a situation such as an ADHD diagnosis and alleviate or minimize ADHD behaviors and symptoms in a drug-free way? That was the subject of an exhaustive 2010 case study, "Functional Medicine and Attention Deficit Hyperactivity Disorder," coauthored by the Institute of Functional Medicine's Mark Hyman and Kara Fitzgerald.[17] The study looked at the case of a twelve-year-old boy (hereafter referred to as LC) who was first diagnosed with ADHD at age five but was also found to be suffering from dysgraphia (learning disability that affects writing), environmental allergies, asthma, insomnia, eczema, canker sores, migraine headaches, muscle cramps, stomach pain, nausea, and diarrhea. The report outlined a pharmacological history of methylphenidate, which the boy took for four years, plus seven other prescription drugs, "an overwhelming pharmacopoeia for a twelve-year-old boy," the report states. "His physical, mental, and behavioral symptoms were still not under control." A concussion, sustained at age five (before the ADHD diagnosis), was also noted, along with food allergies and pronounced increases in weight and sugar intake after being taken off methylphenidate. On top of that, LC "had never received a positive teacher's report. Off the methylphenidate (Ritalin), he continued to be disruptive and unfocused."

Very few people diagnosed with ADHD have ever had their histories so thoroughly reviewed before getting the diagnosis and prescription. It just doesn't happen. To be fair, I'd never seen a workup so thorough, which brings me to the rub: this study was *just beginning*. All of this was from the initial consultation.

After revealing much more in the twelve-year-old's medical history, along with his dietary history and his family's medical *and* household history, the report moved into the action phase. These findings, and the degree of detail, hit me like a trip into the wonderland of future health-care treatment, where we get to the bottom of everything and make our bodies healthy again, and pharmaceuticals need not apply, unless they are the only option. (Functional medicine is not explicitly anti-pharma-ceutical, but rather averse to prescriptions that mask symptoms and toxify the body.) Here are some of this report's findings that make me feel like I've come face-to-face with the vision I've been trumpeting to a quarter million Twitter followers for years:

- Environmental exposure: LC's house had a mold infestation, one of his two determined allergies—the other being tree pollen.
- The boy had a nutrient-poor diet, audio sensitivity, muscle spasms, hives, headaches, stomach problems, immune system problems, and more, for which a battery of blood and nutritional tests were performed.
- To determine toxicity from food, environment, and medicines, LC was administered a six-hour urine toxic metal test.
- To determine hormone and neurotransmitter issues (two core biomarkers of ADHD), LC was tested for neurotransmitter metabolites and plasma amino acids.

Now, for some results, direct from the case study:

"LC was very low in zinc and magnesium; low-normal levels were reported for the rest of the minerals. These findings were not surprising given LC's poor diet, GI inflammation, and cimetidine use. Zinc defi-ciency is implicated in asthma, atopic dermatitis, allergies, *and ADHD* (emphasis mine)"; and, this showstopper:

"Had LC continued with his presenting diet and lifestyle, the plasma fatty acid analysis reveals the likelihood for continued inflammatory conditions as an adult, including possibly heart disease, diabetes, and cancer. Addressing these findings early not only treated his initial com-plaints, but significantly reduced his risk for a future of ill health."

In addition, the tests concluded that LC suffered from hypovitamin-osis, which impacted his immune response, energy, mood, concentra-tion, general development issues, chronic infections, and hypersensitivities. In other words, poor nutrition was slowly choking off his mental and physical health. They tested for ninety different foods, and found positive allergic reactions to peanuts, dairy, and six other items *associated with people diagnosed with ADHD*. His urine test hit upon something equally worrisome: overly high levels of lead, which have been directly tied to cognitive and behavioral problems—and, yes, ADHD. They also find low neurotransmitter turnover and a specific deficiency in serotonin, along with deficiencies in vitamin B6 and magnesium—which synthesize dopamine and serotonin to create hormonal balance in healthy people.

There is much more, but within this battery of tests and the medical and life history workup that preceded it, these specialists found dietary, environmental, pharmaceutical, and other contributors to LC's condition. Not the type of wholesale, life-altering diagnosis and prognosis you hear in a typical office visit to be evaluated off the DSM-V checklist, is it?

As difficult as it is to believe this breakdown of the boy's life with ADHD can't get any better, well, it does. Next up on the functional medicine evaluation were the treatment rationales and recommended steps moving forward. Here is a partial list of treatments that the two authors (an MD and a naturopath)—working in collaboration with dieticians, nutritionists, the boy and his family—sent home with him to help end his eight-year nightmare:

- Multivitamins and minerals with added zinc, magnesium, and vitamin D3
- Omega-3 fatty acids to minimize pro-inflammatory substances
- A modified elimination diet minus dairy, peanuts, gluten, sugar, and trans fats; a reduced saturated fat intake; and whole, minimally processed, organic foods
- Broad-spectrum probiotics to build his immune system and treat intestinal issues and food sensitivities
- After sixty days, start taking DMSA (dimercaptosuccinic acid), a major treatment for lead toxicity, while monitoring to assure kidney and bowel functions are improving
- Start taking 5-HTP, a serotonin precursor, to increase serotonin and help alleviate insomnia

They also recommended follow-up visits at two months and six months.

Highlights from LC's six-month visit included the following: freedom from chronic symptoms of *all* his various ailments; complete cessation of all medications; stabilized mood and behavior, and sharply improved concentration levels; no more hyperactivity symptoms; and complete resolution of his hives, asthma, runny nose and postnasal drip, anal itching, stomachaches, nausea, diarrhea, headaches, muscle cramps, and sensitivity to loud noises. His grades were way up, his social life was strong for the first time, and he slept soundly at night.

Furthermore, his mother took wellness steps for her own life, changed her diet, and cleaned the toxins out of the house. She also wrote in his case study, "This was the first time in his entire schooling history that everything seems to be going well. The input from his teachers was that he is 'a different kid' than they saw in the first half of the year and that they're amazed by the difference."

What a case. What a story. What a result. Can you imagine what would happen if we transposed this type of work onto the current ADHD diagnostic template? I wonder if we'd be able to handle the degree of personal, social, and environmental transformation that would occur. Suffice to say, as more and more people find out about functional medicine and case studies like this, it will become a go-to approach for alleviating ADHD symptoms and behaviors—and creating the dietary and lifestyle changes we need.

However, since we can't shift the poles all at once, there is something we can do, and get our loved ones to do: change our diet. As I just illustrated, the results can be not only life affirming, but life changing.

16

PROBLEM CHILD OR GIFTED CHILD

When I was a kid, going to school offered a much different experience than today. We received plenty of instruction in the "three Rs"—reading, (w)riting and (a)rithmetic—some science, but also recesses, playtime during lunch, and creative time spent drawing, painting, or performing skits.

You've heard my story, which inspired me to look deeper into my ADHD diagnosis and write this book. Now, I'd like to tell you a bit about my co-writer, whose story will surprise many who know of him through his books and magazine articles. It's not something he normally shares.

Bob attended elementary school in the 1960s, and middle and high school in the 1970s. Times were creatively great. In fifth grade, social studies class ended with ten or fifteen minutes of drawing caricatures, spacecraft, and "secret cities," led by the social studies teacher—a former artist at Walt Disney Studios. In middle school, a typical day featured social studies, math, reading, writing, science, music, art, physical education, puzzle building, and problem solving in his MGM (mentally gifted minors) sessions, along with two recesses and a lunch. At his Southern California high school, it was more of the same: he took art, drafting, creative writing, media skills, physical education, Latin, world history, wood shop, and journalism, along with today's common core subjects—science, math, language arts, government, and history.

The result was "a lifelong love of learning," as Bob calls it. I call it the most important gift any teacher can give a student. It fed his creativity, natural curiosity, desire to try new things, and willingness to risk suspending his own beliefs and opinions to learn something new. His first newspaper job came in high school, and along with that came a love of writing and journalism, leading to a professional writing career that marked its fortieth anniversary in 2016.

Bob started exhibiting signs of a fluid mind early on. He began reading at four, and had trouble sitting still, beginning with kindergarten. He bored easily, and always needed something to occupy his mind. When he was nine, he wrote a seventy-page sci-fi piece about sending the girls in his class to Mars on a one-way ride (it was the Space Age sixties, after all). Thankfully, his attitude toward girls changed as he got older! The teachers, decades removed from those aggravating "common core" shackles, worked directly with him to feed his interests. They also made sure he ran off excess energy during recesses.

In today's world, Bob would have been pegged as an ADHD kid by age five, registering positive on seven of the nine major DSM-V guidelines. The resulting prescription would have made him less squirmy in his seat, perhaps more focused—though hard to argue with the focus level of someone who's written or ghostwritten twenty books. What about the latent creativity? The deeper potential? The love of learning, experiencing the fullness of life?

Thankfully, caring teachers and parents, along with a school curriculum that addressed the *full* education of the young mind—part and parcel of life in the sixties and seventies—gave Bob everything he needed to channel his creativity, energy, and attention into studies and projects that engaged him.

SCHOOLS TODAY

Unfortunately, the same cannot be said about a lot of young students these days. Dr. Susannah-Joy Schuilenberg, who specializes in dysfunctional behavior, trauma, anxiety, depression, and unhelpful thinking habits, puts it succinctly:

> Parents are under pressure to deal with the teacher's concerns in the classroom; teachers are under pressure to meet specific educational goals; schools are under pressure to do well on standardized tests, and the whole system makes the child the problem. Teachers see

medication as a way to make the classroom work, and parents see medication as a way to keep the school happy, and to minimize the chaos and conflict that has produced the label of ADHD in the first place.[1]

Doesn't sound like the same happy degree of caring or fully educating the student, does it?

Where are we going to promote the lifelong love of learning over "teaching to the test"? More importantly, how can we return to the dynamic in which educators, parents, and students work together for the *complete* body-mind education and well-being of the student, a simple routine back when ADHD diagnostic rates were 1 percent?

While everything from art and technology schools, magnet schools, STEM-based schools, and charters of various stripes pop up, our public schools continue to die on the vine. That's not all. With massive budget cuts forcing school districts to cut art, music, drama, dance, and even physical education from the school day (and more coming, thanks to the recent shift in U.S. Department of Education policy), young people have fewer options for channeling their creative and intuitive minds. "A child may be distractible in a classroom setting due to ADHD, but just as often that child may be experiencing anxiety, hunger, poor hearing or vision, allergies, boredom, tiredness, a learning disability, or a variety of other conditions that do not allow the child to be fully attentive to the classroom instructions," Dr. Marianne Kuzujanakis says. "A classroom is an artificial environment where kids are required to sit for prolonged periods of time and attend to learning in a uniform, methodical, and rote style. This is more evident in today's classrooms where recess, arts, and music are frequently sidelined in order to pack in more standardized core curriculum learning and test prep."[2]

Those guidelines revolve around an intense diet of English and language arts (and its passive, academic writing versus creative writing), history/social studies, math, science, and technical subjects—the Core Curriculum. The diet begins in elementary school and intensifies through high school. It features standardized testing, involving several weeks of preparatory drills before the actual tests. Why are these tests so important? Because states fund schools in relationship to overall test scores. They also fund schools based on attendance ratios.

When the White House announced that 2014–2015 marked the highest high school graduation rate on record—83.2 percent—it indicated that the huge effort to keep kids in school paid off.[3]

There is a lot to celebrate in this number. It shows the United States fully understands how vital education is to building a competitive workforce in the world. It also shows schools are keeping their kids on campus, and slowing down the dropout rate.

Between these numbers, though, is something else: Schools must post high attendance figures to be funded. Likewise, the more proficient schools are in Core Curriculum and student test scores, the better the funding. Core Curriculum classes are heavily left-brain oriented, with little creativity, thus little brain balance. Countless kids can't cope with that naturally and become fidgety, unfocused, inattentive, and difficult to handle. Then they grow depressed and anxious because they can't keep up. Some lose interest altogether. Others receive ADHD diagnoses, get prescribed a stimulant, and become quieter, more compliant, more focused. But at what cost?

TESTING

Don't get me wrong. Our current educational system trains our young people to be competitive in the global economy, and keeps us technologically proficient. Many great achievements come (and will come) from these students. But, in a system with so many tests, emphasis on sitting still and strict compliance, and such a restrictive, narrow curriculum void of artistic and social education—not to mention *life skills* education—how many would do more? How many would unleash their fullest potential? How many would become so engaged that they focus and actively participate without drawing attention as possible ADHD cases or needing medication?

Dr. Royer believes the current system forms a wicked, tied-to-money triangle: (1) grades and test scores are tied to money, (2) attendance is tied to money, and (3) getting kids to focus on attendance and tests via ADHD prescriptions is tied to money. This emphasis on money in our educational system often comes at a high cost: the neglect of creative minds and the suppression of gifted expression.

If we could fix it [the current educational system], I think we would create more Rembrandts. Because most of these kids that are going too slow [creatively], it's because they are diagnosed with ADHD and then they get put on a stimulant. If we would let these kids be, they are the ones that write the books, paint the pictures, invent the new technology. We've pushed them in a box, and now they can't become what they were made to be. So if we could right that ship—and that's a big question mark—we would see more and more innovation, more disruptive stuff. We would see more art, we would see things that make us kind of drop our jaw—that breathtaking moment. I think we've gotten farther and farther away from, so in an attempt to make the brain more focused, we've lost some of its ability to be as disruptive and artistic as it can be.

To change the course of that, our educational system would have to change. We're basing things on your chronological age rather than your brain's potential, so it messes up the whole system. And we want kids to be more still and less creative; creativity creates problems for the second grade teacher. There are so many different levels to this. I've been in the system for a long time, and I have a lot of great experiences with people getting better, but then I look at the big system that's pushing them. It's tricky.[4]

Like Dr. Royer, my concern lies with each student. The emphasis on Core Curriculum, standardized testing, and high-pressure advanced placement (AP) programs, prompted by ever-tougher college admissions standards, has changed elementary, middle, and high school dramatically. It has also changed the way we learn. The healthiest forms of learning—direct experience, natural curiosity, trying new things, balancing between the arts, core subjects, and physical education—have been replaced by the brain-numbing requirements of testing and getting into school.

BETTER WAYS OF LEARNING?

The "hunter's mind" or "360-degree mind" mentality , the way of natural learning embedded in our DNA since we became human, has been displaced by a linear, tightly focused approach. When kids can't handle it, they become unfocused and disruptive. That's how kids react. When traumatized by home or other events, they often seek greater attachment and direct contact with teachers. They need attention to competencies and self-esteem, and guidance on behavior management, says *Teacher* magazine—which many overwhelmed teachers find too difficult or time-consuming to address.[5] A growing number of parents are putting kids on ADHD meds to improve their performance in school (hence the term, "study drugs"[6]). This is despite warnings from all sides of the health-care world. Consequently, home schooling is thriving, as are charter, satellite, tech, arts, STEM, and other nontraditional public schools.

GIFTED STUDENTS

Where does that leave the precocious, inquisitive child who has talents, gifts, wide-ranging potential, and the capability of doing whatever he or she wants in life but is so bored and fidgety in the classroom that an ADHD diagnosis is bound to happen?

When the Baby Boomer Generation was passing through school, psychologists and teachers routinely spotted gifted children, those far ahead of their peers in various subjects. These kids often were spirited to the psychologist's office, along with their parents, for interviews and IQ tests. In the United States, if a kid's IQ measured at 132 or higher, he or she qualified for MGM—the Mentally Gifted Minors program. "The range of IQ that determines giftedness runs from 120 to 200+," Dr. Kuzujanakis points out. "Within that range are multiple levels of giftedness that frequently are vastly separated from each other by ability and behaviors. A gifted child with IQ 130 may be so starkly different from a gifted child with IQ 180, so as not to think they have anything in common. The outliers of giftedness—those about IQ 160—rarely find age-peers in their classroom, their school, or in their community."[7]

In Mentally Gifted Minors, the kids would spend extra classroom time with a designated teacher, working on complex puzzles of various types, solving multilayered problems, determining hidden meaning, context and subtext of stories, playing chess or other board games, and playing word games. They would also do advanced reading or math work, depending upon their level. Although unstated, the MGM classroom gave them of feeling of community, of belonging; the students realized that they weren't alone among those who thought differently and accelerated in their learning. After that, they would return to their normal classes and, with few exceptions, fit in with their classmates and regular assignments.

Sadly, only thirty-two states mandate gifted identification in schools, and only a small fraction of that includes funding. Only the most exceptional educators, those who can rise above their already overwhelming, strictly regulated jobs, are spotting them.

Not surprisingly, the diagnosis rate for ADHD has jumped nearly a thousand percent since the Baby Boomers were students and identifying gifted children was considered part of being a good educator. As shown over and over again, the ADHD meds are no friends of creative expression.

STRESS, ANXIETY, AND DEPRESSION

Stress, anxiety and depression are killers in anyone's life, and they are prevalent in school settings, especially today. In 2014, suicide rates were the highest in the United States in thirty years, according to the Centers for Disease Control and National Institutes of Health.[8] The increase reflected across all age groups, including those aged five to twenty-four (the window of being a student).

That's not all. In a paper titled "Very Early Predictors of Adolescent Depression and Suicide Attempts in Children with Attention Deficit/ Hyperactivity Disorder," University of Maryland department of psychology professor Andrea Chronis-Tuscano noted that 27 percent of six- to eighteen-year-old boys diagnosed with ADHD also suffer from major depressive disorder (MDD). Ten years later, when Dr. Chronis-Tuscano and her co-writers revisited their test subjects, they found 46 percent had MDD—almost double the initial amount. The girls' stats were even more startling; 5.1 times as many girls dealt with MDD ten years into their ADHD protocols. More alarming, ADHD males were *90 percent* more likely to experience suicidal ideation in high school than the controls, or non-ADHD males, who were part of Dr. Chronis-Tuscano's study. While emotional and mental illness plays into this, I have to ask, what is our current method of educating kids, with its emphasis on testing and high achievement standards in a narrow corridor of subjects, doing to alleviate this? Or stoke it?[9]

Furthermore, why are we considering student anxiety and depression part of an overall ADHD condition in the first place? Anxiety and depression require different treatment protocols from ADHD. They often arise from outer environment, rather than inner behavior. What if a student is anxious or depressed because he's unchallenged? What if she's bored and feels apart from her peers due to her wider interests, for which she's finding no relevant courses or guidance? This is a huge problem on campuses, and no ADHD prescription will solve it.

In Great Britain, the National Children's Bureau (NCB) is focusing on rising stress, anxiety, and depression with a wonderful tool that can and should be adopted in every North American school. In October 2016, the NCB released a study that stated that 55 percent of polled members of the Association of School College Lecturers noticed a large increase in anxiety or stress, while 79 percent reported an increase in self-harm or suicidal thoughts among students. Is it because they're worried about jobs or careers? Keeping up in class? Or are class choices too narrow and emphasis on scores too high?

The NCB has responded by creating "a whole school framework for emotional well-being and mental health"—a self-assessment and improvement tool designed for school leaders. Its framework breaks down like this:

- Stage 1: Deciding to act and identifying what is currently in place
- Stage 2: Gaining a shared understanding and commitment to change and develop
- Stage 3: Building relationships and developing practices
- Stage 4: Implementing and evaluating[10]

This tool focuses on *relationships,* and teachers *caring* about their students. When a student feels a teacher (or coach) cares, they tend to get more focused and perform better. That is a simple fact of life that our standardized educational system seems to keep stripping out. For my money, a sure path to reducing ADHD diagnoses and the influence of ADHD stimulants on our kids and schools is to adopt plans like this, which assure the human touch stays in place.

Now let's go back to our work with gifted children—and all children.

GIFTED CHILDREN REVISITED

Instead of pouring resources into the children Dr. Royer calls "Rembrandts" and, back in the day, were often called (sometimes derisively) "Einsteins," we're diverting toward hitting test scores that deliver matching funds. We're emphasizing performance over student well-being, and completion of mandated course work plus testing over student initiative to excel in the areas in which they show particular talent. In those thirty-two states with existing gifted children programs, such kids are eligible for special needs resources through Individual Education Plans (IEPs) and the 504 Plan for Students with Disabilities. (I'm not sure how giftedness equals disability, but then again, I'm not one of the legislators that passed this law.) However, they are rarely utilized, with emphasis instead placed on remolding the kids into cookie-cutter students, which, sadly, reflects on the ADHD statistics.

Let's advocate for gifted children. Let's take charge of our future society and its direction by unleashing these kids. Let's encourage them to meet their greatest talents, highest potential, and innate ability to innovate, try something new, take risks, and lead us to as-yet-unseen accomplishments. These students are the real change agents, and when they are free to work four and five grade levels above their peers, something wonderful often happens—their peers accelerate, too. When we trust this process, as we did throughout the pre-ADHD hysteria, inspired teachers find the time and energy to spend more direct time with the kids, challenging them in new ways and bringing out their very best—which can be serious outlier stuff, to borrow Malcolm Gladwell's term.

How do we do it? We individualize, rather than systematize. When my coauthor taught writing in Northern California, he had several gifted students, a few ADHD students, and a few others who were twice-exceptional (a couple gifted children/Asperger syndrome, a couple others gifted children/ADHD). He gave them papers, research projects, and term projects specific to their areas of interest, and made them co-creators of part of their own curricula. One student co-developed a course on the Beat Generation, a huge force in American literature in the 1950s and 1960s. Another focused on our fascination with fast cars and racing. A third zeroed in on Persian poetry. Two others started memoirs on their fascinating lives, and tracked and recorded every step of the process (one was published in 2016).

Some forward-thinking high schools are moving in this direction—which, I should add, seemed to work for the most celebrated of all whole-body, whole-mind cultures, the Ancient Greeks, and that was 2,500 years ago. Luella High School, located outside Atlanta, is one such institution. Luella High School principal Jerry Smith said in an interview with KQED-TV, "If you are truly going to reach every student you have to see education as a personal thing for every person who walks into the building, including the adults."[11]

Smith's and Luella High's effort began by putting student relationships with the teacher in the center of the learning process. Then they focused on mastery of content, as opposed to learning enough to get by on standardized testing or a passing grade. I know that when I focus on subjects I am passionate about, I become locked in so deeply that I won't stop until I have uncovered everything about that subject and figured out exactly how it works and can work. That's how I started my social media platform on ADHD issues. This is the mind-set of mastery, of commanding the subject. When you do so, self-esteem and self-worth elevates, and attentiveness and focus levels increase greatly as well. I become totally engaged, and not much distracts me—sounds like the opposite of ADHD, doesn't it? Better yet, with mastery of a subject or a task, the knowledge of having mastered it and how to move forward stays with me for the rest of my life.

Luella High School operates on that premise. They also educate with full engagement in mind, with the variety of subjects pre-Millennials remember, along with requisite advanced placement courses. Teachers rotate *within* subjects; for example, there are three sophomore English teachers at Luella High. One might focus on literature, another writing, and another the assigned project. Students rotate between them, receiving the best of each instructor—and improving their mastery of the subject far more than if one teacher was scattered between all three components of the course. As the students get older, the school gives them a bigger say in their curriculum choices, with questions focused on life, career, and passion, as much as (or more than) AP classes and test scores.[12]

This is a great step that cuts down deeply on classroom boredom and disengagement, two subcurrents of the ADHD problem. Within this discussion lies, I feel, a real solution for slowing down the diagnoses, misdiagnoses, and stimulants pumping into our classrooms: giving kids more direct voice in their educational paths and choices. If a fourth grader can write at her fullest on climate change, why bog her skills down with a book report on a story she didn't like? Let her write about climate change and grade her skills accordingly! Who knows—we might be stoking the fires of a future change agent. If a kid is puzzling over a calculus problem or a trigonometry word problem because he finds the references boring or without application, make them relevant! If the assigned school reading list of dead English poets and writers offers nothing to the bookworm in your room who's keenly interested in world cultures and dreams of being in the Peace Corps or creating a school overseas, let them read about it! If we spend time finding out what impassions and engages our students and creates their dreams, and we modify schoolwork to develop those interests—yes, even Core Curriculum can be modified—then we can revive the school system and launch our future leaders, scholars, change agents, and innovators. Focus and attentiveness will skyrocket, fidgety and (negatively) disruptive behavior will plummet, discussion in the classroom will greatly increase, social behavior will improve, and eyes will shine brightly. We will once again instill the love and joy of pure learning, exploration, and discovery, without involving a diagnosis or drug. When a kid loves to learn, he or she can truly become anything. Look into the psychology of any great achiever—businessman, scientist, salesperson, athlete, educator—and you'll always find a refined love of learning, and undoubtedly, a mentor or two who impressed that on the person.

Impossible, you think? Look back forty or fifty years, before ADHD became a household world. The Baby Boomers not only received whole-person education but saw the value of hard work and maximum potential right before their eyes: America put Neil Armstrong and Buzz Aldrin on the moon with technology less advanced than your mobile device. I yearn again for that time of boundless imagination, possibility, innovation, achievement and potential, when virtually every kid who walked into a school knew they could be anything they put their mind to—and had a school system to help them get there. So let's get there.

We will not fix our ADHD problem until we fix our school system, and stop looking at gifted or precocious children as inattentive, unfocused behavior problems that need to be "settled down." True, some do need the intervention of drug therapy, but as we've heard from one expert after another, most only need to be properly challenged.

17

NUTRITION'S NECESSARY PLACE

I have enjoyed a strong rapport with right nutrition since my teen years. When I was thirteen, I started working out with weights, which led to a keen interest in nutrition for building muscle. I became bulky like a football player (I was eating way too many carbohydrates, since I didn't know any better), but I was beginning to grasp the importance of healthy eating for the purpose of bodybuilding.

With ADHD symptoms such as anxiety, rapid mood swings, quick frustration, and impulsivity a significant part of my adult life, I've used my personal interest in nutrition to make sure I'm feeding my body and brain optimally. I cannot think of a more important way in which can take care of themselves. You will only hear this on a limited basis during exams for ADHD (after all, how much information can they impart in fifteen minutes?), but major research and study shows that more than ever, diet plays a major role in mellowing out the anxiety, stress, impulsiveness, and lack of focus commonly associated with ADHD. The functional medicine case I broke down in chapter 15 spells this out in every conceivable way.

THE RELATIONSHIP BETWEEN DIET AND MOOD

We need to focus strongly on diet, nutrition, and the relationship between what we eat and how it fuels our brains and bodies. If we're to get beyond the highly stimulated ADHD world in which millions find themselves, we can start by taking a look at our diets. Parents, this is doubly important when it comes to your kids, because you can instill eating habits that they will carry them through their entire lives, which explains the "odd kid" who will happily eat fruits, vegetables, and healthy grains while his or her peers are junking out on high-carbohydrate, high-fructose diets. Not surprisingly, the kids eating fruits, vegetables, and other healthier items are less likely to show the behavioral characteristics of ADHD. A part of that has to do with choice of foods, something known to the medical field (but not necessarily followed) since allergist Dr. Benjamin Feingold, the founder of the Feingold ADHD Diet, began changing food choices for hyperactive children in the 1970s.

I've spent the past several years studying nutrition to get it right, which I would recommend for parents, educators, those in a position to influence ADHD kids, and, of course, teens and adults living with this diagnosis. We need to be more cognizant of how we eat, especially with growing health problems associated with poor eating and state-to-state obesity rates ranging from 20.2 percent (Colorado) to 36 percent (Louisiana).[1] Those (like me) with behaviors and symptoms consistent with ADHD need to be even more vigilant.

When I'm eating every few hours with a balance between carbohydrates, proteins, and fats, I do well emotionally. The main biochemical reason: my blood sugar is balanced, and I mix energizing and calming foods. However, if I skip a meal, watch out. My body is so attuned to eating every few hours that any deviation triggers anxiety, as my mind starts leaping to the conclusion that I'm starving myself. Days can quickly spin out of control if I don't honor my eating patterns, something I have in common with many who suffer from anxiety-related or stress-related issues. There's a reason why we seek out warm, often heavy "comfort foods" when anxiety and stress fall upon us. That out-of-control feeling magnifies when we eat "bad" foods, those we should avoid at all costs. For example, if I eat a lot of junk food or processed foods with no nutritious meals to "balance them out," I will get moody, often resulting in high anxiety, exhaustion, and frustration in a vicious cycle.

THE IMPORTANCE OF WATER

I also need a lot of water to feel "good." We all do. Somewhere between a half- and full gallon per day, to be more to the point. If nothing else, bottled water's rise from an occasional treat to an everyday companion has reminded us of the vast importance of hydrating. Water also flushes out impurities and makes us more alert, more receptive to outside stimuli. Not only do we need to store enough water to balance our body chemistries and keep our vital organs and minds strong, but water comprises two-thirds of our bodies. This becomes doubly important in the matter of living healthy with ADHD and other behavioral or anxiety-related disorders.

Furthermore, we live in an increasingly toxic world, exposed to more cancer-causing chemicals and contaminants than ever before, troubling pollution, and the psychological toxins of stress and negativity. The 2015 water supply crisis in Flint, Michigan, drove that point home to all of North America. Water flushes toxins—simple as that. The more good water we drink, whether filtered via "reverse osmosis," which removes a lot of contaminants, or net alkaline (it has been proven that cancer cells cannot grow in an alkaline environment), the better off we are.

A BALANCED DIET

The best way to fight off these toxins daily, and to bolster our overall health, is to strike the right balance of protein, carbohydrates, and good fats. You can do this by adopting a diet of fruits and vegetables, whole grains, and lean meat and seafood. Protein provides the building blocks for our brains and body cells, while carbohydrates convert those proteins into energy.

SUPPLEMENTING THE DIET

How to supplement the diet? In a fine article, Harvard Medical School researchers (and many others in the field) heavily endorse omega-3 fatty acids, which improve cell function, increase immunity, and enhance heart health—*all of which reduce stress*. Even more specific to

ADHD, omega-3s affect transmission of dopamine and serotonin in our brain's neurotransmitters, which help brain cells to communicate. Remember, ADHD involves lack of concentration and attention, often caused by misfiring neurotransmitters. Omega-3 strengthens those. Salmon, tuna, cold-water fish, and some seeds and oils provide a plentiful supply of omega-3, which is also available in capsule or liquid form in any grocery store.

Astonishingly, while nutritional experts, functional medicine practitioners, and dieticians have touted the value of omega-3s to help with ADHD, the medical community has been slow to respond. The American Psychiatric Association has only published one review connecting omega-3s and ADHD, and it was inconclusive. The good news? More clinical trials are coming soon.[2]

What about other minerals and supplements? Researchers have noticed a deficit in minerals such as magnesium, zinc, iron, and Vitamin B6 in children diagnosed with ADHD, as the Functional Medicine study in Chapter 15 showed. Why does it matter? Consider what these micronutrients provide the body, relative to behavior associated with hyperactivity and lack of focus or attention. Magnesium calms the body. Zinc boosts the immune system, helps fight cancer, and aids digestion and hormone production. Iron produces red blood cells and helps metabolize protein. Vitamin B6 helps in the production of neurotransmitters, the conductors of our brains, and helps improve moods. All can be found in any supplement department. However, you can also delight your taste buds to a helping of magnesium (beans and nuts, brown rice, green leafy vegetables), zinc (garbanzo beans, cashews, beef, spinach, shrimp, kidney beans), iron (red meat, dark leafy green vegetables), or B6 (bran, pistachio nuts, fish, potatoes, non-citrus fruit).

EAT AT REGULAR INTERVALS

Eating regularly throughout the day is another big key to success, since mood swings are made worse when blood sugar levels are out of whack. Eating smaller, more frequent meals every three to four hours that include some protein, carbs, and fats will offer the best shot at keeping a level head throughout the day, resulting in better decision-making and cognitive skills. Many people eat smaller servings five times per day, or keep healthy snacks around. I have a friend who stations bowls in his kitchen and office, filled with an assortment of nuts, beans, and seeds that not only satisfy every refueling need, but also crucial mood-balancing micronutrients (zinc, magnesium, B6, iron). The old-school way of eating three huge meals a day not only tires people out, but also teaches the body to store the nutrients as fat, since the body is programmed (by habit) to think that another meal isn't coming for a long time. Program your body in the healthiest way possible by eating smaller but more frequent balanced meals.

WHAT NOT TO EAT

It is just as important to know what *not* to eat. While the exact relationship between diet/nutrition and ADHD is still a research work in progress, at least in the clinical world, researchers and nutritionists note a few "don'ts" that I would recommend copying down and posting on the refrigerator:[3]

Avoid high-fructose corn syrup. This is a tall task, since the American food supply is loaded with it. This began in the United States in 1971 with President Richard M. Nixon's approval of an FDA request to incorporate high-fructose corn syrup into the American food supply in order to bolster corn farming prices.[4] Since then, American adult obesity rates have jumped from 14.9 percent to 30 percent overall, with an estimated 68 percent of American adults and children somewhat overweight—a $147 billion health problem (in 2008 dollars), according to the Centers for Disease Control.[5] Not coincidentally, hyperactivity and ADHD have skyrocketed since. Keep in mind that, in 1971, what we now know as ADHD only affected 1 percent of North Americans (compared with 12 to 14 percent today). Could there be any greater correlation between food and ADHD than fructose, the most addictive and stimulating of all sugars?

Avoid food colorings, preservatives, and dyes. Recently, the United Kingdom's Food Standards Agency (the UK's version of the FDA) asked that food manufacturers remove six artificial coloring agents and the preservative sodium benzoate from foods marketed to kids. (The FDA requires these be listed on packaging but has not requested they be removed.) The Food Standards Agency studied 153 kids, both with and without ADHD, and learned that all 153 displayed elevated levels of hyperactivity after drinking liquids mixed with various levels of sodium benzoate and the coloring agents, including sunset yellow, allura red 4C, carmoisine, tartazine, quinolone, and ponceau 4R. Researchers concluded the liquids accounted for 10 percent of the behavioral difference between hyperactive and non-hyperactive kids. Furthermore, researchers at Columbia and Harvard analyzed fifteen trials, and determined that removing these items from the diet would offer up to *half* of the effectiveness of putting a kid on methylphenidate. What a game-changer![6] You can find these preservatives and food colorings, along with a bountiful supply of high-fructose corn syrup, in most of our packaged and processed food supply.

A quick list of items with dyes and colorings that we eat or use every day shows how pervasive our use is, and how challenging it can be to remove them: toothpaste, vitamins, fruit and sports drinks, hard candy, fruit-flavored cereals, barbecue sauce, canned fruit, fruit snacks, gelatin powders, and cake mixes. Eliminating them would involve completely changing the pantry in many homes. However, consider the clear benefit—a mellower, happier, more focused and less disruptive child or adult.

Be careful with restrictive diets. I eat healthy food—and plenty of it. While restrictive diets can help us lose weight or bring one part or another of ourselves into greater balance, experts and researchers generally agree that they are of limited value. The goal is to balance the diet and biochemistry in our brains and bodies, done to a large degree by simply eliminating fructose, processed packaged foods, and white foods (white bread, bleached pasta, white potatoes, etc.) from our diet. With those three steps, most will likely find weight dropping and health improving without any further dietary restrictions.

Go easy on stimulants such as caffeine—or avoid altogether. Easier said than done; we live in a society that is not only addicted to caffeine, but also economically committed to promoting it. Coffee and sugar can really do harm to our moods and physical health, since both are very heavily connected. While I enjoy a cup of coffee every morning (two, in fact), we must each be aware of our patterns, what we eat, and notice our reactions to certain foods. For many, caffeine can make us more alert, but also quicken our heartbeat, raise our blood pressure, and induce more stress and impulsive behavior. Not good if you're dealing with ADHD. An easy way to tone down the caffeine intake without giving it up altogether is to switch from coffee to tea, from coffee beans to cacao (dark chocolate, a benign natural caffeine source), or from black tea to green, white, or red teas. Best of all, make drinks with natural, benign stimulants such as maca, cayenne pepper, ginseng, chia seeds, coconut oil, gotu kola, or guarana.[7]

Avoid or minimize unsaturated or trans fats, along with rapidly digested carbohydrates (like potato chips) and fast food. I realize I might be causing heart palpitations for some with this statement, but we can feel health benefits quickly just by reducing our intake of these items. A well-publicized and subsidized effort has created thorough awareness of unsaturated and trans fats, leading to reduced consumption. Likewise, one of the breakthroughs in the fast food world this decade has been the adoption of healthier menu items. For people like me who deal with mental health, anxiety, and stress issues, such as ADHD, this is of even greater importance.

Watch for allergens. Allergens appear in healthy foods, but cause reactions in many people that can affect brain function, most especially hyperactivity and inattentiveness, two bellwether signs of ADHD. Allergens are found in wheat, milk, peanuts, tree nuts (such as almonds and pecans), eggs, soy, fish, and shellfish.

Salicylates.[8] During the 1970s, Dr. Feingold, creator of the Feingold Diet for ADHD, claimed a 30 to 50 percent improvement in his hyperactive patients when he removed salicylates, natural anti-inflammatories used in aspirin and pain-relieving medications. This is part and parcel of the Feingold Diet, in which foods with salicylates, preservatives, dyes, and colorings are eliminated, and replaced with foods not containing them.[9] The premise? It's the same as functional medicine: the fewer toxins and unnatural agents in our system, the less stressed our brains and systems will be. Dr. Feingold, who died in 1982, found that while salicylates are beneficial for most of the population, they tend to stoke stress in those prone to hyperactivity. Many who treat ADHD by natural means, including diet, subscribe to his approach. This means reducing or eliminating foods such as red apples, almonds, cranberries, grapes, and tomatoes.

I've put it all together into a tidy list that feeds our bodies; provides much greater fuel to our brains; reduces food-induced stress, anxiety, and mood disruption; and keeps harmful foods away (or at least reduces them):

Foods to Increase

- Trans-dermal magnesium
- Seeds, nuts
- Almond milk
- Peanut, almond or cashew butter
- Bananas
- Probiotics (for optimal nutrition absorption for those with gut issues)
- Zinc
- Iron
- Vitamin B6 and the entire B-complex
- Fresh vegetables
- High-protein grains (quinoa, teff, spelt, buckwheat)
- Spirulina
- Whole, natural foods
- Hormone-free proteins
- Good fats (avocado, nuts, seeds)
- Omega-3s

Foods to Avoid or Reduce

- Fish from areas with high mercury levels (which are tied to behavioral issues)
- Sugar, especially sucrose and fructose
- Dairy
- Gluten
- Wheat
- Fruit juices
- Many cereals
- High-fructose corn syrup
- Pre-packaged foods
- Food colorants
- Frozen vegetables
- Cake mixes/frostings

- Energy drinks

I make proper eating a huge priority, knowing the potential for negative effects. That said, I'm not obsessive. I love food, and I enjoy fast food here and there as well (as I also enjoy a glass of wine), but I keep it generally healthy choice-wise. I know what works for me and what doesn't. That's key—learning how your body reacts to different foods.

18

SHAKING OFF THE LABEL

My approach to the ADHD label began differently from most. I wanted to know as much about my diagnosis as possible—and not just from the doctor treating me. So, I took to social media to find the existing ADHD community, as well as doctors, parents, educators, and others chattering about the disorder and what it means moving forward. In a sense, I took the label and ran fully with it in order to peel it off of me forever.

My destination turned out to be much different than originally thought. As my journey makes clear, the thousands of conversations, comment exchanges, and discussions I had with skeptical medical professionals, my followers, and others converted me from a man promoting his ADHD label to seek answers into a skeptic. When my questioning of the way we treat ADHD grew into questions about the diagnosis itself—particularly the near-universal acceptance of the DSM-V checklist—I found myself really wondering.

I'm one of the lucky ones. I originally bought into the diagnosis after my 2011 suicide attempt, but the first inkling that I may not have ADHD came when my stimulant medication did absolutely nothing (except leave me as anxious as I already was). Also, and I must emphasize this, medication "working" does *not* confirm an ADHD diagnosis. People are easily misled into that belief without being told about the deeper science into amphetamines and what to watch out for. There needs to be a continuous ruling out of other actual root causes for symptoms and behaviors. In hindsight, I happened upon a growing, mammoth issue in North America (and, gradually, the rest of the world): the diagnosis and label called ADHD. I could not have known what would happen.

SPEAKING OUT ABOUT ADULT ADHD

In 2013, I decided to speak out more publicly about having adult ADHD. I began on Twitter and then started a video blog (v-log), as well as posting on Facebook. I shared my experiences and the tools, tips, and support that people like myself needed to thrive despite this "difference." However, as time passed and I learned more about ADHD, I became aware of the huge number of things that mimic (and are easily misdiagnosed as) ADHD. I grew increasingly conflicted: "What if I didn't actually have ADHD, but there were other reasons for my patterns of behavior and thought?"

That really weighed on me during later 2014 and onward, until Dr. Royer helped me see that my testing scores and background didn't fit the ADHD standard that he's studied for decades. After receiving such an in-depth, eye-opening and mind-blowing confirmation and validation of my concerns, a new line of inquiry was born within me. Since then, I have sought to expose and discuss these diagnostic and treatment issues on a global scale so we can look beyond ADHD, and the way we understand it, stigmatize it, assess for it, label it, and internalize it both in our identities and assessment and (sadly) judgment of others.

ADHD AND LABELING

As humans, we've labeled the objects of our surroundings, desires, and lives since we learned language. It helps us identify, define, assign, and group traits and characteristics; it makes sense of things. A bear is different than a lion; when we hear the label "bear," we know we're not looking at a large feline roaming the savannah. Likewise, we think of bears as fearsome, bloodthirsty man-killers, especially when we see them in the wild. However, they are much more than that, particularly when viewing their role in the animal kingdom, their striking beauty, and their great physical and spiritual value in the Native American world. They are beneficent animals in many, many ways. But when I wrote "bear," you weren't necessarily thinking of the good things first, were you?

That's the downside of labeling. We attach a label to something, then it grows into whatever our thoughts make of it. If we view the object positively, then it's a label that gives us pleasure or feeds our success; for example, "professional athlete" or "CEO" is a good label to have. But if we draw negative conclusions, well, all hell can break loose in our minds or worlds. If you label someone a "divorcee" when they're trying to work through a marital separation, that's not good. How do you feel when someone tags you as "stupid" or "ignorant," two popular labels these days—even though you are neither?

Now let's take our labeling of things onto social media. What happens when we state our opinions online or define someone's actions or ways? Someone else runs with it, then it branches out; eventually, in little more than the blink of an eye, the recipient of all this noise has been defined or redefined in a different way from who they really are or from the deeper truth of their actions. They have been publicly labeled. Unless you're being labeled a "superstar" or "great musician" or "super mother" or "expert craftsman," chances are you'll wear that label like a lead weight. Especially inside your mind and heart, where it can really cause some damage.

Some people adopt existing labels to help make better sense of a subject or to feel a part of something larger. Some turn it the other way, trying to make sense of others or situations by resorting to their labels. That gives them access to information familiar to them—something they heard, read, discussed—in order to define that person. But what if the situation is much more complicated and the person much deeper and more diverse than the label or lens through which we view them?

"It's a bit concerning that in my experience most people are able to label and describe ADHD yet struggle with describing symptoms or contributing factors of depression and anxiety or acknowledging reactive adjustments to significant stressors and trauma," Australian mental health therapist Erica Dametto noted.[1]

That's my issue with labels—especially at a time when everything we say, do, eat, or breathe seems to have a hashtag or name attached to it. And when it involves medical conditions with mental health components, fuzzy diagnostics, and constant media coverage and discussion—

not to mention rumors and gossip, especially on school campuses—well, I think we're really doing people a disservice.

We're also doing ourselves a disservice, because by labeling, we're pretty much suggesting that we are done learning about that subject. Why read or talk about the incredible amounts of work sports superstars put in when we just view them as "lucky, spoiled, richer-than-hell superstars"? Or in a real hot-button subject, "If you believe in socialized medicine, you're a liberal." "If you believe in gun rights, you're a conservative." And just like that, you're tagged—even though those views might be the only ones that match one side or the other. Labeling can be a hard, dark slog through a complete misunderstanding of each other, made worse because by labeling someone or something, we thought we could gain instant comprehension!

Most of us don't explore further. We define, log it in our brains, and make it the way we look at that person or subject. Also, it's hard to swallow our pride when we choose to dig beyond the label or question the way we view something and find out there's a big, wide world out there we knew nothing about, with another side to the story, fresh facts and insights, a lot of reasons for us to either change or deepen our view. Some of us take that uncomfortable leap. A few are nonjudgmental, innately curious, and ignore labeling. However, most of us accept labels and give them the strength and support of our minds.

This led me to look at my own ADHD label, as well as the way it affects others, from a fresh set of eyes. When you have 20 million to 25 million people carrying the same label in their medical files, it's worth exploring this issue to determine the impact.

Turns out it is a really big deal—and getting bigger. Many may think it's cool to joke, when someone is acting bizarre, overly excited or hyperactive, "He's so ADHD," or "Guess her meds haven't kicked in yet." All of us have heard these comments; maybe we've made them a few times with no harm intended. However, these comments help to slather tar and feathers onto that person's view of themselves, not to mention what we think of them publicly. It reinforces the idea that "I've got ADHD; there is something wrong with me."

Then there's the professional side. Quick question: if you're an employer for a machine shop, would you hire someone who identifies as ADHD or someone you learned was ADHD when doing a medical check? Would you hire someone who, despite having ADHD, keeps it well-hidden from you? Chances are the label is going to impact your decision in such a way that you lean away from the person who is honest about his or her ADHD. Chances are decades of hearing and reading about it in newspaper articles have formed a pretty strong impression of ADHD in your mind. You're now affected by the label, but you're not alone.

"Misdiagnosing and labeling a patient with ADD has major societal and individual consequences, and unfortunately this happens much too often," Dr. Jeffrey Hirschfield says. "Most significantly, a misdiagnosis of ADD has the label of mental health stigma and often, unintended consequence stem [from] this stigma, as parents and teachers chalk these children off as 'lazy' or 'less intelligent.' The label may also impact the child's ability to exhibit any strong sense of self-esteem, resulting in poor peer relationships and personal mental state."[2]

Dr. Hirschfield could just as easily be speaking about adults as well. Most of us know how it is to live under the label of someone else's definition of us, and to live with it for years or decades even. Feels pretty shitty, doesn't it? It happens in all walks of life, from personal relationships—"He just can't keep a relationship together; why would it change now?" (one I've heard about me before); to the business world—"She's never pushed her ideas forward; she's a quitter; she won't amount to anything"; or worse—"She's the best person for the job in the company, but she's a woman, and we don't hire women executives."

"IT'S JUST THE ADHD KICKING IN"

Now imagine the person diagnosed with ADHD. First of all, if they were diagnosed in a clinician's office with a brief visit and the DSM-V checklist as the existing tools, the diagnosis has roughly a 50/50 chance of being correct—as experts throughout this book have pointed out. Secondly, when we're labeling a person as "so ADHD" or "unreliable, because they have ADHD and they can't pay attention," what are we really labeling? Their impulsiveness? Inattentiveness? Difficulty in functioning normally? Constant zest for trying new things or having new experiences? Trouble socializing with others? High anxiety? Depression? Trouble focusing on things that don't interest them? This is the DSM-V grab bag, and I for one think it's really fucked up that we rope all of these very different behaviors or medical conditions into a giant sack, tie it around a person's neck, and say, "Yeah, it's just the ADHD kicking in."

Let me show you how much we shortchange ourselves with the ADHD label, and how much we discredit and possibly harm the person we label. Take inattention, one of the best-known "markers" in an ADHD evaluation. I mean, if you or your kid can't pay attention, it's gotta be the ADHD kicking in, right?

Here is what Dr. Schuilenberg says about that:

> There are many children referred in the past five years with issues of attention, who have "fractured focus" rather than inattention. They have grown up in a digital world where the screen changes every ten to fifteen seconds (or sooner if they are gamers). . . . Additionally, the children of today are often texting, listening to music, have the TV or a movie on, and then have a "boring" print textbook in front of them for math class. They believe (erroneously) that they are "multitasking" when in fact they are spending mere seconds focusing in turn (or by demand) on each of these tasks. They have never learned what it means to "pay attention," and their neurological wiring expects constant, ever-changing stimulation.[3]

Her comment blows out the standard view of "inattention" within the ADHD label, doesn't it? It has been remarks like these, made to me by countless medical, social, and behavioral experts over the past few years, that have caused me to turn on the ADHD label and look for a way beyond it.

Dr. Schuilenberg didn't stop there. When I asked her to break down the impacts of ADHD labeling on young people (which could pertain to any condition, really), she responded with a list of bullet points that should give one reason to question any label:

- Incorrectly prescribed medications
- Inappropriate academic/behavioral interventions
- Mislabeling following the child through school
- Marginalization in school and by peers
- Delayed physical growth/development
- Poor sleep habits (due to stimulant medications)

- Suppressed appetite
- Increased risk of cardiovascular event from medication(s)
- Development of psychological/habitual dependence on pills to manage life

When I asked her about the danger of going into a medical assessment with the ADHD label implanted in your mind, she followed up with this: "There's a *lot* of other conditions and circumstances that conspire to produce the behavior which is often labeled 'ADHD.'"

> Somewhere south of forty-plus other disorders, conditions, circumstances, and/or experiences can produce what *looks* like ADHD. In my experience, upwards of 80 percent of the referrals from schools for assessment were because the teacher/administration believed the child had ADHD. In fact, the referral often came with this "diagnosis," which I was expected to confirm. In reality, only five to seven percent of these children actually met the clinical threshold for a diagnosis of ADHD, any type. The rest? All something else, and often not a disorder at all, but a response to the child's family dysfunction. The observed *behaviors* seemed to be ADHD, but they were caused by something else entirely.[4]

Dr. Brock Eide and Dr. Fernette Eide, both neurologists, wrote an amazing piece for the *New Atlantis* (thenewatlantis.com), a science and technology journal, concerning the impact of kids mislabeled for ADHD. It covers many reasons other than ADHD for why a kid might lose classroom focus and exhibit unacceptable behaviors, and also why function might be impaired. Then it discusses the traumatic, damaging effects of being labeled, right down to accepting the label for something they are not—in this case, truly ADHD. The Eides add, "Understanding why a particular child is struggling with attention involves more than simply documenting certain behaviors. It requires completely assessing the physical, medical, neurological, cognitive, behavioral, emotional, educational, and psychological aspects of the child's development, to see where breakdowns in the child's attentional or behavioral control mechanisms are occurring." Then, at the end of their article, they note, "The development of a child's mind is a kind of unfolding or flowering that we can't wholesale create but can nurture into fullest bloom. The metaphor is the garden, not the factory farm and certainly not the neurochemist's laboratory."[5]

I should add that the Eides wrote this piece in 2006—more than a decade ago. Clearly, their message has yet to sink into our society in a meaningful way.

CHECKLIST LABELING

When you look at our minds, and our children's minds, this way, how in the world can we resort to checklist labeling? I see a problem here, don't you?

Among other experts, Dr. Marianne Kuzujanakis sees an issue with the almost *laissez-faire* attitude surrounding public knowledge of ADHD diagnoses and treatment. She explained that once the doctor makes the diagnosis, then the label exists. Once recorded on a medical chart, the document can be reviewed by parents, schools, and doctors—step one of how labeling spreads. When an ADHD diagnosis gets out at school, or in the workplace, the label can feed into our preconceived notions. "I constantly worry about health-care providers who succumb to external pressures from parents or teachers, or provide a quick diagnosis of ADD from superficial symptoms alone," she added. [6]

DIGGING DEEPER

We need a much deeper inquiry not just into each individual, but in our institutions and conventional wisdom, to understand the full impact of an ADHD label. That inquiry begins with doing what we used to do all the time socially—getting to know the person. Sure, they may have been diagnosed for ADHD, and may show some (or all) of the checklist characteristics, but do you know their favorite hobbies? Their greatest passions? Their fashion or interior design preferences? The most memorable book they read or movie they watched—and why? The one or two things they cannot live without? If you didn't know me, and saw my Twitter feed, you'd immediately tag me with an ADHD label. But if you also knew I'm into cats, love nature, played ten years of top-league youth hockey, and rooted for the Cleveland Indians in the 2016 World

Series, and if you thought about those things, I doubt you'd think of me so much as "that crazy social media guy with ADHD" anymore. Likewise, any labels or prejudices I might have formed about you would evaporate once I took the time to get to know you better.

That's where we need to meet this problem: at the personal, face-to-face, heart-to-heart level. We need to open up to those who label or are labeled by the powers that be, and get to know them better. When we do, our perception changes, and three important things happen that, I believe, can partially write our ticket out of this ADHD biosphere:

1. We stop thinking of "that person with ADHD," seeing him or her as an individual with unique gifts, passions, likes, and dislikes.
2. We want to know them better, perhaps we make a new friend— not "that person with ADHD." A little more of the label dissolves.
3. We carry this attitude into the world and encourage others to really get to know the people they might be labeling. Just get to know them!
4. Finally, at some point, "them" becomes "one of us." Or, "them" becomes no big deal at all, nothing worth pointing out negatively.

My coauthor told me a great story about this. One of the kids on his high school cross country team is diagnosed ADHD. Bob nicknamed him "The Weatherman" because of his ability to know weather patterns. He and the young man also go back and forth about car racing; the kid can already rebuild many different engines, and can identify dozens of makes and models by sound alone, including vintage cars. Going into the season, Bob knew the kid's medical background. He easily could have labeled him "that ADHD runner" and let him flounder. (Some coaches do.) Instead, he got to know the kid better. He also found a unique task for this spirited young man—having him lead the team cheer to close every practice and to start every competition. By the end of the season, he had become a team leader.

This quick little story illustrates the upside of dissolving labels. You and I have the power every moment to see each person as a unique imprint of humanity. When we start getting to know people as individuals, the ADHD or any other label starts shredding faster than a shady politician disposing of questionable documents.

OUR INSTITUTIONS

We can start shredding the ADHD label immediately. Unfortunately, the same is not true for our institutions; to be more fair, the actions of a few will take a while to become the actions of many. The obstacles are numerous. The three biggest institutions in the ADHD world today are the school system, the doctor's office, and the pharmaceutical manufacturers. As we've shown, schools do not function properly if kids aren't quiet, don't fit in with classmates, and are not compliant. But kids aren't built to be compliant; they're built to be individual, unique, and expressive. Schools revolve on the decision-making triangle of parents, teachers, and administrators, and when they are in lock-step with something, things move forward. Such is the case with the ADHD diagnosis, which is almost universally accepted at the school level. With school revenue tied to tests scores, test scores tied to attentiveness, and attentiveness tied to ADHD, it behooves schools to do everything to promote good behavior and attentiveness. So kids are referred to doctors to the tune of 14 percent of the population. Most walk out of the clinic with the ADHD label. That's fucked up. But it's a reality of life on campus that will take a lot of time and the dedicated collaboration of influential people to overcome.

Then there are the doctors' offices. Doctors are in the business of examining patients and diagnosing diseases, disorders, and other medical issues. It is their Hippocratic duty to diagnose as accurately as possible and set a course of treatment that promotes the best possible chance of healing of *body, mind, and soul* (emphasis mine). Sadly, with ADHD, we're only treating a set of behaviors and sending millions back into the world, most with prescriptions, and all with the stigmatizing news that they have ADHD. Many of us wonder how we can change doctors' offices. Well, we need the help of the medical profession to do that. One by one, as you've seen from the professionals in this book, plus many others I've talked to, health-care experts are starting to shift. I believe as we get our diagnosing more precise, and the number of people who actually *have* ADHD plummets—which it will—then we can get beyond the labeling within doctors' offices themselves.

CHANGING LABELS

However, to change language or labeling, you need to believe in the direction you're headed, which can be very hard when the majority of media coverage supports and promotes ADHD. (Not too surprising in this day and age, since pharmaceutical companies spend billions on advertising, and the barriers between editorial and advertising content have all but disintegrated.) For instance, a 2010 article in *ADDitude* magazine sounded off about ADHD labeling—but then talked about how ADHD is not only a real disorder but also covered by the Americans with Disabilities Act. Later, the article asserted that ADHD will be defended, successfully, as a true disability.[7] When you're trying to get beyond the label, who wants to replace it with another label? I find it disempowering and troubling to label those diagnosed with ADHD as "disabled," when in fact, most are probably highly gifted!

However, the media thrives on labels. The more, the merrier. It's not a criticism, but a fact of how they create instant connection and interest with their readers, as well as headlines and lead stories to sell papers, magazines, ads, and TV commercial time. We've adopted it on social media, too: how else to describe hashtags but a matter of us putting labels on things and drawing interested viewers to add to them? We've very much a culture and society of labels in the twenty-first century, and our media is a reflection of who we are. This makes it all the more important for the media to address the labeling and mislabeling of ADHD and other conditions directly and often, such as in "The No-Label Movement," the awesome 2013 piece from the *New Yorker* in which the writer, Amanda Schaffer, ominously notes about labeling, "Financial incentives also shadow this terrain in ways that surely lead to more labeling."[8]

RESPONSIBLE LABELING

Ultimately, labeling needs to be controlled more responsibly. Pharmaceutical companies are in the business of labeling and marketing. They label every drug they manufacture with the proper med description and cautions; they also market those products by giving them catchy or at least simpler names than their complex laboratory names.

For the sake of being an integral part of our health-care system, pharmaceutical companies are experts at labeling and branding. They are so expert, in fact, that one of the two signature drugs for ADHD is built on the acronym itself: Adderall is code for ADD-for-all. Now I ask, if the labeling is that deeply embedded in the very culture of diagnosing and prescribing for ADHD, to one of its two signature prescribed drugs, how are we going to rise beyond it and into a society that views individuals over labels? When we're talking about millions of people on the receiving end? When the business sector's sales and profit margins depend on that label flashing in neon lights on all fronts—in your doctor's office, on your TV set, and in the workbooks your ADHD kids get from school as part of the special education component set up for ADHD?

This is a really tough one, because a multi-billion dollar industry isn't going to do anything to jeopardize its multi-billion dollar revenue streams. Since most media coverage is either pro-ADHD or neutral, doctors continue to dispense in ever growing numbers, teachers spot-diagnose for what they believe to be ADHD in classrooms, and parents are just trying to do whatever will get their kids focused, more functional, and more adept at school, it's pretty much the perfect storm for this wheel to keep on turning—sweeping up kids and adults for life, in some cases.

THERE IS HOPE

But there is hope for people who want to celebrate the value of every person: manufacturers have been openly promoting healthy lifestyles to go along with whatever prescription you're taking. Obviously, I'd rather they go easy on the second part, but they're not going to hurt their own business. At least they're not just saying "take this" anymore. They're starting to put a lifestyle improvement slant to it. As I see it, if you're a healthy person living with ADHD, why bother with the ADHD part? That's another way to shed a label—just *shed it!*

We need to halt our own labeling, and in doing so, show another way of looking at this. It's one thing to be diagnosed with ADHD. It's another for everyone around you to suddenly look at you and think, "She's got ADHD; how messed up is that?"

We need to find ways to teach people to look beyond the label and diagnosis of ADHD for their own sake. It's in our hands—as is much else as we move out of the gravitational force of ADHD and into a place beyond it.

19

THE WORLD BEYOND ADHD

You've made it this far. Thank you for exploring ADHD with me, and some ways of digging deeper into what's actually happening in our world so we can grow together and thrive beyond ADHD in the future. Obviously I don't have a crystal ball, but there are some key ways to improving the current mess associated with ADHD, the varied societal perceptions of it, and the diagnosing and the treatment as well.

IN NEED OF AN OVERHAUL

Our education systems desperately need an overhaul (or at the very least, alternatives that focus more on teaching different types of learners and learning styles; none of us learn the same way, nor are we interested in the same topics). Yes, we need a solid foundation of basics across the board, but where should the line be set for that? Shouldn't a fundamental part of the curriculum be to learn self-care, wellness, and coping strategies for the world that children are going to inherit?

Our parents and the educational system form a great sacred trust in our society—working together to raise and instruct our children. However, their front-line role as early "pseudo-diagnosers" of ADHD needs to be eliminated. They are just that, parents and educators, not health-care professionals, and their wishes to see kids settle down, behave better, or conform to classroom instruction or lesson plans is not just cause for influencing overstretched doctors to issue such a profound, possibly life-changing diagnosis, and the prescription that goes with it. Nor does it allow a thorough assessment of everything else that could be affecting the child, as Drs. Schuilenberg, Royer, Quaid, and Kuzujanakis, among others interviewed for this book, have illustrated. "I can only speak to my own process for assessment, but having been responsible for supervising clinicians in a multicultural environment, assessing children from all over the world, I worked with other stellar professionals to develop an assessment protocol that allowed for effective and accurate diagnosis," Dr. Schuilenberg says.

> This protocol included standardized forms such as the Connors Behaviour Rating Scales [CBRS] completed by teachers, parents, and/ or nannies; one- to two-hour developmental history interview with [preferably] both parents; completion of the Connors Continuous Performance Test [CPT] or the TOVA [Test of Visual Attention], a computer-based objective measure of the ability to sustain focus; age-appropriate completion of self-assessment, and finally assessment using a hands-on format, such as the Test of Everyday Attention for Children [TEAC]. This process was completed over two or three 2-hour sessions and usually involved at least two experienced therapists. The final results were collated, and a senior clinician evaluated whether or not the threshold had been met, and whether or not additional assessments to rule out other possible causes were needed (almost always this was the case).
>
> Eventually, when the *team* was satisfied that there was little or no ambiguity to the results, I would write an eight- to twelve-page report. Finally, I would meet with the parents (and often the school admin) to develop a plan to address the issues that generated the referral in the first place. In rare cases, this meeting also included a referral to a psychiatrist for assessment with regard to possible medication, because *sometimes*, it is the best answer to the problem.[1]

In my opinion, maintaining personal wellness is one of the most important skill sets we have, because it can and often does propel us to greater success, achievement, and fulfillment. It seems a no-brainer to me, yet we're still so dominantly focused on "teaching for the test" that we lose sight of what means most in life, regardless of how much money someone makes, how big their house is, and how many followers they have on social media channels.

Current levels of understanding need to improve when it comes to the diagnosis of ADHD. We need to nail down and laser in on what ADHD is and what it isn't. As we've pointed out, the diagnosis today consists of a very subjective set of observed behaviors—with just as many opinions as to its hold on people's lives. Some folks see it as a "gift," while others see it as a curse, a disorder to avoid (such as in the hiring process).

I'm not the only one advocating for us to get beyond the ADHD label, and in fact to retire it—not by a long shot. You've heard from well-respected health-care experts and concerned citizens, all of whom feel that the rush to diagnose and prescribe is both rash and ill-fated. An October 2016 *Psychology Today* blog ran under the heading "Is It Time to Retire ADHD?" The article drew a connection between ADHD and the United States' epidemic of opiate and heroin abuse, and made the somewhat astonishing (for a national publication) comment that ADHD thought leaders have "promoted a false sense of value and safety of ADHD drug treatment."[2] It talked of messaging that ADHD medication is safer than aspirin, that underdiagnosis is more the issue rather than overdiagnosis, that brain scans reveal anatomical markers of ADHD (as Dr. Royer's work with me bore out, there *are* brain wave differences, but they don't need an umbrella label), and that anyone criticizing ADHD is a "fringe doctor" or "social critic."[3] The article's conclusion was a harsh one: those health-care professionals spreading the prevailing message of ADHD are taking action that runs afoul of their Hippocratic oaths and other ethical vows they took. This raises the question: is ADHD something the medical profession created and built to justify sets of behaviors or is it a biological disorder? When you unpeel the onion, the answer might surprise you.

DECONSTRUCTING ADHD

Where do we even begin to deconstruct ADHD, and follow a vision toward a world that looks beyond a label and digs to the many deeper, actual root causes for these patterns? We take it one step at a time, from the foundation up. To effect real, lasting change in this area, modern psychiatry (and psychology) must change. That is easier said than done. Popular opinion, or "conventional wisdom," is heavily influenced by the media, advertisers, and corporations with billions of dollars available and budgeted to direct-market to the masses. In order to create a massive change across the globe, we have to mastermind a way to permeate the population, just like the media does.

Then there is the whole question of what is better in education—nurturing creativity and self-expression or making everyone proficient in the same Core Curriculum, heavily steeped in math, science, and technical subjects? Why should people who absolutely thrive in creative, alternative learning styles be forced into a diagnosis due (in part) to how our society's institutions (such as education and industry) are structured toward the amassing of greater revenues and profits? Isn't there a way we can come to a new and evolved win-win scenario for all involved?

You're darn right there is, but this is only one piece of the big picture. Factors such as poor nutrition, lack of proper sleep, technology inundation, and anxiety-inducing social media channels and email notifications (as well as bright screens constantly in our faces) also play a massive role here, as you've read throughout this book.

In a society that is increasingly losing the ability to relax, sit with one's self (without the instinctive desire to check email or text), and enjoy the moment, we risk losing ourselves in the mix. This will cause even more anxiety, depression, toxic stress, and a loss of fulfillment and joy in life (even toward the simple things). Our views can easily become "skewed" toward a more robot-like existence, or a mindless society that follows authoritarian rule without question a la Huxley's *Brave New World*, but we aren't man-made instruments. We are made of flesh and internal organs, we possess hearts and souls to go with our minds, and we have hopes, dreams, and other emotions that make us the magical, flawed, glorious beings we are.

"Society today has become more fast-paced, more demanding, more interconnected and wired," Dr. Kuzujanakis points out.

> No one seems to have time to just do nothing. People make lists of the 100 places to go to before they die, the 100 things to do before they die, while taking endless selfies and sharing constantly on social media. There is a definite pressure on many kids to keep up, to be productive, and to excel. Some students without ADHD take ADHD stimulants as a means to simply compete (a dangerous, sad reality in itself). They sometimes mimic symptoms to obtain prescriptions or

share medications with friends. Other kids, especially those without the support or means to keep up, may have other outlets including illegal drug use. All in all, the stress of today's society may propel children and young adults to experiment with medications to alleviate self-perceived weaknesses in productivity with some saying, "I need something because I feel so ADHD today!" Sometimes the stress of today's society alone can exacerbate symptoms of anxiety that may mimic ADHD.[4]

GETTING "BEYOND ADHD"

With ADHD so deeply embedded in our culture, educational system, and the minds of stressed-out teens trying to keep up, how do we truly get "Beyond ADHD"?

I have a few solutions, but we're going to need to (1) believe in the ability to change society by speaking out and creating movements; and (2) remain open to looking beyond the status quo that currently exists in many parts of the world (or embracing it, if that system benefits people of all learning and personality types in constructive ways). Bearing these two things in mind, I'd like to suggest the following.

Education Systems Must Evolve in New Ways

The system must evolve in new ways beyond a band-aid approach, such as "special needs" labeling and adding unnecessary stigma to diagnoses and lives. It simply isn't necessary. We need more educational options for families, options that work toward a strengths-focused approach, while teaching the basic fundamentals needed for self-stability and sufficiency in society and life. The concept of "teaching to the test" doesn't work for a significant percentage of students. We need to not only be OK with that reality but also embrace the fact that we all have talents and abilities that need to be discovered, recognized, and nurtured. We need to infuse in our students a lifelong love of learning, one that spills into everything they do in life.

We need fresh, inspired innovators with courage to lead this return to whole-mind learning by brainstorming a blueprint for how we might incorporate this more into the classroom. This is indeed a mammoth task and endeavour, but if there's one thing we've learned from this world, it's that great, game-changing achievement is always possible—always.

We Need to Overhaul the Psychiatric System

We need an overhaul of the current psychiatric "system," especially in North America. Well-meaning people venture into this area, but the issues are glaring when it comes to big pharmaceutical companies having too much influence in daily practices across the psychiatry realm. We need to find a way to keep the advertisers and greedy profit-seekers in check while also treating people as human beings, with past traumas, hopes, dreams, struggles, and the desire to live some semblance of a successful and fulfilling life.

A more holistic approach is desperately needed. We've shared examples of this approach in action, all of them offering new directions and more thorough treatment and understanding of those diagnosed with ADHD. However, the fact that millions of humans can't afford the wellness care and programs that would teach them coping strategies and self-sufficiency must change. We need to bring these programs further into the pipeline and somehow price them into an affordable range.

Let's Explore Deeper Causes

We need to rein in the drive to diagnose children and adults for ADHD without exploring deeper causes. Fifteen-minute clinical visits achieve nothing. We need to readopt the once-standard way of medicine, ruling out all other causes, before making an ADHD diagnosis and subjecting the person to powerful stimulant medication or other courses of therapy. Better yet, we need to treat for the individual aspects of the diagnosis—which, in at least half the cases, as we've shown, are the real issues[5] —and we need to seriously focus on doing so in as drug-free an approach as possible.

"A misdiagnosis of ADD has the label of mental health stigma and often, unintended consequence stem this stigma, as parents and teachers chalk these children off as 'lazy' or 'less intelligent,'" Dr. Jeffrey Hirschfield warns. "The label may also impact the child's ability to exhibit any strong sense of self-esteem, resulting in poor peer relationships and personal mental state. The societal consequence of wrongly prescribed stimulant medications lies primarily in the increased illegal trafficking of these drugs on our streets, within our neighborhoods, in high school parking lots, and in college dormitories."[6]

Pay More Attention to Nutrition

Nutrition must be addressed. Basic courses will go a long way toward showing people why they need to be aware of the effects created by what they put into their bodies. We also need to make good, quality foods more affordable in general. Media and advocacy groups can join forces to continue focusing on the huge detriment of sugar in our diet, for instance, and to promote foods and supplements that relax, reduce stress, build core strength, feed the brain, minimize blood sugar crashes and mood swings, and reduce allergens and reactions.

Address Technology and "Fractured Focus"

Technology and "fractured focus" must be addressed in every family, with every connected human being on the planet. Everyone is different, but anyone with symptoms of what we call ADHD must consider the amount of time they spend looking at screens (as we indicated, estimates run at up to eight hours per day for teenagers, and an hour a day for *two- to four-year-olds*). We need to make much more time to get outside, play, or sit in nature, and to be with ourselves in solitude or with others socially. It's time to get real—as in, get to the real heart and essence of who we are as human beings connected to this planet.

Bring Back Exercise and Creative Outlets

Exercise and creative outlets must return full-force into the educational paradigm and working world. We need time to "switch off" from the hectic 9 to 5 rush (or 8 to 8, as it is for more and more hardworking men and women) and take some deep breaths, remembering that self-care is crucial for a fulfilled, rewarding life. Corporations must close the gap between focusing solely on profits and nurturing their employees, feeding their strengths and their sense of ownership and value in their work. It is well proven that an employee that feels like (or is) a stakeholder is a happier, more focused, and more purposeful employee. When employees feel purposeful, you don't see many ADHD-like behavioral challenges in the office. A "win-win" scenario can be put into place that will benefit *all* involved over the long-term.

Consider the Environment

The environment: this is yet another factor. We must continue to research the damage to the environment caused by tap-water exposures and pesticides, as well as emissions, gases, lead, and climate change. Make no mistake—as we pointed out in chapter 15—many ADHD diagnoses stem from misdiagnosed environmental impacts on our bodies, such as toxicity. Furthermore, we need to embrace our relationships to the environment, feel more a part of the natural world and our surroundings instead of finding more ways to separate from it.

Encourage Different Personality Types

Encouragement for all types of personalities, brain "processing speeds," and learners is well overdue. In fact, the entire concept of ADHD (and other "disorders") needs an overhaul. While there will always be a small percentage who need medication to function optimally, we need to review each case individually rather than lumping so many under one high-flying acronym and starting them on powerful stimulant prescriptions. We've had such disempowering brainwashing on the dangers and differences of people labeled with one form of mental health "difference" or another that the burden of living with that stigma has destroyed the potential of millions of very capable people in our midst— more than we might like to admit or recognize.

Teach Self-Awareness and Wellness Learning

Self-awareness and wellness must be taught from a very early age. This needs to be ingrained, instead of depending on pills to solve problems. As evidenced by the frightening opioid epidemic and suicide rates, society needs to embrace a greater emphasis on therapy, personal communication, and digging for deeper causes to grow beyond medication (for those who can) and into a truly empowered culture. As a man who shares his story openly and vulnerably, it has become clear to me that regardless of whether someone needs medication or not, self-knowledge, self-compassion, and adopting a growth mind-set helps us transcend our pasts and realize new achievements, fulfillment, and a deeper sense of belonging.

We Need to Slow Down

We adults need to slow down. We need to chill! We push so hard to drive our kids so far forward, to make them better than we were or are (as every caring parent wants), that we often forget to see the world through their eyes. We need to pay more attention to their emotional needs, focus more on *their* interests and innate abilities, give them more space to be themselves, restrict their time on devices to reduce anxiety and increase self-reflection, and keep their lives in perspective. The more we slow down and relax, and not pin every emotional hope on the next test or game, the more our kids will slow down and reduce their anxiety and stress.

CONCLUSION

I didn't ask for ADHD to be a part of my life. It was delivered to me in a hospital room, bagged, tagged, and stigmatized. From it, however, I saw an opportunity to learn more about myself and the ADHD community, and ran into an incredible group of dedicated health-care professionals, educators, therapists, concerned parents, and forward thinkers. For me to say that my ADHD diagnosis hurt me (though it was an incorrect diagnosis, ultimately) is unfair. It actually prompted me to start taking charge of my life, one where I no longer need to associate with this label—except to help others see the many ways beyond it, too.

When we can shed the label as a society, we will awaken to what we are truly all about: achieving the heights of our own potential, loving and caring for each other, treating each person as an individual with unique gifts and abilities, living in vibrant health, feeling much more secure and less anxious, conquering our social obesity and dependency issues, using prescriptions *only* as a last resort, promoting self-esteem and self-worth over needing others (or prescriptions) to help us along, and creating a much gentler world for future generations.

It all begins by paying attention—and focusing more on ourselves and our children.

NOTES

I. A NEW DOCTOR'S OFFICE

1. The Neurocore Brain Performance Centers, headquartered in Michigan, work with adults and children on a variety of neurological disorders and issues. Licensed clinical specialists, client advocates, and "brain coaches" focus on ADHD, autism spectrum disorder, traumatic brain injury, PTSD, Alzheimer's, dementia, anxiety, stress, and other neurological issues. To quote the website on ADHD, "We recognize that every child is unique, and our diagnosis identifies why your child is experiencing his or her specific behaviors. Our innovative treatment program features the best in applied neuroscience. We work with a child's natural ability to learn, helping them reach their full potential." For more information, go to https://www.neurocorecenters.com/treatment/adhd/.

2. From *Burning Out Rembrandt,* a book in progress by Dr. Timothy Royer, 2016. Reprinted by permission of the author.

3. See http://www.cdc.gov/ncbddd/adhd/data.html.

4. See http://www.amenclinics.com/treatments/qeeg/.

5. September 15, 2016, phone interview with Dr. Tim Royer, and authors Jeff Emmerson and Robert Yehling. The interview, conducted more than a year after Dr. Royer began working with me, covered topics specific to our work. It also branched into a larger discussion on the diagnosing, prescribing, and labeling of ADHD. Excerpts appear throughout the book.

2. PEEKING BEHIND THE ADHD CURTAIN

1. The *Diagnostic and Statistical Manual of Mental Disorders* is the American Psychiatric Association's diagnostic resource for physicians and mental health professionals. Its first edition was published in 1952. In 2013, the APA released DSM-V, which includes a standard checklist of behaviors and symptoms by which most ADHD diagnosing takes place. See http://dsm.psychiatryonline.org/doi/book/10.1176/appi.books.9780890425596.

2. From an interview with Dr. Royer and the author, October 1, 2015.

3. Clay Marzo and Robert Yehling, *Just Add Water* (Boston, MA: Houghton Mifflin Harcourt, 2015).

4. From *Just Add Water,* video documentary produced by Quiksilver, Inc., 2009.

5. D. T. Max, "The Secrets of Sleep," *National Geographic*, May 2010, http://ngm.nationalgeographic.com/2010/05/sleep/max-text.

6. Alice Boyes, *The Anxiety Toolkit: Strategies for Fine-Tuning Your Mind and Moving Past Your Stuck Points* (New York: Perigee, 2015).

7. According to an article in *Naturally Savvy*, "[W]ithin the last half century, our food has drastically changed. Things we eat now are not the same as they once were. . . . [N]early 80 percent of all processed foods in the U.S. contain genetically modified ingredients. They're full of artificial colors, flavors, and sweeteners." See Jill Ettinger, "Food Then and Now: How Nutrition Has Changed," *Naturally Savvy*, http://naturallysavvy.com/eat/food-then-and-now-how-nutrition-has-changed.

8. Robert Yehling, "Forging New Directions in Cardiovascular and Stem Cell Therapies," *Innovation & Tech Today* 2, no. 4 (Winter 2014–15).

3. OPTIMAL HEALTH, INTERRUPTED

1. Arthur Hughes et al., "Prescription Drug Use and Misuse in the United States: Results from the 2015 National Survey on Drug Use and Health," *SAMHSA NSDUH Data Review*, September 2016, http://www.samhsa.gov/data/sites/default/files/NSDUH-FFR2-2015/NSDUH-FFR2-2015.htm.

2. Centers for Disease Control and Prevention, "Attention-Deficit / Hyperactivity Disorder (ADHD),"http://www.cdc.gov/ncbddd/adhd/data.html.

3. Philip Hickey, "ADHD: The Hoax Unravels," *Behaviorism and Mental Health* (blog), May 10, 2016. In this article, Dr. Hickey exhaustively broke down all sides of the ADHD structure—diagnostics, prescriptions, treatment, prevalence in schools and society—and concluded by describing ADHD as "an

unreliable and disempowering label of arbitrarily chosen and vaguely defined behaviors." No matter your views on ADHD, this article is enlightening. See http://behaviorismandmentalhealth.com/2016/05/10/adhd-the-hoax-unravels/.

4. AbleChild.org, "50 Conditions That Mimic ADHD," http://ablechild. org/resources/information-for-help/help-for-parents/50-conditions-that-mimic-adhd/.

5. The Centers for Disease Control and Prevention provides the DSM-V checklist on http://www.cdc.gov/ncbddd/adhd/diagnosis.html.

6. Jeffrey M. Jones, "In U.S., 40% Get Less Than Recommended Amount of Sleep," *Gallup*, December 19, 2013, http://www.gallup.com/poll/166553/less-recommended-amount-sleep.aspx.

7. The Institute for Functional Medicine, "Case Studies," https://www. functionalmedicine.org/functiona-medicine-in-practice/casestudies/. This magnificent case study describes in great deal how a functional medicine approach not only helped a long-diagnosed ADHD patient gain full health without medications but also details the complex web of what an ADHD diagnosis can incorporate—and what it can miss.

8. Constance M. Moore et al., "Differences in Brain Chemistry in Children and Adolescents with Attention Deficit Hyperactivity Disorder with and without Comorbid Bipolar Disorder," *American Journal of Psychiatry* 163(2006): 316–318, https://www.ncbi.nlm.nih.gov/pmc/articles/PMC4068129. This is an excellent National Institutes of Health report on the comorbid relationship between ADHD and early onset bipolar disorder.

9. From Ariana Cha, "CDC Warns That Americans May Be Overmedicating Youngest Children with ADHD," *The Washington Post*, May 3, 2016, https://www.washingtonpost.com/news/to-your-health/wp/2016/05/03/cdc-warns-that-americans-may-be-overmedicating-two-to-five-year-olds-with-adhd/.

10. Tony Schwartz, Jean Gomes, and Catherine McCarthy, *The Way We're Working Isn't Working: The Four Forgotten Needs That Energize Great Performance* (New York: Free Press, 2010). Tony Schwartz has written extensively on our addiction to distraction, including his book, *The Way We're Working Isn't Working*. Schwartz became part of the U.S. political discussion in another way in 2016 as the credited and oft-interviewed co-writer of *Trump: The Art of the Deal*.

11. Kostadin Kushlev, "Can Addiction to Smartphones Trigger ADHD?" *Newsweek*, May 15, 2016, http://www.newsweek.com/can-addiction-smartphones-trigger-adhd-459362.

12. These and other comments from Thom Hartmann come from an August 2002 interview with co-writer Robert Yehling, originally published in *Sierra Dove In Motion*, an online magazine (2001–2004).

13. This opening line to the poem "The Men That Don't Fit In," by Robert Service (1874–1958), is quoted often when early historical references to hyperactivity and ADHD are made. The first stanza continues,

There's a race of men that don't fit in,
A race that can't stay still;
So they break the hearts of kith and kin,
And they roam the world at will.
They range the field and they rove the flood,
And they climb the mountain's crest;
Theirs is the curse of the gypsy blood,
And they don't know how to rest.

4. OPTIMAL HEALTH, INTERRUPTED

1. Alexandra Ossola, "The Surprising Amount of Time Kids Spend Looking at Screens," *The Atlantic*, January 22, 2015, http://www.theatlantic.com/education/archive/2015/01/the-surprising-amount-of-time-kids-spend-looking-at-screens/384737/.

2. Jane Wakefield, "Children Spend Six Hours or More a Day on Screens," *BBC News*, March 27, 2015, http://www.bbc.com/news/technology-32067158.

3. See Google search results: https://www.google.com/?gws_rd=ssl#q=average+time+kids+spend+in+front+of+screens+and+devices+daily.

4. Tamar Lewin, "Screen Time Higher Than Ever for Children," *New York Times*, October 25, 2011, http://www.nytimes.com/2011/10/25/us/screen-time-higher-than-ever-for-children-study-finds.html.

5. Daniel F. Connor, "Problems of Overdiagnosis and Overprescribing in ADHD," *Psychiatric Times*, August 11, 2011, http://www.psychiatrictimes.com/adhd/problems-overdiagnosis-and-overprescribing-adhd.

6. From Luke Whelan, "Sales of ADHD Meds Are Skyrocketing," *Mother Jones,* February 24, 2015, http://www.motherjones.com/environment/2015/02/hyperactive-growth-adhd-medication-sales.

7. According to data provided by Better Policies for a Healthier America in its report, "The State of Obesity," all fifty U.S. states have obesity rates exceeding 20 percent, with four—Louisiana, Alabama, Mississippi, and West Virginia—topping out above 35 percent. Fully half the states have obesity rates of 30 percent or higher. Not surprisingly, there is a correlation between obesity rates and ADHD prescription rates. See http://stateofobesity.org/adult-obesity/.

8. Emily Morman, "25 Years of Parenting: A Look Back and Ahead," *Me-troParent*, January 8, 2015, http://www.metroparent.com/daily/parenting/parenting-issues-tips/25-years-parenting-look-back-ahead/.

9. Christopher McDougall, *Born to Run: A Hidden Tribe, Superathletes, and the Greatest Race the World Has Never Seen* (New York: Vintage, 2011). McDougall's revelation speaks to Thom Hartmann's view that we are at our most powerful, aware, and natural when we operate with an instinctive, "hunter's mind," or full awareness of our surroundings. This is more prevalent in children diagnosed with the hyperactive branch of ADHD. High movement and high alertness, though natural to our state of being, are being threatened by today's social dynamics.

10. Thomas S. Dee and Henrik Sievertsen, "The Gift of Time? School Starting Age and Mental Health," *National Bureau of Economic Research*, October 26, 2015, http://www.nber.org/papers/w21610.

11. Maria Konnakova, "Youngest Kid, Smartest Kid?" *The New Yorker*, September 19, 2013, http://www.newyorker.com/tech/elements/youngest-kid-smartest-kid.

12. See http://www.additudemag.com/adhd/article/1975.html.

13. Susan Dermond, *Calm and Compassionate Children* (Berkeley, CA: Celestial Arts, 2007). Ms. Dermond's comment is from a 2015 interview for this book (emphasis mine).

14. See http://www.additudemag.com/adhd/article/1975.html.

15. See http://www.edmontonadhd.com/educational-performance-program. The Edmonton ADHD educational performance program runs under the auspices of Zone Performance Psychology, and features neurofeedback training to increase patient focus and concentration in problem solving.

5. SO EASY TO DIAGNOSE, SO TRICKY TO UNDERSTAND

1. NCADD, "Too Many Young Children with ADHD Receiving Medicine as First Treatment: Report," May 5, 2016, https://www.ncadd.org/blogs/in-the-news/too-many-young-children-with-adhd-receiving-medicine-as-first-treatment-report.

2. ADHD Institute, "DSM-5TM," http://www.adhd-institute.com/assessment-diagnosis/diagnosis/dsm-5tm/.

3. Right Diagnosis, "Misdiagnosis of Attention Deficit Hyperactivity Disorder," http://www.rightdiagnosis.com/a/attention_deficit_hyperactivity_disorder/misdiag.htm.

4. Shadia Kawa and James Giordano, "A Brief Historicity of the *Diagnostic and Statistical Manual of Mental Disorders*: Issues and Implications for the

Future of Psychiatric Canon and Practice," January 13, 2012, https://www.ncbi.nlm.nih.gov/pmc/articles/PMC3282636/.

5. On the official DSM website, http://dsm5.org, there are a number of excellent articles, guideline breakdowns, and descriptions of how the DSM task force and committees arrive at the published guidelines for various disorders, including ADHD.

6. See http://dsm5.org.

7. Kimberly Holland and Valencia Higuera, "The History of ADHD: A Timeline," *Healthline*, February 26, 2015, http://www.healthline.com/health/adhd/history#19524.

8. See https://www.ncbi.nlm.nih.gov/pmc/articles/PMC3000907/.

9. R. A. Barkley and H. Peters (November 2012). "The earliest reference to ADHD in the medical literature? Melchior Adam Weikard's description in 1775 of attention deficit (Mangel der Aufmerksamkeit, Attentio Volubilis)." Of the various historical threads assigned to ADHD, Weikard's description appears to be the first rendered by a doctor in western medicine and was familiar to Sir Alexander Chilton when he was writing more extensively on the subject at the turn of the nineteenth century. For a definition of cinchona, see *Wikipedia*, https://en.wikipedia.org/wiki/Cinchona.

10. See http://dsm5.org.

11. Gerald Beals, "The Biography of Thomas Edison," *ThomasEdison.com*, http://www.thomasedison.com/biography.html.

12. Centers for Disease Control and Prevention, "Attention-Deficit/Hyperactivity Disorder (ADHD)," http://www.cdc.gov/ncbddd/adhd/data.html.

13. Email from Dr. Allen Frances to Jeff Emmerson.

14. Ibid.

15. Centers for Disease Control and Prevention, "Attention-Deficit / Hyperactivity Disorder (ADHD)," http://www.cdc.gov/ncbddd/adhd/data.html.

16. Dr. Hinshaw made these comments in a webinar cosponsored by *ADDitude* magazine, http://www.additudemag.com/RCLP/sub/10741.html. It should be noted that while he and other experts such as Dr. Tim Royer put the average doctor's visit for an ADHD diagnosis at fifteen minutes—the figure most often cited when reviewing ADHD diagnoses—the American Psychiatric Association estimates the average time at ten to fifteen minutes. Suffice it to say, the amount of evaluation time for each patient is, I feel, dangerously little.

17. Leonard Sax and Kathleen Kautz, "Who First Suggests the Diagnosis of Attention Deficit/Hyperactivity Disorder?," *Annals of Family Medicine*, vol. 1, no. 3 (September 2003).

18. The Child Advocate website offers a helpful article to understand ADHD's place in the IDEA act and resources available to ADHD children because of this classification: http://childadvocate.net/adhd-under-idea/.

19. Hart's comments are part of a provocative article on the Sober Forever website: "FYI, ADHD is BS," September 30, 2015, http://www.soberforever. net/addictionblog/index.php/fyi-adhd-is-bs/. It explores the ADHD market, diagnostic world, and culture through the eyes of long-practicing specialists who have become skeptical.

20. Ilina Singh, "ADHD, Culture and Education," *Early Child Development and Care* 178, no. 4 (May 2008): 347–61.

6. WHY PERSONAL HISTORY MATTERS IN DIAGNOSING

1. Dr. Patrick Quaid in discussion with Jeff Emmerson, February 22, 2017.

7. THE LARGER PROBLEM OF MISDIAGNOSIS

1. Dr. Susannah-Joy Schuilenberg, interview with Jeff Emmerson, June 14, 2016.

2. Dr. Tim Royer, phone interview with Jeff Emmerson and Robert Yehling, September 15, 2016.

3. Nicole Brown, "How Childhood Trauma Could Be Mistaken for ADHD," *The Atlantic,* July 7, 2014, http://www.theatlantic.com/please-support-us/?next=http%3A%2F%2Fwww.theatlantic. com%2Fhealth%2Farchive%2F.

4. Caroline Miller, "How Anxiety Leads to Disruptive Behavior," from the Child Mind Institute. Dr. Rappoport's comments concerning both inattentiveness and anxiety appear in this informative piece: http://childmind.org/article/how-anxiety-leads-to-disruptive-behavior/.

5. Peter R. Breggin, "ADHD Is a Misdiagnosis," *The New York Times,* October 13, 2011, http://www.nytimes.com/roomfordebate/2011/10/12/are-americans-more-prone-to-adhd/adhd-is-a-misdiagnosis.

6. Crystal Lewis, "How Many Children Are Misdiagnosed with ADHD a Year? The Numbers Are Ridiculous," *Romper.com*, August 11, 2016, https://www.romper.com/p/how-many-children-are-misdiagnosed-with-add-adhd-a-year-the-numbers-are-ridiculous-16240.

7. See Centers for Disease Control and Prevention, "Attention-Deficit / Hyperactivity Disorder (ADHD)," http://www.cdc.gov/ncbddd/adhd/data. html.

8. Lydia Furman, "Wondering about Disparities in ADHD Diagnosis and Treatment," originally appeared in *Pediatrics,* September 7, 2016, http://www. aappublications.org/news/2016/09/07/ADHD-diagnosis-and-treatment-socio-economic-disparities-pediatrics-0816.

9. ADDitude, "Is It ADHD? Use Our Checklist of Common Symptoms," http://www.additudemag.com/adhd/article/621.html. The ADHD symptom checklist on ADDitudeMag.com is one of several online checklists available for adults and children to predetermine if they might have ADHD. Given the strength and potentially addictive qualities of the stimulant medication most often prescribed, I highly advise not using these checklists to influence any decision but to first talk with professionals in the field.

10. DreddyClinic.com, "50 Conditions That Mimic ADHD," November 9, 2003, http://www.dreddyclinic.com/online_recources/articles/disease/adhd. htm.

11. Dr. Susannah-Joy Schuilenberg, interview with Jeff Emmerson, June 14, 2016.

12. Jordan Raine, "Big Pharma and ADHD: Stop the Overprescription of Harmful Medication," *The Unapologists.com,* http://theunapologists.com/big-pharma-and-adhd.

13. Dr. Jeffrey Hirschfield, interview with Jeff Emmerson and Robert Yehling, August 16, 2016.

14. Ibid.

15. Dr. Marianne Kuzujanakis, interview with Jeff Emmerson, October 20, 2016.

16. Ibid.

17. Ibid.

18. Dr. Susannah-Joy Schuilenberg, interview with Jeff Emmerson, June 14, 2016.

19. Erica Dametto, interview with Jeff Emmerson, July 15, 2016.

8. PRESCRIBING IN AN OPEN OCEAN

1. This figure is cited in the lead paragraph of a May 3, 2016, *Washington Post* article by Ariana Eunjung Cha, "CDC Warns That Americans May Be Overmedicating Youngest Children with ADHD," https://www. washingtonpost.com/news/to-your-health/wp/2016/05/03/cdc-warns-that-

americans-may-be-overmedicating-two-to-five-year-olds-with-adhd/?
postshare=9221462383247926&tid=ss_fb.

2. From Anouk Schrantee, Hyke G. H. Tamminga, Cheima Bouziane et al., "Study Finds ADHD Drugs Alter Developing Brain," *JAMA Psychiatry*, September 2016, http://archpsyc.jamanetwork.com/article.aspx?articleid=2538518.

3. Dr. Tim Royer, phone interview with Jeff Emmerson and Robert Yehling, September 15, 2016.

4. Vyvanase, Adderall, Concerta, Metadate, Focalin, Daytrana, and Ritalin are seven of the top eleven drugs prescribed for ADHD. The others are Methylin, Strattera, Kapvay, and Intuniv. For parents unsure about the exact properties and effects of each, *Consumer Reports* issued a helpful report, "Evaluating Prescription Drugs Used to Treat Attention Deficit Hyperactivity Disorder," http://consumerhealthchoices.org/wp-content/uploads/2012/08/BBD-ADHD-Full.pdf.

5. Dr. Susannah-Joy Schuilenberg, interview with Jeff Emmerson, June 14, 2016.

6. Luke Whelan, "Sales of ADHD Meds Are Skyrocketing. Here's Why," *Mother Jones,* February 24, 2015, http://www.motherjones.com/environment/2015/02/hyperactive-growth-adhd-medication-sales.

7. Dr. Susannah-Joy Schuilenberg, interview with Jeff Emmerson, June 14, 2016.

8. John Fauber and Kristina Fiore, "Drugs for Treatment of Adult ADHD Carry Risk of Dependence, Abuse," *Illness Inflation: A Watchdog Report*, May 22, 2016, http://archive.jsonline.com/watchdog/watchdogreports/drug-for-treatment-of-adult-adhd-carries-risk-of-addiction-abuse-b99725282z1-380007321.html.

9. Whelan, "Sales of ADHD Meds."

10. Cha, "CDC Warns That Americans May Be Overmedicating Youngest Children with ADHD."

11. See Kimberly Holland and Elsbeth Riley, "ADHD by the Numbers: Facts, Statistics, and You," September 4, 2014, http://www.healthline.com/health/adhd/facts-statistics-infographic#1; and Mayo Clinic, "Attention-Deficit/Hyperactivity Disorder (ADHD) in Children," http://www.mayoclinic.org/diseases-conditions/adhd/basics/complications/con-20023647.

12. Steven Francesco, *Overmedicated and Undertreated: How I Lost My Only Son to Today's Toxic Children's Mental Health Industry* (United States: Francesco International, 2015). His website can be found here: http://stevenf.workfolio.com.

13. Matthew Holden, "FYI, ADHD is BS," *Saint Jude Retreats*, September 30, 2015, http://www.soberforever.net/addictionblog/index.php/fyi-adhd-is-bs/.

14. The article inspired by this statistic, "The Drugging of the American Boy" by Ryan d'Agostino, appeared in the March 27, 2014, issue of *Esquire* magazine. I consider it one of the most well-written, significant treatments of this subject ever to appear in an American lifestyle magazine. The article can be found here: http://www.esquire.com/news-politics/a32858/drugging-of-the-american-boy-0414/.

15. Fauber and Fiore, "Drugs for Treatment of Adult ADHD Carry Risk of Dependence, Abuse."

16. This testimony was reported in Stuart A. Kirk, Tomi Gomory, and David Cohen, *Mad Science: Psychiatric Coercion, Diagnosis, and Drugs* (New Brunswick, NJ: Transaction Publishers, 2013), 217.

17. Blaire Briody, "The Shocking Cost of Your Child's ADHD," *The Fiscal Times*, April 1, 2013, http://www.thefiscaltimes.com/Articles/2013/04/01/The-Shocking-Cost-of-Your-Childs-ADHD.

18. Makiko Kitamura, "American Adults Surpass Children in Taking Drugs to Stay Focused," *Bloomberg.com*, June 22, 2015, http://www.bloomberg.com/news/articles/2015-06-22/american-adults-surpass-children-in-taking-drugs-to-stay-focused.

19. Ibid.

20. Denise Roland, "Shire's Profit Falls Sharply, ADHD Drug Sales Rise," *MarketWatch*, February 11, 2016, http://www.marketwatch.com/story/shires-profit-falls-sharply-adhd-drug-sales-rise-2016-02-11.

21. Nicolas Rasmussen, *On Speed: The Many Lives of Amphetamine* (New York: New York University Press, 2008).

22. Klaus W. Lange, Susanne Reichl, Katharina M. Lange, Lara Tucha, and Oliver Tucha, "The History of Attention Deficit Hyperactivity Disorder," *National Institutes of Health*, November 30, 2010, https://www.ncbi.nlm.nih.gov/pmc/articles/PMC3000907/.

23. Julie Donohue, "A History of Drug Advertising: The Evolving Roles of Consumers and Consumer Protection," https://www.ncbi.nlm.nih.gov/pmc/articles/PMC2690298/.

24. Rebecca Robbins, "Drug Makers Now Spend $5 Billion a Year on Advertising. Here's What That Buys," *STAT*, March 9, 2016, https://www.statnews.com/2016/03/09/drug-industry-advertising/.

25. MapLight, http://maplight.org/us-congress/interest/H4300/view/all.

26. Sheila Kaplan, "Exclusive: Investments Give Lawmakers Personal Stake in Biotech, Health Care," STAT, December 1, 2015, https://www.statnews.com/2015/12/01/congress-pharmaceutical-investment/.

27. Dr. Jeffrey Hirschfield, interview with Jeff Emmerson and Robert Yehling, August 16, 2016.

9. WHAT WE'RE UP AGAINST

1. Dr. Susannah-Joy Schuilenberg, interview with Jeff Emmerson, June 14, 2016.

2. Meghan Keshavan, "Tasty and Easy to Take, a New ADHD Drug Alarms Some Psychiatrists," *STAT*, May 23, 2016, https://www.statnews.com/2016/05/23/adhd-drug-concerns/.

3. Ibid.

4. Michael Allen, "Doctors Giving Kids ADHD Drugs to Improve Grades," *OpposingViews.com*, August 3, 2016, http://www.opposingviews.com/i/health/doctors-giving-poor-kids-adhd-drugs-improve-grades.

5. Alan Schwarz, "Attention Disorder or Not, Pills to Help in School," *New York Times*, October 9, 2012, http://www.nytimes.com/2012/10/09/health/attention-disorder-or-not-children-prescribed-pills-to-help-in-school.html.

6. Allen, "Doctors Giving Kids ADHD Drugs to Improve Grades."

7. Dr. Susannah-Joy Schuilenberg, interview with Jeff Emmerson, June 14, 2016.

8. Dr. Tim Royer, phone interview with Jeff Emmerson and Robert Yehling, September 15, 2016.

9. Dennis Thompson, "ADHD Meds May Pose Heart Risks for Some Kids," *HealthDay News*, June 1, 2016, http://www.webmd.com/add-adhd/childhood-adhd/news/20160601/adhd-meds-may-pose-heart-risks-for-some-kids#1. One of the best developments in 2016 has been the publishing of an increasing number of reports tying heart and other vital organ risks to the stimulant properties of ADHD drugs—as well as their impacts on developing bodies. I expect this trend of watchdog reporting to intensify in the coming years.

10. Ashlee Loughan and Robert Perna, "Neurocognitive Impacts for Children of Poverty and Neglect," *CYF News*, July 2012, http://www.apa.org/pi/families/resources/newsletter/2012/07/neurocognitive-impacts.aspx.

11. Justin Karter, "ADHD Drugs Linked to Psychotic Episodes in Children," *Mad in America*, December 30, 2015, https://www.madinamerica.com/2015/12/adhd-drugs-linked-to-psychotic-symptoms-in-children/.

12. Justin Karter, "Study Finds ADHD Drugs Alter Developing Brain," *Mad in America*, August 23, 2016, https://www.madinamerica.com/2016/08/study-finds-adhd-drugs-alter-developing-brain/.

13. Ibid.

14. Marco A. Bottelier, Marieke L. J. Schouw, Anne Klomp et al., "The Effects Of Psychotropic Drugs on Developing Brain (ePOD) Study," February 19, 2014, http://bmcpsychiatry.biomedcentral.com/articles/10.1186/1471-244X-14-48.

15. National Institute of Mental Health, "Multimodal Treatment of Attention Deficit Hyperactivity Disorder (MTA) Study," https://www.nimh.nih.gov/funding/clinical-research/practical/mta/multimodal-treatment-of-attention-deficit-hyperactivity-disorder-mta-study.shtml.

16. Dr. Tim Royer, phone interview with Jeff Emmerson and Robert Yehling, September 15, 2016.

17. Ibid.

18. Arianna Yanes, "Just Say Yes? The Rise of 'Study Drugs' in College," *CNN*, April 18, 2014, http://www.cnn.com/2014/04/17/health/adderall-college-students/.

19. Dr. Susannah-Joy Schuilenberg, interview with Jeff Emmerson, June 14, 2016.

10. THE ADHD BUY-IN

1. Allen Frances, "Keith Connors, Father of ADHD, Regrets Its Current Misuse," *The Huffington Post*, March 28, 2016, http://www.huffingtonpost.com/allen-frances/keith-conners-father-of-adhd_b_9558252.html. I found this particular article both troubling and personally redeeming, in that Dr. Frances, the chair of the DSM-IV Task Force, had spoken his grave concerns about the expansion of the ADHD age-range parameters in DSM-V.

2. American Psychiatric Association, "Diagnostic and Statistical Manual of Mental Disorders (DSM-5)," http://www.dsm5.org/Pages/Default.aspx.

3. Jeffrey R. Lacasse and Jonathan Leo, "Consumer Advertisements for Psychostimulants in the United States: A Long History of Misleading Promotion," *Psychiatric Times*, February 26, 2009, http://www.psychiatrictimes.com/articles/consumer-advertisements-psychostimulants-united-states.

4. An online copy of the 185-page *The ADHD Workbook for Kids* can be found at https://www.scribd.com/doc/139395621/The-ADHD-Workbook-for-Kids. This book is distributed as a resource to schoolchildren covered by the ADHD designation of the Americans with Disabilities Act.

5. Alan Schwarz, "The Selling of Attention Deficit Disorder," *The New York Times*, December 14, 2013, http://www.nytimes.com/2013/12/15/health/the-selling-of-attention-deficit-disorder.html?r=0.

6. Meghana Keshavan, "Tasty and Easy to Take, a New ADHD Drug Alarms Some Psychiatrists," *STAT*, May 23, 2016, https://www.statnews.com/2016/05/23/adhd-drug-concerns/.

7. Schwarz, "The Selling of Attention Deficit Disorder."

8. Ariana Eunjung Cha, "CDC Warns That Americans May be Overmedicating Youngest Children with ADHD," *The Washington Post*, May 3, 2016,

https://www.washingtonpost.com/news/to-your-health/wp/2016/05/03/cdc-
warns-that-americans-may-be-overmedicating-two-to-five-year-olds-with-
adhd/?postshare=9221462383247926&tid=ss_fb.

9. ADHD and You, "Adults: What Are the Symptoms of ADHD?," https://
www.adhdandyou.com/adhd-patient/symptoms-of-adhd. Shire is among several companies that post checklists with suggestive questions or statements like
"Check to See If You Have ADHD." I find that troubling, in that ADHD
should be considered serious enough to be diagnosed by a medical or behavioral expert, preferably working with others.

10. Dr. Jeffrey Hirschfield, interview with Jeff Emmerson and Robert Yehling, August 16, 2016.

11. Centers for Disease Control and Prevention, "Attention-Deficit /
Hyperactivity Disorder (ADHD)," http://www.cdc.gov/ncbddd/adhd/
guidelines.html.

12. "ADHD Market Will Be Worth $25 Billion in 2024, Report Predicts,"
The Pharma Letter, July 9, 2016, http://www.thepharmaletter.com/article/
adhd-market-will-be-worth-25-billion-by-2024-report-predicts.

13. Dr. Marianne Kuzujanakis, interview with Jeff Emmerson, October 20,
2016.

14. Dr. Jeffrey Hirschfield, interview with Jeff Emmerson and Robert Yehling, August 16, 2016.

15. Ibid.

11. WHAT ABOUT OUR BOYS?

1. Caroline Miller, "The Disturbing Link between ADHD and Conservative Education Reform," *Alternet,* March 2, 2014, http://www.alternet.org/
education/disturbing-link-between-adhd-and-conservative-education-reform.
First published in *Salon* magazine.

2. Erica Dametto, interview with Jeff Emmerson, July 15, 2016.

3. Alan Schwarz and Sarah Cohen, "A.D.H.D. Seen in 11% of U.S. Children as Diagnoses Rise," *New York Times*, March 31, 2013, http://www.
nytimes.com/2013/04/01/health/more-diagnoses-of-hyperactivity-causing-
concern.html.

4. See http://hmi.ucsd.edu/howmuchinfo.php. Every day, it seems, we
learn more about the capacity of brain—and also, how much information we
absorb on a daily basis. I feel this is vital to understanding just how much
stimulation and information our brains can handle, as well as our children's
brains. The *type* of information and stimulation our kids absorb demands our
fullest attention.

5. Richard Alleyne, "Welcome to the Information Age—174 Newspapers a Day," *The Telegraph*, February 11, 2011, http://www.telegraph.co.uk/news/science/science-news/8316534/Welcome-to-the-information-age-174-newspapers-a-day.html.

6. Shea Bennett, "Social Media Overload—How Much Information Do We Process Each Day?," *Social Times*, July 31, 2013, http://www.adweek.com/socialtimes/social-media-overload/488800.

7. Jennifer Schuessler, "Too Much Information about 'Information'?," *ArtsBeat*, March 23, 2011, http://artsbeat.blogs.nytimes.com/2011/03/23/too-much-information-about-information/.

8. Tony Schwartz, "Addicted to Distraction," *The New York Times,* November 28, 2015. I consider this one of the most important recent articles to address this day and age, and especially the underlying causes of attention deficit—which bolsters my contention that if we change society, we erase much (if not all) of ADHD. http://www.nytimes.com/2015/11/29/opinion/sunday/addicted-to-distraction.html.

9. Nicholas Carr, *The Shallows: What the Internet Is Doing to Our Brains* (New York: W.W. Norton, 2011). This book was a finalist for the 2011 Pulitzer Prize in General Non-Fiction. If you want to know how the Internet influences you or your child's thinking patterns and way of perceiving and relating to the world, and what has happened to deep thinking as a result, read this book (http://books.wwnorton.com/books/The-Shallows/).

10. Richard A. Friedman, "A Natural Fix for A.D.H.D.," *The New York Times*, October 31, 2014, http://www.nytimes.com/2014/11/02/opinion/sunday/a-natural-fix-for-adhd.html.

12. WHAT IS WITH MY BRAIN?

1. Dr. Tim Royer, phone interview with Jeff Emmerson and Robert Yehling, September 15, 2016.

2. Ibid.

3. Ibid.

4. Ibid.

5. Ibid.

6. Ibid.

7. Ibid.

8. Jared Friedman, "The Neurobiological Origin of ADHD," *PsychCentral*, http://psychcentral.com/lib/the-neurobiological-origin-of-adhd/. The 60 percent figure is not a high estimate, by any means. *ADDitude* magazine, the

informative, pro-ADHD publication for parents and educators, estimates that 75 percent of children will go on to exhibit ADHD behaviors as adults.

9. James Randerson, "How Many Neurons Make a Human Brain? Billions Fewer Than We Thought," *The Guardian*, February 28, 2016, https://www.theguardian.com/science/blog/2012/feb/28/how-many-neurons-human-brain. The actual number of neurons has been adjusted several times during the past ten years, as neuroscience advances and studies become more refined. Most credible estimates put the figure at somewhere between 80 billion and 100 billion.

10. From *Burning Out Rembrandt* by Dr. Timothy Royer (unpublished manuscript, 2016). Reprinted by permission of the author.

11. Ibid.

12. William Dodson, "Secrets of Your ADHD Brain," *ADDitude* magazine, October 2013, http://www.additudemag.com/adhd/article/10117.html. Dr. Dodson runs the Woodburn Pediatric Clinic, which is dedicated to treating ADHD and other behavioral disorders. Information can be found at http://woodburnpediatric.com. Another related article on the subject is available at http://woodburnpediatric.com/adhd-and-the-nervous-system.

13. Dr. Tim Royer, phone interview with Jeff Emmerson and Robert Yehling, September 15, 2016.

14. From *Burning Out Rembrandt* by Dr. Timothy Royer (unpublished manuscript, 2016). Reprinted by permission of the author.

13. EXPLORING THE DEEPER CAUSES

1. "Autism Prevalence," *Autism Speaks*, https://www.autismspeaks.org/what-autism/prevalence.

2. Susanna N. Visser, Benjamin Zablotsky et al., "Diagnostic Experiences of Children with Attention-Deficit / Hyperactivity Disorder," *National Health Statistics Report*, September 3, 2015, http://www.cdc.gov/nchs/data/nhsr/nhsr081.pdf.

3. Gil Press, "Internet of Things by the Numbers: Market Estimates and Forecasts," *Forbes,* August 22, 2014, http://www.forbes.com/sites/gilpress/2014/08/22/internet-of-things-by-the-numbers-market-estimates-and-forecasts/#2ffa4f542dc9.

4. "Family Stressors and Traumatic Childhood Experiences Linked to ADHD Diagnoses in Children," *ScienceDaily*, October 11, 2016, https://www.sciencedaily.com/releases/2016/10/161011130010.htm.

5. Ibid.

6. Understood, "Understanding Social Communication Disorder," https://www.understood.org/en/learning-attention-issues/child-learning-disabilities/communication-disorders/understanding-social-communication-disorder.

7. Ibid.

8. The American Speech-Language-Hearing Association has an excellent website and series of assessment tools to help determine the social communication skills of our kids—and, more importantly, to help work with any issues specific to SCD, rather than lumping them under the ADHD umbrella. See "Social Communication Disorders in School-Age Children," *American Speech-Language-Hearing Association*, http://www.asha.org/PRPSpecificTopic.aspx?folderid=8589934980&section=Assessment.

9. "Study Reveals Everyday Items Contain Chemicals That Cause Cancer, ADHD, and Autism," *7News*, October 19, 2016, https://au.news.yahoo.com/a/32944210/study-reveals-everyday-items-contain-chemicals-that-cause-cancer-adhd-and-autism/#page1.

10. Jonathan Leake, "Diesel Fumes Poison Babies in the Womb," *The Sunday Times*, March 27, 2016, http://www.thesundaytimes.co.uk/sto/news/uk_news/Health/article1682266.ece. Scientists have increasingly pegged environmental causes to behavioral and emotional disorders, as we've begun doing with autism and ADHD. It should come as no surprise; after all, many forms of cancer are directly linked to environmental causes.

11. Richard A. Friedman, "A Natural Fix for A.D.H.D.," *The New York Times,* November 2, 2014, http://www.nytimes.com/2014/11/02/opinion/sunday/a-natural-fix-for-adhd.html.

12. Larry Rosen, "ADHD and Technology: Helping Our Children Reclaim Their Focus and Attention," *The Huffington Post,* January 5, 2015, http://www.huffingtonpost.com/dr-larry-rosen/adhd-and-technology-helpi_b_6096168.html.

13. Fellerman & Van Essen, "Distributed hierarchical processing in the primate cerebral cortex," *Cerebral Cortex, 1991.* https://www.ncbi.nlm.nih.gov/pmc/articles/PMC3306444/#R37.

14. Pennsylvania College of Optometry, "Randomized Clinical Trial of Treatments for Symptomatic Convergence Insufficiency in Children," https://www.ncbi.nlm.nih.gov/pubmed/18852411.

15. Dr. Patrick Quaid, interview with Robert Yehling, February 5, 2016.

16. Paul Stone, "Adults With History of TBI Have Higher Chance of ADHD Diagnosis," *NRI*, August 20, 2015, http://www.traumaticbraininjury.net/adults-with-history-of-tbi-have-higher-chance-of-adhd-diagnosis/.

17. Larry Maucieri, "Why Do Brain Injuries Look Like ADHD?," *Psychology Today*, October 6, 2015, https://www.psychologytoday.com/blog/the-distracted-couple/201510/why-do-brain-injuries-look-adhd.

14. NEW WAYS OF WORKING WITH ADHD

1. Kimberly Leonard, "Parents: Don't Start with ADHD Medication," *U.S. News and World Report*, May 3, 2016, http://www.usnews.com/news/articles/2016-05-03/cdc-encourages-behavior-therapy-for-preschoolers-with-adhd.

2. Dr. Tim Royer, phone interview with Jeff Emmerson and Robert Yehling, September 15, 2016.

3. Katherine Davis, "White Matter Similarities Found in Children with ADHD, OCD, Autism," HealthImaging, July 29, 2016, http://www.healthimaging.com/topics/molecular-imaging/neuroimaging/white-matter-similarities-found-children-adhd-ocd-and-autism.

4. NEBA Health, "FAQ," https://nebahealth.com/faq.html.

5. Sabrina Tavernise, "Brain Test to Diagnose A.D.H.D. Is Approved," *The New York Times*, July 15, 2013, http://www.nytimes.com/2013/07/16/health/brain-test-to-diagnose-adhd-is-approved.html.

6. "De Novo Classification Request for Neuropsychiatric EEG-Based Assessment Aid for ADHD (NEBA) System," https://www.accessdata.fda.gov/cdrh_docs/reviews/K112711.pdf.

7. Timothy Egan, with Casey Egan, "Can the Selfie Generation Unplug and Get into Parks?" *National Geographic,* October 2016, http://www.nationalgeographic.com/magazine/2016/10/unplugging-the-selfie-generation-national-parks/.

8. Stephen P. Hinshaw and Katherine W. Ellison, *ADHD: What Everyone Needs to Know* (New York: Oxford University Press, 2015).

9. Dr. Marianne Kuzujanakis, interview with Jeff Emmerson, October 20, 2016.

10. Kat Heagberg, "This Is Your Brain on Yoga," *Yoga International*, January 15, 2014, https://yogainternational.com/article/view/this-is-your-brain-on-yoga.

11. Yoga Alliance, "2016 Yoga in America Study Conducted by Yoga Journal and Yoga Alliance Reveals Growth and Benefits of the Practice," *PR Newswire*, January 13, 2016,http://www.prnewswire.com/news-releases/2016-yoga-in-america-study-conducted-by-yoga-journal-and-yoga-alliance-reveals-growth-and-benefits-of-the-practice-300203418.html.

15. TOWARD COLLABORATIVE DIAGNOSING AND CARE

1. Dr. Tim Royer, phone interview with Jeff Emmerson and Robert Yehling, September 15, 2016.

2. Susan R. Barry, *Fixing My Gaze: A Scientist's Journey into Seeing in Three Dimensions* (New York: Basic Books, 2009).

3. Dr. Patrick Quaid, *Seeing Is Believing* (unpublished manuscript).

4. NEBA Health, "FAQ," https://nebahealth.com/faq.html.

5. Dr. Tim Royer, phone interview with Jeff Emmerson and Robert Yehling, September 15, 2016.

6. Andre De Los Rosas, interview with Jeff Emmerson, July 1, 2016.

7. Michael Silverstein, L. Kari Hironaka, Heather J. Walter et al., "Collaborative Care for Children with ADHD Symptoms: A Randomized Comparative Effectiveness Trial," March 2015, http://pediatrics.aappublications.org/content/early/2015/03/17/peds.2014-3221.

8. Ibid.

9. "ADHD Overdiagnosed," *Cedarbrook Center*, November 29, 2016, http://www.cedarbrook.us/~cedarb9/index.php/adhd/100-adhd-overdiagnosed. This is yet another example of the fairly mountainous amount of data that shows a misdiagnosis rate of at least 50 percent for ADHD. I've cited several different sources throughout the book to illustrate how, while the numbers may vary a bit, they paint the same compelling story: we overdiagnose, misdiagnose, and prescribe far too much to mask other, deeper causes.

10. "The Tornado Programme: A Collaborative Approach for the Treatment of ADHD in Dutch Children," ADHD Institute, July 2016, http://www.adhd-institute.com/expert-scientific-insight/scientific-insight/the-tornado-programme-a-collaborative-approach-for-the-treatment-of-adhd-in-dutch-children/.

11. Ibid.

12. Melissa McGonnell, Penny Corkum, Margaret McKinnon et al., "Doing it Right: An Interdisciplinary Model for the Diagnosis of ADHD," November 18, 2009, https://www.ncbi.nlm.nih.gov/pmc/articles/PMC2765379/.

13. Ibid.

14. Ibid.

15. "The Functional Medicine Niche," internal report issued to potential practitioners (Institute of Functional Medicine, 2015).

16. "About Functional Medicine," *Institute for Functional Medicine*, https://www.functionalmedicine.org/what_is_functional_medicine/aboutfm/.

17. Kara N. Fitzgerald and Mark Hyman, "Functional Medicine Case: Attention Deficit Hyperactivity Disorder," *Institute of Functional Medicine*, 2010, https://www.functionalmedicine.org/files/library/adhd-case-study_002.pdf.

16. PROBLEM CHILD OR GIFTED CHILD

1. Dr. Susannah-Joy Schuilenberg, interview with Jeff Emmerson, June 14, 2016.

2. Dr. Marianne Kuzujanakis, interview with Jeff Emmerson, October 20, 2016.

3. The White House announced on October 17, 2016, the highest U.S. high school graduation rate on record at 83.2 percent in the 2014–2015 school year, although significant disparities still exist between groups of students. According to the National Center for Education Statistics, every group—from race to low-income students to those with disabilities—had increases in graduation rates, although the numbers vary from group to group.

4. Dr. Tim Royer, phone interview with Jeff Emmerson and Robert Yehling, September 15, 2016.

5. Mollie Tobin, "Childhood Trauma in the Classroom," *Teacher Magazine*, July 27, 2016, https://www.teachermagazine.com.au/article/childhood-trauma-in-the-classroom.

6. Nancy Shute, "Neurologists Warn against ADHD Drugs to Help Kids Study," *National Public Radio*, March 14, 2013, http://www.npr.org/sections/health-shots/2013/03/13/174193454/neurologists-warn-against-adhd-drugs-to-help-kids-study.

7. Dr. Marianne Kuzujanakis, interview with Jeff Emmerson, October 20, 2016.

8. Sabrina Tavernise, "U.S. Suicide Rate Surges to a 30-Year High," *The New York Times*, April 22, 2016, http://www.nytimes.com/2016/04/22/health/us-suicide-rate-surges-to-a-30-year-high.html?_r=0.

9. Andrea Chromis-Tuscano et al., "Very Early Predictors of Adolescent Depression and Suicide Attempts in Children with Attention-Deficit/Hyperactivity Disorder," *General Psychiatry* 67, no. 10 (2010): 1044–51. Dr. Chromis-Tuscano heard of our work on this book from her colleague at the University of Maryland, Dr. Andre De Los Rosas, and offered this paper for our review and use. The paper illustrates yet again, in stark and sobering terms, why behavioral therapy must be the major way to work with children living with behaviors we characterize as ADHD.

10. "New Toolkit Launched to Help Schools Deal with Mental Health Issues in Children and Young People," *Mental Health Today*, October 24, 2016, https://www.mentalhealthtoday.co.uk/new-toolkit-launched-to-help-schools-deal-with-mental-health-issues-in-children-and-young-people.aspx.

11. Katrina Schwartz, "Why a School's Master Schedule Is a Powerful Enabler of Change," KQED News, *Mind/Shift* magazine, October 24, 2016, https://ww2.kqed.org/mindshift/2016/10/24/why-a-schools-master-schedule-is-a-

powerful-enabler-of-change/. I find this not only an inspiring story, but also a road map that other schools can use to rework their schedules toward greater whole-mind engagement with students, as well as focusing more on the social and health portions of a well-rounded education. Combine these three areas and you have engaged, eager, ambitious students, with less likelihood of focus, attentiveness, or behavioral problems. Simply put: a happy student is a focused student.

12. Schwartz, "Why a School's Master Schedule Is a Powerful Enabler of Change."

17. NUTRITION'S NECESSARY PLACE

1. "Adult Obesity Rate by State," The State of Obesity, September 1, 2016, http://stateofobesity.org/adult-obesity/. This study was a big shock to me because it assigned 20 percent obesity rates even to health-conscious states like California. No U.S. state fell below 20 percent, and half of them reported obesity rates of 30 percent or higher. The correlation between the American diet—with its processed foods and high fructose corn syrup sweetening the supply—reduced daily exercise, obesity rates, and rise in diagnosed ADHD cases is no accident: kids need to have a way to burn off extra energy, especially from potentially harmful sugars.

2. "Diet and Attention Deficit Hyperactivity Disorder," Harvard Health Publications, Harvard Medical School, 2016, http://www.health.harvard.edu/newsletter_article/Diet-and-attention-deficit-hyperactivity-disorder.

3. Angela Ayles, "Managing ADHD: 15 Foods to Avoid," Activebeat.com, http://www.activebeat.com/diet-nutrition/managing-adhd-15-foods-to-avoid/. There are numerous lists of foods to avoid online, but I like this list the best. The author not only lists the items, but specifically points out ways they affect attention, focus, functionality, behavior, and energy.

4. Alexander Le Tellier, "Blame Nixon for the Obesity Epidemic," Los Angeles Times, June 27, 2012, http://articles.latimes.com/2012/jun/27/news/la-ol-nixon-obesity-epidemic-corn-20120627.

5. Centers for Disease Control and Prevention, "Adult Obesity Facts," https://www.cdc.gov/obesity/data/adult.html.

6. D. McCann et al., "Food Additives and Hyperactive Behaviour in 3-Year-Old and 8/9-Year-Old Children in the Community: A Randomised, Double-Blinded, Placebo-Controlled Trial," Lancet 370, no. 9598 (November 3, 2007): 1560–67.

7. Colleen Carteaux, "10 Natural Stimulants," Med Health Daily, http://www.medhealthdaily.com/natural-stimulants/. One of the easiest first steps to

take for any of us who have anxiety, stress, hyperactivity, or tension issues is to stop drinking coffee and black tea. Rather than going cold turkey, which creates stressors of its own, substitute with a natural stimulant from this list.

8. Jane Hoppe and Rena Goldman, "5 Food Items to Avoid with ADHD," Healthline, http://www.healthline.com/health/adhd/foods-to-avoid#Overview1.

9. "What Is the Feingold Program?," The Feingold Association of the United States, http://feingold.org/about-the-program/what-is-the-feingold-program/.

18. SHAKING OFF THE LABEL

1. Erica Dametto, interview with Jeff Emmerson, July 15, 2016.

2. Dr. Jeffrey Hirschfield, interview with Jeff Emmerson and Robert Yehling, August 16, 2016.

3. Dr. Susannah-Joy Schuilenberg, interview with Jeff Emmerson, June 14, 2016.

4. Ibid.

5. Brock L. Eide and Fernette F. Eide, "The Mislabeled Child," *The New Atlantis,* Spring 2006, http://www.thenewatlantis.com/publications/the-mislabeled-child.

6. Dr. Marianne Kuzujanakis, interview with Jeff Emmerson, October 20, 2016.

7. Linda Roggli, "Think beyond the Label: Accepting ADHD as a Disability," *ADDitude*, 2010, http://www.additudemag.com/adhdblogs/8/7070.html.

8. Amanda Schaffer, "The No-Label Movement," *New Yorker*, October 2, 2013, http://www.newyorker.com/tech/elements/the-no-label-movement.

19. THE WORLD BEYOND ADHD

1. 1 Dr. Susannah-Joy Schuilenberg, interview with Jeff Emmerson, June 14, 2016.

2. Gretchen L. Watson, "Is It Time to Retire ADHD?," *Psychology Today*, October 3, 2016, https://www.psychologytoday.com/blog/extraordinary-people/201610/is-it-time-retire-adhd.

3. Ibid.

4. Dr. Marianne Kuzujanakis, interview with Jeff Emmerson, May 11, 2016.

5. Dr. Jeffrey Hirschfield, interview with Jeff Emmerson and Robert Yehling, August 16, 2016.

6. Ibid.

BIBLIOGRAPHY

Amen, Daniel G. *Healing ADD: The Breakthrough Program That Allows You to See and Heal the 7 Types of ADD*. New York: Berkley, 2013.

Archer, Dale. *The ADHD Advantage: What You Thought Was a Diagnosis May Be Your Greatest Strength*. New York: Avery, 2016.

Barkley, Russell A. *Taking Charge of ADHD: The Complete, Authoritative Guide for Parents*. 3rd ed. New York: Guilford Press, 2013.

Barkley, Russell A. *Taking Charge of Adult ADHD*. New York: Guilford Press, 2010.

Boyes, Alice. *The Anxiety Toolkit: Strategies for Fine-Tuning Your Mind and Moving Past Your Stuck Points*. New York: Perigee, 2015.

Carr, Nicholas. *The Shallows: What the Internet Is Doing to Our Brains*. New York: W.W. Norton, 2011.

Dermond, Susan Usha. *Calm and Compassionate Children*. Berkeley: Celestial Arts, 2007.

Doidge, Norman. *The Brain's Way of Healing*. New York: Viking, 2015.

Hallowell, Edward M., and John J. Ratey. *Driven to Distraction: Recognizing and Coping with Attention Deficit Disorder*. New York: Anchor, 2011.

Hartmann, Thom. *The Edison Gene: ADHD and the Gift of the Hunter Child*. Rochester, VT: Park Street Press, 2003.

Hyche, Karen, and Vickie Maertz. *Classroom Strategies for Children with ADHD, Autism and Sensory Processing Disorders: Solutions for Behavior, Attention and Emotional Regulation*. Eau Claire, WI: PESI, 2014.

Kirch Debroitner, Rita, and Avery Hart. *Moving Beyond A.D.D./A.D.H.D.: An Effective, All Natural, Holistic, Mind-Body Approach*. Kill Devil Hills, NC: Transpersonal Publishing, 2007.

Larsen, Stephen. *The Neurofeedback Solution: How to Treat Autism, ADHD, Anxiety, Brain Injury, Stroke, PTSD, and More*. Rochester, VT: Healing Arts Press, 2012.

Maiquez, Adonis. *Modern Medicine for Modern Times: The Functional Medicine Handbook to prevent and treat diseases at their root cause*. The Functional Medicine Protocol Series. CreateSpace Independent Publishing Platform, 2015.

Martin, Jeremy. *ADHD: Beyond the Meds*. Maitland, FL: Xulon Press, 2011.

Marzo, Clay, and Robert Yehling. *Just Add Water*. New York: Houghton Mifflin Harcourt, 2014.

McDougall, Christopher. *Born to Run: A Hidden Tribe, Superathletes, and the Greatest Race the World Has Never Seen*. New York: Vintage, 2011.

Meyer, Martin. *ADHD Diet: The Cure Is Nutrition Not Drugs*. CreateSpace Independent Publishing Platform, 2016.

Miliken, Kirsten. *PlayDHD: Permission to Play . . . a Prescription for Adults with ADHD*. [N.p.]:BookBaby, 2016.

Quaid, Patrick. *Seeing Is Believing*. [Forthcoming, 2017].

Robbins, Jim, *A Symphony in the Brain: The Evolution of the New Brain Wave Biofeedback*. New York: Grove Press, 2008.

Royer, Timothy. *Burning Out Rembrandt*. [Forthcoming, 2017].

Schwarz, Alan. *ADHD Nation: Children, Doctors, Big Pharma, and the Making of an American Epidemic*. New York: Scribner, 2016.

Schwartz, Tony. *The Way We're Working Isn't Working: The Four Forgotten Needs That Energize Great Performance*. New York: Free Press, 2011.

Shapiro, Lawrence. *The ADHD Workbook for Kids: Helping Children Gain Self-Confidence, Social Skills, and Self Control*. Oakland, CA: Instant Help, 2010.

Yehling, Robert. "Forging New Directions in Cardiovascular and Stem Cell Therapies," *Innovation & Tech Today* 2 (Winter 2014–2015), Innovative Properties Worldwide, Denver, CO.

Zylowska, Lidia. *The Mindfulness Prescription for Adult ADHD: An 8-Step Program for Strengthening Attention, Managing Emotions, and Achieving Your Goals*. Boston, MA: Trumpeter, 2012.

INDEX

360-degree Mind (also Hunter's Mind),
27, 58, 164, 191

AbleChild.Org, 29
acupressure, 170
acupuncture, 170
ADD, 54, 59, 81, 83, 95, 97
ADDitude Magazine, 45, 47, 141, 219
ADHD: adult-onset, 6, 210; child-onset,
6, 121, 159; distractions, positive, 128;
distractions, unhealthy, 127–128;
effects, television viewing, 38; energy,
excessive, 43, 44, 45, 46–47; epidemic,
33; history of, 53, 87, 95, 174; labeling
(stigmatism), 10, 15, 24, 84, 90, 122,
150, 209–221; 'No Label Movement,'
219, 225; novelty, positive impacts of,
128, 129; prescription rate, 28, 48, 129;
societal impact, 59, 77, 84, 213, 223,
226, 228; stress, impact, 13, 15, 26, 30,
31, 43, 46, 57, 85, 100, 123, 143, 148,
150, 152, 165, 168, 170, 193, 194, 200,
201, 205, 226; 'textbook traits,' 6, 14,
23, 216; youth sports, importance of,
68, 123, 124
ADHD: Diagnosis, 3, 6, 17, 31, 33, 39, 51,
55, 59, 63, 75, 77, 83, 84, 107,
121–122, 130, 136, 139, 142, 145–146,
159–160, 173–174, 225; accuracy,
need for increased, 142, 162, 181, 215,
225; collaborative care, 178–179,

179–180; collaborative diagnosis,
necessity of, 115, 116, 173–175,
176–177, 177; combined type, 107;
definition of, 55; "Diagnosis of Last
Resort," 91–92, 109; diagnostic
checklist, 17, 22, 29, 33–34, 55, 78, 93,
112, 136, 142, 174; diagnostic levels,
142, 145; fear, impact of diagnosis, 62,
84, 130, 216; fractured focus, vs.
inattentiveness, 214, 229; Hyperactive
Type, 107, 108; Inattentive Type, 51,
77, 78, 107, 118, 215; indication of
other conditions, 78–79, 81, 86, 183,
184–185, 215; medical history,
importance of, 80, 183, 184–185;
misdiagnosis, 9, 10, 75, 77, 77–78, 78,
86, 174, 215, 228; overdiagnosis, 59,
60, 62, 76, 91, 122, 225; personal/
family history, importance of, 63, 104,
146–147, 183, 184–185; "Right
Diagnosis," 85, 89; rise in, 10, 39, 113,
114; straight-line diagnosing, 130, 136
ADHD: What Everyone Needs to Know,
60, 165
ADHDandyou.com, 78
Adverse Childhood Experiences (ACEs),
85, 146–147, 147–148
advertising, impact of, 114, 117, 126
Adweek, 126
allergies, 31
Alles, Gordon, 94

ABOUT THE AUTHORS

Jeff Emmerson is a mental health advocate, popular video blogger, and leading social media figure focused on reframing how we view ADHD. He has a passionate mission to prevent mis- and overdiagnoses and to help people whose lives are impacted by the condition. He has over 400,000 followers (and counting) on his Twitter account, 15,000-plus LinkedIn connections, a large viewership on Periscope and YouTube, and is continuously growing his platform at a strong and steady pace. His e-mail list has over 50,000 subscribers. Emmerson is aligned with a number of leading medical, neuroscience, and behavioral experts, many of whom are quoted prominently in his book. He has written for *EverydayHealth.com*, *AdditudeMag.com*, and *AOL Health*, and has been interviewed on NPR.

Robert Yehling is the author of twelve books and ghostwriter of nine others. He focuses on nonfiction titles pertaining to mental health, behavior, and fitness. His most recent title, *Just Add Water*, the biography of autistic surfing great Clay Marzo (2015), has been nominated for the Dorothy Gray Children's Literature Award and an International Book Award. He also works with author Kevin Hines, whose *Cracked, Not Broken* (2013) is revered worldwide for its treatment of bipolar disorder and suicide prevention. Yehling has also edited published titles on traumatic brain injury, vision therapy, post-traumatic stress disorder, and autism. A professional journalist since 1976, Yehling was the recipient of the 2007 Independent Publishers Book Award for *Writes of Life: Using Personal Experiences in Everything You Write*. He also has won national awards for his newspaper, magazine, and online journalism, as well as a Bank of America Liberal Arts Award for creative writing. Yehling teaches cause-based writing and other topics at conferences and workshops throughout North America.